One Hundred Yea
The History and Chronology or the North
Dakota Developmental Center

by Brent A. Askvig

with assistance from Ana Novosel

May, 2004

Cover photo from the State Historical Society of North Dakota, item #0164-25.

The development of this text was supported in part by the North Dakota Center for Persons with Disabilities (NDCPD), a University Center of Excellence at Minot State University, Minot, ND. The opinions expressed here are those of the author and do not necessarily reflect the opinions or policy of the NDCPD or Minot State University.

Copies of this book may be obtained through
North Dakota Center for Persons with Disabilities
500 University Avenue West
Minot, ND 58703
701/858-3580

Published by
North American Heritage Press
P.O. Box 1
Minot, ND 58703
701/852-5559

Dr. Kolstoe

*Hope you enjoy
this bit of ND
special education
history!*

Brent A. Askvig

Thank You!!

Obviously no book is the work of a single individual. This work was no exception. Many people helped in the development, design, production and completion of the book. I am thankful to all that are listed here. Hopefully I've not forgotten anyone!

Ana Novosel, an MSU graduate student, assisted me greatly in the development of this book. Ana provided a great sounding board for the initial outlines and drafts of early chapters of this book. She was also a wonderful set of eyes and ears on her first visit to Grafton in January, 2003. Ana's great library skills were invaluable in putting together the chronology of the laws related to the institution. Also, Ana found nearly all of the biennial reports upon which the book is based.

Terri Senger and Gina Fradette, also MSU graduate students, gave up nearly two weeks of study time to pull together the last pieces of the North Dakota laws. Your help in compiling the appendix of laws on the institution is much appreciated.

Bryce Fifield, Executive Director of the ND Center for Persons with Disabilities, was always supportive of my work on this book. His encouragement, insight, and thoughtful editing were always helpful in getting the job done.

I want to thank Mike Williams for his time and materials. On a snowy, cold January morning, Mike graciously gave access to his materials from the ARC lawsuit. In addition he spent over two hours talking about the history behind the class action lawsuit. I learned so much. Thanks Mike!

Thank you to my colleagues at the ND Center for Persons with Disabilities. You endured my weekly reports and findings during the writing of the book. Thanks!

Thanks so much to Phyllis Butler, Susan Anderson, and Renee Olson for covering for me when the deadlines came, and other work began piling up. I could not have done this without your help! Also Susan was extremely helpful in printing the photographs from my digital archives.

To all of my colleagues, friends and acquaintances with disabilities and their families, current and past, thank you. I have learned so much over the years about the resiliency of people. This book reinforces that, and hopefully we are all better for it.

To the staff members of the State Historical Society of North Dakota, Sharon Silengo, Photo Archivist, and Larissa Harrison, Archives Specialist. Sharon helped so much in obtaining the digital photos or archived materials. Larissa made sure that the materials were always available and organized, even when I gave very little notice. Thanks!

Thanks to Sue Foerster, Ken Weisen and Paul Kolstoe of the ND Developmental Center. Your openness and time spent with me was invaluable. Sue was so supportive of the idea of the book. Paul encouraged me as if I was writing another dissertation, and frankly it felt like that at times. And Ken was such a help with additional archival materials from the Developmental Center files. I'm forever thankful to each of you for your hospitality and gracious support of this book.

To my friend and colleague, Neil Scharpe. Thanks for the forward to the book, and thanks for your interest and enthusiasm in this endeavor. Over the year I have immensely enjoyed our discussions about the politics and delivery of services for people with disabilities. Your dedication to persons with disabilities is truly admirable.

Thanks to my parents for instilling me with the desire to learn and to do the best job possible. It was quite a struggle at times, especially when the short-cut would save time and headaches. However, I always knew you'd want me to do the best job possible. I hope I have.

To my sons, Josh and Ethen, thank you also. You have both grown into great young men and I am a very proud father. You two have shown me the resiliency of children and young adults. And if you saw that blank stare on my face and ever wondered what I was thinking about all those evenings, this is it!

Finally, to my wife Stacy, thanks! Thank you for being such a good friend and life partner. Thanks for putting up with the barking dogs while I was too busy to feed them, with the messy den at home, with the endless ranting of "here's another new thing I found out", and the evenings and weekends you spent alone while I worked on the book. Your support and encouragement was a lifesaver.

This book is dedicated to Ron Archer, teacher and mentor.

Table of Contents

Thank You ii

Table of Contents..iv

Foreword...v

Introduction..1

A Historical Chronology of the ND Developmental Center.......................................6

The People 53

The Institutional Landscape: Buildings and Facilities...69

Education and Training..80

Laws and Legislation of the Institution...91

The Institutional Farm...102

Science and Research at the Institution..109

Appendix A – Site Plan of the ND Developmental Center 122

Appendix B - Photographs...124

Appendix C – State Laws on the ND Developmental Center..................................133

References..175

Foreword

Most states in the union have one or more "institutions", designed to serve an identified population with similar needs. Everyone, at one point in their life or another, deals with an institution. For most of us, it is confined to a school or an educational institution. My first experience with a state institution was a visit to the School for the Deaf in Faribault, Minnesota in the early 70's. It was a short visit that propelled me into a lifetime of service to people with disabilities.

In 1976, I spent the summer guiding high school students enrolled in the Youth Service Corps who had volunteered to work at Grafton State School and San Haven State Hospital. We spent four weeks living and working on the grounds of Grafton State School. Old Main was our home, and Wylie Hall, North A and B was where we spent our days. Working with high school students who saw this field of service/study as a rewarding career enhanced my own desire to finish my degree and contribute in a different manner.

It was while I was enrolled at Minot State University pursuing my master's degree in Special Education that I met Brent Askvig. We spent many hours discussing the service delivery system for people with disabilities. One of our instructors was Dr. Ronald Archer, a past superintendent at Grafton State School. During Dr. Archer's tenure at Grafton, the focus of treatment switched from a medical model to a behavioral and educational model. Dr. Archer gave us an interesting perspective on the evolution of the state facility.

Dr. Askvig's historical review of the North Dakota Developmental Center is a great tool. It allows us to look back on the ever-evolving service delivery system for people with disabilities. You will note that there are few qualitative judgments made throughout this review. Dr. Askvig is passionate about how services should be delivered, but has reserved those comments for another time.

For those who have had an interest in the North Dakota Developmental Center, you will find this historical perspective very enlightening. Dr. Askvig traces the expansion of services through buildings and programs. He notes changes in population, which denotes society's perception of how people with severe disabilities should be treated.

The study of historical information should be done to review what was done correctly and what could have been done differently or better. As you read this book, remember that decisions were made with the knowledge and resources at the time. The past twenty-five years have seen dramatic changes in how services are provided for people with severe disabilities. The institution continues to provide services, but with a completely different focus.

The future is always just over the horizon, and the look of that landscape will be designed by today's parents, professionals and by the people who are being served. As Dr. Askvig and I get together for coffee to discuss this picture, I hope in some small way we can assist in the positive evolution of services in North Dakota for people with severe disabilities. The history that Dr. Askvig prepared in this book will be very beneficial to future planning. Enjoy an interesting look at North Dakota history.

A friend and colleague,
Neil Scharpe, M.S. in Special Education

One Hundred Years

Chapter One

Introduction

This book *is not* about whether persons with mental retardation (or any other disability) should be institutionalized. Many people, with much better experiences and credentials than I, have made eloquent arguments for over 150 years on both sides of this issue. Rather, this is a historical chronology and review of one particular institution, the North Dakota Developmental Center (a.k.a., North Dakota Institution for the Feeble Minded, or Grafton State School).

Brief History of Institutions for Persons with Mental Retardation

Before describing why I went into depth chronicling one particular institution, it might be helpful to review the general history of institutions for persons with mental retardation. Richard Scheerenberger wrote perhaps the most complete history of services for persons with mental retardation in his 1983 book, *A History of Mental Retardation*. While the text focused on many aspects of the history, including influential people, historical and theoretical ideas, prevalence, and etiology, his documentation of the development and operation of various institutions is fascinating.

Residential facilities for persons with mental retardation are a relatively new phenomenon, having been around for only about 200 years. (Consider that hospitals and schools, for example, have been around for over 1,000 years.) However, the pre-cursors to institutions were begun in the 15th and 16th centuries. The Mansur Hospital in Cairo, Egypt used a Middle Eastern style of care for individuals with disabilities. This care included two nurses per resident, musicians to put patients to sleep, Koran reciters, and dancers, actors and storytellers for entertainment.

The Gheel (Belgium) Hospital provided a family style hospital for persons with mental or physical disabilities in 16th century Europe. Residents lived in homes with others and engaged in family activities such as gardening and baby-sitting.

In 1606, the king of France ordered that the Hotel Dieu in Paris care for persons with mental illness and mental retardation. Although priests and nuns provided the care, the over-crowding and unsanitary conditions made it a horrible place to live. In the mid 1600s the Bethlem Hospital in London England provided residential care. However the conditions were so terrible, and the use of chains, manacles and stocks so prevalent, the hospital became known as "Bedlum". A variation of this term now connotes chaotic horror.

The first public school for children was the Institution National des Sourds-Muets in Paris. Established in 1760, the school served those who were poor and those who were deaf. Charles Michel, l'abbe de L'Epee, the founder of the school was also a promoter of manual systems of communication (sign language) for deaf children.

The early 1800s saw a great reduction in the size and in the services provided by many European institutions for persons with mental retardation or mental illness. Although well intentioned, the staff were only able to provide stone floors, straw beds, and poor food to the residents. The prevalent thought at the time was that people with disabilities were incurable, and thus only required the basic necessities until their lives mercifully ended.

In 1842 Johann Guggenbuhl, a Swiss physician, opened Abendberg, the first residential facility exclusively for persons with mental retardation. In 1836, Guggenbuhl became interested in and extensively studied cretinism, a particular form of congenital retardation. Convinced he could cure cretinism with good care, clean air and education, he built the Abendberg institution in the Swiss mountains. Unfortunately Guggenbuhl's claims of cure were unfounded, the institution fell into disrepair, and Abendberg closed 25 years later.

Samuel Howe and Edouard Sequin started the Institution for Feeble-Minded Youth in Barre, Massachusetts in 1848. This was the first U.S. school for children with mental retardation, and the staff used Sequin's methods of sense and physiological training. Coupled with Howe's medical training and treatments, the Barre institution served as a model for most US institutions. By the late 1800s many smaller, family style institutions were replaced by larger facilities. Administrators who originally accepted only children began accepting adults, which resulted in over-crowding and more custodial treatments of the residents. Many used 'colony plans' which included a training school, and industrial, custodial and farm departments.

By 1900 there were 9,334 persons with mental retardation in residential programs in the U.S. Over the next 30 years that number would grow to 68,035. During this time, nearly every state-funded institution increased in size. The philosophy was protective paternalism – keeping individuals with disabilities comfortable, safe, and away from the general public.

From 1940 to the late 1960s the institutional resident populations continued to increase. By 1969 there were nearly 250,000 persons with mental retardation in state-run institutions. Most were large, medically oriented, custodial facilities. In rural states the institutions depended upon farming operations to support the limited state funding.

By the late 1960s family members, media, and activists began to speak out against institutionalization for persons with mental retardation. Since the early 60s federal legislation supported research for better services. Advocates began to use these research results and their legal and political influence to produce change. By 1985 nearly every state legislature or administration had dealt with a lawsuit or state law forcing greater community inclusion, or at least more comprehensive service systems, for all U.S. citizens with mental retardation.

In the next 15 years states saw a sometimes gradual, sometimes dramatic decrease in institutional services, and a mass exodus into community-based services. By 2002 nine state had completely eliminated state supported institutions for people with mental retardation, and another eight states had fewer than 200 individuals in institutions (Braddock, 2004). Presently, there are less than 45,000 people with mental retardation or developmental disabilities in state operated institutions across the U.S.

Why Write About the North Dakota Developmental Center?

I became interested in institutions and the ND Developmental Center as a 20-year-old college student at Minot State. In 1979, Dr. Ronald Archer was a professor of special education at Minot State College. As one of his students, I participated in a field trip to Grafton State School. Dr. Archer had just completed his tenure as superintendent of the institution and he wanted to make certain that his students in the mental retardation training program understood people with mental retardation, services for those individuals, and the institution in particular. Later, Ron would urge me to read through the state reports on the history and processes that had shaped the institution. His direction to those state reports was the impetus (and now the basis) for this book.

The institutional visit was a life-impacting event for me. I had a chance to travel through the campus tunnels, speak to the direct care workers and department heads of the institution, and walk around the campus grounds. I met many individuals with mental retardation in the institution, some who invited me to spend time with them or to eat lunch with them, and others who were occupied with self-abuse and self-stimulation and paid absolutely no attention to me.

I was profoundly moved by what I call the "human factor" of the institution. For me the institution was about real humans, real people. There were interactions, emotions, movements, thoughts and lives. Staff, residents, administrators were all attempting to make human connections and establish humane conditions. Some of the human conditions and experiences were positive, and others were not. Without going into the specifics, suffice it to say that I was able to look past all the activity, lack of activity, bureaucracy, buildings, services, and staff to see the people. And they amazed me.

In subsequent years, first as a direct care staff member for persons with developmental disabilities, and later as a public school teacher, and then university professor, I learned first-hand about institutions from people who lived and worked there. And the stories were fascinating. Here was a place where dreams were dreamed, and lives changed, both positively and negatively. But it was the lives, the lived human experiences that moved me. And I wanted to know more about them.

Over the years, lawyers, reporters, court observers, and public and private agencies have written and reported about the ND institution, and what has and has not happened to people with developmental disabilities. These stories were all very moving; yet they were often used to forward a particular social, political, or legal point of view. Certainly these were necessary, or at least thought to be necessary for achieving those specific outcomes, but I don't think they really told the whole story. Instead, I chose to take a different viewpoint of the institution, one that is directed neither toward a positive and optimistic stance, nor one that is meant to attack the people, the systems or the politics of institutions. Rather, this book is about the history of a place and of people. I believe it is a story that can teach us much about what we have been, what we have done, and where we may need to go in the future.

History is a powerful teacher. Historians take the approach that, with proper documentation, we might more clearly understand past events, past lives, and perhaps even future events. Examining what has happened also gives us insight into our future work and ourselves.

I have tried to take this historical perspective in writing this book. The book is primarily based on previously written documents. Most documents are historical works in themselves. Much of the detail comes from published state reports on the institution, while other information comes from the ND Century Code and the published Laws of North Dakota. Still other information comes from the ND State archives, institutional newsletters and documents, and newspaper clippings. Thus, it has been an attempt to construct the history from what is published, rather than oral histories, interviews, and the like.

A Comment on Terminology and Services

One may notice the variations in language and terminology used throughout the book. In many cases I have used the terminology of the time, particularly in the quotations from the various documents. While my comments are generally in the typical person-first language commonly used today, the use of older, non-traditional terminology in not meant to be demeaning or derogatory. Rather it is used to give a flavor of the approaches and perspectives of the laymen and professionals of the time. The terminology patterns and changes in themselves are educational.

Likewise, one may find that the education and training practices described here are archaic, out-dated, or even barbaric. Please remember that in most instances these methods were often viewed as exemplary, state-of-the-art procedures in their times. In very few instances did I find definitive evidence that institutional staff, administrators, or elected officials used procedures specifically to harm persons with mental retardation. Most often they were doing the best that they knew how.

Overview of this Book

This book contains eight chapters each designed to describe a particular feature of the ND Developmental Center. After this introduction the second chapter provides a chronology and history of the institution. The origin of the institution is described, and then an era by era portrait of the institution is presented. I have labeled the eras based on my interpretations of the documents of these time periods. Obviously these interpretations are based on my knowledge of general history of the state and on the specific history of mental retardation services. To the extent that my knowledge may be limited in these areas, these interpretations may or may not be accurate representations of actual events. If mistakes are made, they are wholly mine.

Chapter three presents a picture of the people in the institution. Here I discuss the various institutional superintendents and their contributions, the other institutional employees, and the residents. In each case a view of their typical duties and schedules is presented to give the reader an overview of what life was like at the institution.

Chapter four describes the buildings and facilities of the institution. Much of the early work was centered on the construction, repair, and re-organization of buildings and space to serve persons with developmental disabilities. The records show the superintendents' continual pleas for more and better facilities. Later, the state acquired the tuberculosis sanatorium at San Haven to serve individuals with more significant disabilities due to over-crowding, limited space and lack of services at Grafton. Finally, the current facilities are examined and compared to those with the initial buildings and grounds, and the changing purposes of the institution.

Throughout it's history, the ND Developmental Center has provided educational, habilitative and rehabilitative services to people with DD. Chapter five describes many of the historical educational approaches, including farm work, Sloyd training, and the vast array of other academic and vocational programs. The curricula used in the early years is described, along with the models and philosophies used by institutional staff to teach persons with developmental disabilities to be productive, educated citizens.

The sixth chapter describes the laws and regulations that were promulgated to open and operate the institution. Readers will find this section particularly interesting and a nice reflection of the political and sociological views of people with developmental disabilities throughout the last 100 years.

The institutional farm was very important in the early operation of the institution. Chapter seven provides a brief picture of the farm and farming operations. Persons with developmental disabilities often provided the manpower to run the farm, which was essential for assuring that all persons, including staff, were provided necessary sustenance. In this section we also see that many of the early training efforts were linked to the farm operation.

The last chapter describes the scientific approaches and research programs implemented at the institution. Throughout the earliest years the staff relied upon a limited amount of research and writing on persons with disabilities to guide their work. Later, they implemented their own studies to help guide them in their work.

Various appendices are provided to assist the reader in further understanding the institution. Photographs, both current and historical, are presented to show the landscape of the institution. A map is provided to show the current facilities, and a listing of the various legislative actions for the institution is presented. A multitude of references is provided to guide the reader into further study of the institution.

There is no intention to demean persons with disabilities, staff, administrators, or general citizenry in this book. Rather one should view the narrative as a historical, interpretive picture of what has occurred in our state regarding the provision of institutional services to persons with developmental disabilities. Perhaps one can see the learning that has occurred during the past 100 years as we all became more cognizant of the support needs of persons with mental retardation.

Chapter Two

A Historical Chronology of the North Dakota Developmental Center

The Origin of the Institution in North Dakota

The story of the inception of the ND institution for persons with developmental disabilities is an interesting and unexpected one. In 1889, when the Dakota Territory was split into the states of North and South Dakota, the US Congress wanted to assure that each state had at least some equal share of the accumulated resources. At the time, South Dakota had the territorial federal penitentiary in Sioux Falls while there was no comparable facility in North Dakota. During the division of resources prior to statehood, Congress appropriated $30,000 for a penitentiary and land in North Dakota.

Over the next four years, as the new state government developed and defined itself, citizens nearly forgot about the new prison. However, in 1893, the state legislators realized that the prison was to be a state prison, not a federal facility. Since a state penitentiary had already been constructed in Bismarck and another was not needed at the time, legislators were uncertain as to what to do with the federal money and land near Grafton.

At about this same time, ND State Hospital for the Insane's Superintendent, Dr. Archibald, reported to the governor that there *"were one hundred twenty-five (125) feeble minded children in the State of teachable age"* (Sixth Biennial Report of the Institution for the Feeble Minded, 1914). Many of these individuals were in the general population at the State Hospital and the facility was becoming crowded. Archibald proposed that some method for serving these individuals be established, considering that such a method not include keeping the feeble-minded in Jamestown.

Authorizing the Institution

Recognizing the opportunity to serve those with mental retardation, and to provide an economic benefit to his home area, Senator J.C. Cashel from Walsh County proposed that the state build an institution for the feeble minded in Grafton. Thus, the state passed Senate Bill Number 186 in 1901 to build a facility on the western edge of Grafton.

However, the ND State constitution still contained a component requiring that the land and funds were to be dedicated to a penitentiary. Thus, the 1901 ND Legislature amended the state constitution by a concurrent resolution. The amendment was made to subdivision 8 of section 215 of the constitution, and read, *"...to include institution for feeble minded to be constructed on penitentiary site lands given to state and held by U.S. Secretary of the Interior"* (Laws of ND, 1901).

The 1901 ND Legislature then passed Chapter 36 of the Laws of ND and appropriated just over $31,000 for the development of the institution. Finally, S.B. #4, again sponsored by Cashel, was passed, establishing a Board of Trustees and outlining the purpose of the institution, *" For the relief and instruction of the feeble minded and for the care and custody of the epileptic and idiotic of the state..."* (Laws of ND, 1901).

The original Board of Trustees members were W.C. Treumann, President of the Board; G.J.E. Gray, Secretary of the Board; Grant S. Hager; W.J. Price; and B.T. Kraabel. The Board had at its disposal $31,516 for the planning and construction of the institution. These funds came from an original $30,000 disbursement from Congress. In 1891 the state purchased a forty-acre plat near Grafton for $3,000. This was originally designated as the spot for the federal penitentiary. Over the years, the remaining $27,000 increased through interest and the rental of the land, thus amounting to the $31,516 total available for the institution.

Constructing the Institution

In 1902, the Board hired an architectural firm, the Hancock Brothers of Fargo, to lay out the property and to design the institutional buildings. The original plans were to erect a structure that could accommodate 125 residents and staff. Nollman and Lewis were hired as the primary contractors for the buildings. Construction began in 1902, first with the sinking of an artesian well in June 1902, the sewer system installation in July and August, and then the site survey for the building site in late September 1902. Construction began in the late fall of 1902 and in December 1903, the Nollman and Lewis Company handed over the keys to the institution, officially opening the ND Institution for the Feeble Minded. The total cost of the construction was $28,638.04.

Over the next five months the institution prepared to receive it first residents. Dr. Louis D. Baldwin was hired as the first superintendent of the facility. Previously the assistant superintendent of the Hospital for the Insane in Jamestown, Dr. Baldwin began his duties with enthusiasm on December 16, 1903. He began by hiring staff, and then going to Minneapolis to order furniture and supplies.

Even though the building was constructed, there was much work to be done in preparation for receiving residents. Laundry equipment originally purchased in December 1903 did not arrive at the site until the middle of February 1904, and was not installed until the end of March 1904. The artesian well water was found to have too much sand and was too cold for use in the boiler. Thus, the boiler was outfitted with a feed water heater, a purifier, and an oil separator and filter.

The boiler house was not designed to store coal, and so to preserve the quality of the coal from deterioration by the elements, a small coal shed was built next to the boiler house. But perhaps the most pressing issue was the construction of an adequate sewer system. Originally, the sewer outlet for the main building discharged to the surface and emptied into a slough just a few hundred feet east of the main building. The stench was unbearable in the warmer days, and the system was generally unsanitary. Thus, in the spring of 1904 a cesspool was built near the sewer outlet to allow the trapping of solids and a more manageable flow of institutional waste. While it was better than the old surface method, the sewage system would continue to be an issue for the next several years.

Opening its Doors

On May 2nd of 1904 the ND Institution for the Feeble Minded (NDIFM) received its first residents. While the original patient record ledger does not contain their names, only six young men and women were admitted that day. More people gradually entered the doors throughout the first few months. The first recorded entry in the patient ledger was John, an 8 old year old boy labeled mentally deficient due to measles who arrived on May 4th. Ruth, a five-year-old girl who had contracted cerebro-spinal meningitis was admitted on May 11. By order of Governor John White, 27 men and women from the School for the Insane in Jamestown were transferred to Grafton on May 28, 1904. These included Samuel, age 24; Milbert (age unknown); John (38); Anna (age unknown); Margaret (51); Mary (43); Gunild (31); Maria (age unknown); Marion (32); Cora (37); Agnes (39); Isabel (53); Philipina (age unknown); Kristie (35); and Annie (28). One of the last to be admitted that day was Zilla, a 26-year-old young woman who was diagnosed as feeble minded due to congenital causes. Zilla had spent quite some time in Jamestown, and from the day of her admittance on May 28, 1904 lived at the institution until her death in 1961 at the age of 83. In his first report to the Board of Trustees and to the Governor, Dr. Baldwin reported that between May 2nd and November 1st of 1904, 75 individuals had been admitted to the institution. In the first six months the institution was already reaching the limits of its resident capacity.

First Years of Operation: 1904 - 1910

During its first six years, the NDIFM established standard operating procedures and went through a period of general organization. It was also a growth period for the superintendent and for the state itself. Prior to the opening of the institution, individuals with mental retardation were either served by their families or were placed in hospitals (if they had medical complications) or in the Hospital for the Insane in Jamestown. According to the standards of the time, the institution was to be a model for the citizens of North Dakota.

The Board of Trustees, appointed by the governor, hired Dr. Louis Baldwin on December 16, 1903 as the first superintendent. His job was to organize the institution for its inaugural opening. The first six residents were admitted when the institution opened on May 2, 1904. With a few staff and residents, the ND Institution for Feeble Minded was operational.

A specialized training program was begun on September 1, 1904. Miss Alice B. Scott was hired as the first teacher. Previously the principal of the Indiana School for Feeble Minded Youth, Miss Scott started the first classes for the residents. She started with 26 children in a 'kindergarten' type program, and gradually moved to 30 by November 1904. Dr. Baldwin described the purpose of this training program as follows, *"the aim is to so train and develop him, that his life in the institution may be useful and that the greatest amount of happiness and comfort may be realized by him. The training therefore is of the most practical nature and is largely individual, being adapted to the possibilities of each case"* (First Biennial Report, 1904, p. 10).

Throughout the first six years, the institution and physical plant changed. Along with the original Main building, boiler house and smokestack, other buildings took shape. In 1908 the west wing of the Main building was constructed. Also the powerhouse and smoke stack were added that same year. In 1910 the first hospital (later called Midway) was constructed. This was primarily done to assure that many of the infectious diseases of the residents were more effectively confined. Disease and death were a problem in the institution. In the first six years, 78 deaths occurred at the institution, mostly due to highly contagious pulmonary tuberculosis.

Dr. Baldwin was superintendent until 1907 when he resigned and was replaced by Dr. H.A. LaMoure. Dr. LaMoure was instrumental in making improvements in several areas, and pressed for changes in some of the state laws regulating the institution. First, he asked for equipment and funds to introduce Sloyd work into the training program. Sloyd was a type of manual training originally designed in Sweden, and used by rural Swedish farmers during the long cold winters. Sloyd work focused on the use of manual craftwork such as basketry, weaving, network, and woodwork to improve eye hand coordination while building useful and profitable items.

Second, Dr. LaMoure recommended allowing wages be paid to the residents who worked on the farm. While not an expensive proposition, he rationalized that the wages would be a reward and further incentive for the hard work they displayed in support of the institution. This was clearly in direct support of Baldwin's idea of useful work for the residents. Finally, LaMoure worked hard to improve the condition of the institution through the development of the farming operations. He continually pressed for better housing for the farm workers, more and larger farm buildings for the cattle and horses, and more and better equipment for the farm.

LaMoure was also quite the marketer. His biennial reports were the first to include photographs of the buildings and the residents at Grafton. In 1908 he hosted Governor Burke on a visit of the institution, and later held many open houses and tours, often hosting over 100 persons on the campus each month. While his message was generally the same as Baldwin's (protect society from these incurable idiots), he used his reports, the state legislature, and his community interactions to continue developing the institution and promoting its cause.

1910 – 1920: Standardization to Consolidation

Two distinctly different periods, early growth and standardization, and then consolidation marked the first full decade of the institution's operation. From 1910 to about 1916, the institution population expanded greatly. By 1910, the institution was already at capacity. Initially built to house 100 to 125 residents, the June 30, 1910 report showed 165 individuals on the record. Even though the hospital had been in service since February 1910, it did little to alleviate the overcrowding at Grafton. Taking up where his predecessors had left off, Dr. A.R.T. Wylie began his tenure as superintendent in December 1910 requesting additional buildings, particularly for housing the residents.

Growth and standardization. By June 1916, the population had grown to 260. The male residents were now housed in the new Dormitory A, later known as North A. Completed in 1911, this building was state of the art for its time. Dr. Wylie noted particularly that the building would be a much safer residence that the Main building, primarily because North A was a brick structure with reinforced concrete floors and roof and iron stairways. Dr. Wylie believed it was safer in another respect also. He saw the separation of male and female residents as a necessary feature of the institution. He said of North A, "*It is the intention to use this building for the boys, leaving the Main Building for the use of the girls. In thus separating the sexes we can not only add much to their comfort, but also add much to the ease of caring for them*" (Fifth Biennial Report, 1912, p. 159).

This early period was characterized by several major changes in operations, procedures and oversight. In 1911 the state legislature dissolved the Board of Trustees and established the Board of Control of State Institutions. This board provided oversight to many institutions including the hospital for the insane, the state penitentiary, and the institution for the feeble-minded. While seen as a cost saving feature, the superintendents now had a less personal relationship with the governing and advisory bodies in charge of the institutions. This would prove to be both beneficial and detrimental.

The institution was instrumental in requiring all counties and schools conduct a census to determine the rate of feeble mindedness in the state. The first published instance of this census appears in the Fifth Biennial Report. Here Dr. Wylie showed that only fifteen counties conducted a census, and the results suggested that at least another 38 individuals had been identified as feeble minded. However, Wylie was concerned about the lack of reporting and suggested that, along with the 168 residents in Grafton and the 38 identified through the census, there were likely another 1,800 individuals in North Dakota who would need to be institutionalized. (Wylie used population estimation rates developed by researchers in the eastern United States and England to arrive at the overall estimated number of 2,000 *"persons in North Dakota eligible to the care and training of this institution"* (Fifth Biennial Report, 1912, p. 160).

Training and education for the residents expanded greatly during this time. The institutional staff began to use the new Binet-Simon tests of mental ability to classify residents. Then, using these classifications, those with greater abilities were provided education through the main divisions of the training department, either in primary classes, kindergarten classes, or in the manual training program. The teachers did not follow a prescribed curriculum but instead tried to individualize their programs for the students. They used dramatization and experiential learning activities in their lessons. By 1914, nearly 100 residents were receiving some education or training. Even though many could not make adequate progress in basic academic skills, the residents were still exposed to other training procedures. *"Those who are not able to benefit by the school work proper, are taught to care for themselves – drilled in their personal habits, then when they learn this, to care for other of their less fortunate comrades"* (Sixth Biennial Report, 1914, p. 396).

The residents were also involved in many other activities such as attendance at weekly dances, holiday celebrations, and the circus, presentations by local community bands, and participation in plays. An important part of each week was the participation in weekly religious services. Sunday school was a regular occurrence, and local pastors and priests routinely provided church services or mass for the residents.

The fast paced growth during this time brought with it additional challenges for the staff. First, the legislature was somewhat reluctant to allocate funding each biennium for the institution. They had listened to the superintendents and other experts who maintained, that with proper farmland and operational management, the institution could be relatively self-supporting. However, the institution was not yet allowed to purchase large enough plots of land to produce the amount of foodstuffs needed to feed over 200 residents and staff. Thus the superintendent relied increasingly on individual or county assessments for placing residents at Grafton. Originally, the monthly fee for placing a resident at the institution was $12.00. However, by 1911 this amount was insufficient, and the legislature raised it to $15.00 per month. Unfortunately, both parents and guardians, and county governments were notoriously late or deficient in their payments.

The superintendent spent considerable time with the state and local governments attempting to collect the fees for the residents.

Along with the rapid increase in the number of residents was the rise in illness and disease. Each year there was a mortality rate of 10 to 15% of the total institutional population. This was brought about by such close confinement and interaction, both amongst the residents and the staff. While the new hospital helped somewhat with isolation and treatment of the ill, it still did not totally contain the spread of disease. This was evident in the April 1913 measles outbreak when 41 of the approximately 160 residents contracted the disease. Six of the residents died from measles. This, along with the nearly 90 total deaths from 1910 to 1916 created problems for the efficient operation of the institution.

Because of the rapid increase in numbers of residents and the need to be more efficient, along with the transfer of oversight to the Board of Control of State Institutions, Superintendent Wylie and his staff began to standardize operational procedures. First, they began to codify many of their processes. The Sixth Biennial Report of 1914 includes an addendum of rules and regulations, including fire regulations, purpose and structural organization of the institution, terms for admission and payment, duration of attendance, discipline, medical care, access and overview of education, and procedures for visitation. These regulations clearly show the standards of control that Dr. Wylie wanted to maintain. For example, while the parents were able to visit their children at Grafton, they were required to do so between 2:00pm and 5:00pm only on Monday, Wednesday or Friday. Parents were not allowed to give food or articles directly to the residents, but rather were required to drop them off at the main office. Also, the parents were directed to go through the superintendent for any matters dealing with the residents. "*All business matters should be transacted at the office and all letters concerning the children should be sent to the Superintendent*" (Sixth Biennial Report, 1914, p. 435).

Many regulations pertained to the staff. For example, staff were not allowed to interact with the parents or guardians of the residents. Wylie said, "*Employees are forbidden to correspond with relatives of inmates. This is important, and if observed, will prevent many misunderstandings.*" (Sixth Biennial Report, 1914, p. 435).

The fire regulations were particularly explicit and directed to the staff. The regulations implored them to maintain order for the safety of the children and of the institution. "*In case of fire keep cool – make no outcry. Do not create a panic. If you are a man stamp out a commencing fire, using any sort of woolen goods such as a blanket or throw the whole burning mass out of the nearest window. If you are a woman try to do the same only use great care not to allow the fabrics of your dress to ignite. ...Keep cool under the most direful circumstances. Keep cool – all that can be saved will be saved by keeping cool*" (Sixth Biennial Report, 1914, p. 431).

Along with the formal regulations for running the institution, the superintendent also pressed the state legislature for more direct control of certain institutional operations. Along with the previously mentioned increase of the monthly fee for care of the residents, Dr. Wylie also asked for, and received more changes in the laws regarding the institution. As early as 1913, the legislature, at Dr. Wyilie's request, passed a law banning the marriage of persons who were feeble minded. In addition, the state authorized sterilization. In 1917 the legislature changed the laws regarding commitment and discharge from Grafton. Now, no individual could be released from the institution without the superintendent's permission.

Consolidation. The latter part of this decade was marked by a consolidation of institutional operations. The superintendent had little success in gaining larger appropriations for the institution. By 1917 the United States was involved in World War I, and many national resources were directed to this effort. While the institutional population rose rapidly in the first five years of the decade, it remained nearly constant in the last five years. The total population in 1918 was 271, and in 1920 was 292, up only thirty people from 1916. The war had an impact on staff and administration as well. Dr. Wylie was involved in the Walsh County war board, and was the chair of the community Red Cross organization. Further, the war effort removed staff from the institution, as eight direct care staff members and countless community members went to war.

The daily education and training programs had become more standardized, and the biennial reports show detailed schedules of activities for the residents. However, staff hires were few, which resulted in fewer residents attending classes. Resident mortality was still high (e.g., 31 deaths from 1918 to 1920, a rate of over 10% of the resident population), as tuberculosis and pneumonia were still the major causes of death. The institution was able to obtain funding for a refectory (cooking and dining) building, but again the war made materials allocations difficult and delayed construction. A new x-ray machine was obtained for the hospital and it was helpful in diagnosing tuberculosis and pneumonia.

However, Dr. Wylie noted that the institution was still overcrowded and faced several major challenges in the years ahead. By 1920 requests for admissions had reached an all time high with nearly four or five requests each week. The cow barn had burned, and while it was replaced with labor furnished by the institution, the milk production and handling systems were inadequate, having been reviewed and condemned by the state inspector. The institution was still not connected to the Grafton city water system, the existing water boiler system was not sufficient for the needs of the institution, and staff wages and the prices of various products had risen to new highs, making the balancing of the books difficult. The next decade would be a difficult one without some intervention on the state level.

1920 – 1930: Paternalism and Protectionism

The Roaring Twenties was a time of paternalism and protectionism for the ND institution for the feeble-minded. Dr. Wylie began to write less about the operations of the institution and more about the education and training programs. He also began to use case studies to convey the message that more and more feeble-minded were likely present in the state, and those individuals were in need of the care and treatment that only the institution could provide. However, with the continual over-crowding, the institution was in need of new facilities. The superintendent frequently demonstrated that the paternalistic attitude was the correct attitude toward persons with mental retardation.

One example of the paternalism of the time was the superintendent's report of 1922. Dr. Wylie wrote about the lack of school and county compliance in getting an accurate census of feeble-minded persons in the state. Previously he had presented figures suggesting that there were about 2,000 feeble-minded people in the state. However, in this report he stated that there were likely 6,000 persons who would be potential residents of the institution. Using the statistics provided by Massachusetts, he said *"As a result of this investigation they have the names of 15,000 feeble-minded children in their public schools, or 45,000 feeble-minded in the whole population, which is practically one per cent. We have no reason to believe that the rates would be any different in North Dakota. So we can estimate the number of feeble minded in North Dakota at 6,000"* (Tenth Biennial Report, 1922, p. 2491). Later Wylie makes some adjustments to that number, or at least the number that might be reasonably housed at Grafton. In 1924 he wrote, *"From surveys and investigations that have been made it is now pretty generally agreed that the feeble-minded comprise one per cent of the population. This gives our state a feeble-minded population of 6,000. According to the experience of the states that have been longer in the work of caring for their feeble-minded, there never will be a demand for institutionalizing this whole number. But there is a demand for institutionalizing ten per cent of this population. Since this institution has to care for both the feeble-minded and epileptics plans should be made to enlarge this Institution to care for 1,000 inmates"* (Eleventh Biennial Report, 1924, p. 2116).

During this decade, Dr. Wylie made several attempts to assure that legislators and the general public received the message of the dangers of feeble-minded people. In two different reports he spoke particularly of the need for institutionalization and care of women with mental retardation. In 1922 Dr. Wylie asked for additional funds for another dormitory for female residents. Here he wrote, *"The demand for the admission of girls is particularly urgent. And when we call to mind the fact that the feeble-minded women out in the world is the great source of illegitimacy, delinquency and mental defect, this urgency should be especially recognized and additional room be made for them here"* (Tenth Biennial Report, 1922, p. 2496).

Two years later his message was nearly identical. *"We have been able to care for the boys on account of our increased accommodations, but not for the girls. We have thirty-seven girls on the waiting list now – nearly all low grade cases. Some of these have been waiting as long as five years for admission. Many of them are of a most urgent character, and although we have kept our girls' side crowded we have been unable to furnish relief. Feeble-minded women out in the world are the source of illegitimacy, delinquency and mental defect"* (Eleventh Biennial Report, 1924, p. 2121).

Dr. Wylie tried to personalize the impact of the institutional experience for state leaders. He frequently used case stories to emphasize his points. Three are particularly relevant here. In the 1922 report, he spoke of the benefits of the training program at Grafton. He used the stories of Metro and Ottne to illustrate this. Metro's story is repeated here.

The Improvement of Metro

"Four years ago this little boy with his two brothers and mother came to us from the children's Home at Fargo. Nothing of interest seems to be known concerning the father except his name. Mentally he was probably mediocre and socially the scum of the earth.

Metro with his blue eyes, light hair and rather pitiful face soon won a place for himself in the hearts of the teachers and attendants. From the teacher's test at entry we learned he could help himself; speech imperfect; voice thick; memory fair; attention poor; sight and hearing good; nervous; could throw a ball; habits good; obstinate. He had received absolutely no school work so was entered in the kindergarten class. Here he soon learned to match colors and form, string beads, cut paper by lines, weave first over one, under one and by the end of the first year was able to do the hardest weaving problem, cut a design of his own, paste it, and sew the most difficult card. He had learned the value of numbers to twenty and could count and write numbers to one hundred. He became good in sense work and especially good in games.

At the beginning of his second school year he was promoted to the Primary class. Here he began regular grade work. Was given careful drill in phonics as well as writing and number work. He at first scribbled on black board and paper, bit the points off his pencils and was careless, but gradually learned to be more quiet, keep his seat and grew quite exact about his writing, drawing and hand work. During this year he completed the first grade work, developed quite an imagination and became a good errand boy. He was given training in the net and basket classes; became very accurate and independent about the net work and could make a hammock and laundry bag from start to finish. He learned the lazy squaw stitch but could not shape a raffia basket very well. He liked to be busy and was willing to work at one thing until it was finished.

During the third and fourth years he has improved steadily. He is now doing third grade work. He reads quite well in the third reader and recognizes more words, but it is hard for him to get expression. He talks a great deal. His speech is much improved and his voice is clearer and more musical. The "th" sounds are still difficult for him. He writes very well and can compose and write a fairly good letter. Now he knows the value of numbers and can do easy work in addition, subtraction, and multiplication. Last year he went to the physical culture, basketry, net and manual training classes. In the manual training class he at first did brush work. He learned to make polishing, vegetable and scrub brushes and now makes a perfect brush. The brush work became monotonous for him and he wanted to make things in wood. So he was taught the use and care of tools. He can now lay out his own work having learned measurements very quickly. He has also learned how to square up wood. He made ten toys, several kites, and a birdhouse. As metro grows older, he will make a good wood worker because he is accurate and careful. He improved a great deal in basketry, learned the "figure eight" stitch, keeps a design straight now and shapes a basket very well. He has a real boys aversion to sewing carpet rages, but sewed faithfully as his teacher urged him one afternoon each week. He has learned to tell time, is active, has a good sense of rhythm and dances nicely. For one year he has had fifteen minutes in class practice with the band teacher. He showed some much skill and application that he was given work on a cornet. His tones are quite pure. His range for both reading and playing is from middle C to high F. He knows the value of every kind of note and promises to become a good cornet player.

Metro has an enormous appetite, especially for potatoes and we have not been able to teach him even a semblance of table manners. He is so anxious to satisfy his appetite that he simply forgets everybody else and crams. He makes a good bed, can polish and scrub floors, sew on buttons, and helps take care of the crippled children in his class. At times he becomes boisterous but is easily disciplined. He is truthful, generally obedient and usually kind and thoughtful with new boys. A recent Binet test place Metro 8-5. This shows an advancement of 3-1" (Tenth Biennial Report, 1922, p. 2493-2494).

Dr. Wylie's story of Ottne carried the same message. If you place feeble-minded children at the institution in Grafton, the staff will perform an important duty for the state, and take care of these individuals. In the end, the resident's lives will be better.

His third story, told in his 1928 report, conveys the same message, but through the failure of the system to control a young woman named Barbara. Wylie's story tells of a sixteen year old girl who entered the institution from a poor home background. After making progress through training and education at Grafton, she was released, against the judgment of the superintendent, to her parents who promptly married her to a local farm hand. One year later she was divorced, and then later remarried, having four children with the second husband.

Wylie described how the children were poorly cared for, and how they were having trouble in school. To end the story he said, *"From all appearances there is little hope that any of Barbara's children will develop normally. The city will eventually have to support the family. The moral to the story is plain"* (Thirteenth Biennial Report, 1928, p. 1322-1323). The stories helped reinforce the message that institutionalization was important in saving the person with feeble-mindedness from harm, and perhaps more importantly, saving society from the ills of those who were feeble minded.

Health protection. The institution struggled to provide appropriate health care for the residents during the 1920s. There were several major and minor epidemics during this time. In 1922 there was a scarlet fever outbreak. Thirty-two residents came down with the fever, and one died as a result. In the fall of 1923 there was a measles epidemic at the institution with 78 residents contracting the disease and six deaths occurring from the illness. The fall of 1925 saw a German measles outbreak with 31 cases and no deaths. This was followed by a minor chicken pox contagion with 18 cases and no deaths. In the fall of 1929 there was another chicken pox outbreak with 33 residents contracting the disease. In the spring of 1930 thirteen residents came down with whooping cough. There were no deaths in these later epidemics.

However, this was still a deadly decade for residents of the institution. There were 180 deaths on the campus at Grafton. The most frequent cause of death related to upper respiratory infections or diseases, with tuberculosis accounting for 51 deaths. The institutional staff were gravely concerned about these numbers and sought more effective ways to protect the residents. The superintendent frequently asked for a new hospital and better housing for the residents. Medical staff were at a premium after the war, yet there was always at least one or two other physicians on staff, along with the superintendent who was a medical doctor. In addition the institution obtained its own x-ray equipment to diagnose upper respiratory illness and disease, and to more carefully monitor patient progress. Finally, in 1925 all institutional residents were vaccinated to protect from the spread of some of the more common and deadly contagious diseases.

Reliance on classification. During the 1920s the institutional staff increasingly used the Binet-Simon tests to diagnose and classify residents upon admission to the institution. All of the superintendent's reports during this time contain numerous tables showing the mental ages of the residents, classified according to age, mental age, nationality, county of birth, and even the type of manual training or hand work demonstrated by residents with various mental ages.

Protection through education. The reports of the 1920s show increasing attention to education and manual training at the institution. Each report contains narrative explaining the types of education and training activities afforded the residents. The 1930 report contains several actual lesson plans used by the teachers. The following is a lesson plan used in a custodial classification classroom.

Lesson Plans – Custodial
May 19 – 23, 1930
Subject: The Horse

Aim: To teach value of the horse and as a motive for interest in daily work.
General talk about horses on Monday morning – where horses live, their uses, their feed, etc.
Show pictures of horses and have children make short sentences about pictures.
Memorize, "the Little Gray Ponies."
Word Drill: Unfamiliar words taken from reading lessons.
Reading: Read two stories about horses found in the Beacon Primer, pages 26 and 50. For review, write a short story on the board using some words as in the book, but different sentences.

Number work is correlated with games, languages and reading, which consists of counting. Count the number of times the same word occurs in the lesson. Let children take turns about counting the number of ponies to go in the circle.
Rhythms: Let children make believe they are horse and let them run and jump, which they can do. Teach them to gallop to the music of "Away Go the Ponies."
Games: "the Little Gray Ponies." This is a singing game with the language and rhythms as a base.
Handwork: Cut out pictures of horses. Color horses. Trace around cardboard silhouettes and color and cut out. (From the Principal's report, Fourteenth Biennial Report, 1930, p. 2952-2953).

Two final instances show the paternalistic and protectionist approach of the institution in the 1920s. First was the hiring of a social worker who established a program of mental hygiene and community service. In 1929 the institution hosted a six-week summer training session for teachers of children with mental deficiency. One result of this training was the establishment of traveling clinics. Institutional staff went to Jamestown, Wahpeton, Mandan and Bismarck with their Mental Hygiene Clinic. These clinics were one to two day sessions with school staff, physicians, psychologists, nurses, and local women's clubs designed to assess and identify persons who had mental retardation. Wylie reported, *"In all, 112 persons were examined. There was a high percentage of mental deficiency, some personality abnormalities and a number of medical cases. So the schools and social agencies of these cities were shown the mental and physical conditions of their retarded and problem cases and suggestions were given for handling them"* (Fourteenth Biennial Report, 1930, p. 2954). Clearly the institutional staff were attempting to demonstrate the numbers of those with mental retardation and the potential harm for the local communities.

The final example of the prevailing attitude of the time was the attempt at renaming the institution. During the 1920s decade, Dr. Wylie and his staff came under criticism for the title of "The Institution for Feeble Minded". The primary worry was that families and communities wouldn't send residents to the institution. Wylie said, *"The term feeble minded is resented by many of our inmates. Parents hesitate about sending their children to an institution with such a name. It is particularly antagonistic to the epileptics. On account of this, many institutions over the country have had their names changed to a less suggestive one. In conformity with this, I suggest that the name be changed to Grafton State Village"* (Fourteenth Biennial Report, 1930, p. 2954).

1930 – 1940: Era of Social Control

The decade from 1930 to 1940 can easily be characterized as one of social control. While the early part of the decade in North Dakota was spent in overcoming the results of the depression and drought, the latter part of the decade was spent in recovery from these conditions. Wylie successor, Dr. John Lamont, characterized the work of the institution in this manner in the forward to his first biennial report; *"The principles underlying the care of mental deficiency have to do with the amelioration of the burden of society, in a group who are crippled or helpless, and if possible to protect future generations from an equal or greater burden; also, humane treatment and future happiness of the children themselves is a prime consideration"* (Nineteenth Biennial Report, 1940, p. 1215).

Population and health. In July of 1930 the institution had 625 residents. By June 1940 there were 970 residents enrolled at Grafton. There were 219 deaths during this decade, again, most caused by infectious diseases such as pneumonia or tuberculosis. The first Grafton resident was transferred to San Haven in 1938 for treatment of severe tuberculosis, and to prevent a widespread outbreak at the institution.

In 1931 and 1932 there were two major epidemics. First was the mumps contagion during the fall and winter of 1931-32. One hundred seventy two residents contracted the disease. Then there was the influenza outbreak in the winter of 1931-32 that affected over 150 residents. The 1932 – 1934 biennium had numerous other residents who contracted infectious diseases, with 412 getting influenza, 45 contracting chicken pox, and 49 getting scarlet fever. No one died from these diseases.

Institutional staff continually begged for newer hospital facilities even as they added staff and services. Dr. Frank Deason, the institutional superintendent in 1938, reported on the overcrowding of the facilities, particularly the hospital. He was concerned that if epidemics similar to those in the early 1930s occurred again, there would be no place to house the ill. In 1939 the institution added a one half time registered pharmacist to the staff. While a pharmacy existed since the construction of the hospital in 1909, there was no regular registered pharmacist to prepare the medications or manage the office and inventory. The physicians or nursing staff had generally handled this duty. With the addition of the pharmacist, new medications were tested on the residents, and the physicians were more able to administer medical care to the residents.

The residents also needed dental care, and prior to 1930 local dentists assisted part time as often as they could. During this decade, though, the institution had the full time services of Dr. R.W. Kibbee. He performed thousands of examinations and procedures each year, yet was able to only provide the most basic dental services due to lack of space and appropriate equipment.

By 1939 the institution hospital had a laboratory staffed by a medical technician. This allowed the physicians to run a variety of tests to assist in the diagnosis and treatment of residents. This new procedure, however, brought with it some new complications. The introduction of the Wasserman and Kahn tests at admission and during general population screenings resulted in the discovery of syphilis and gonorrhea in a number of the residents. This finding both sparked concern about the morality of the residents and further fueled the desire for more control over their behavior.

Eugenics comes alive at Grafton. Many vestiges of the eugenics movement came to fruition during the 1930s. A major force in shaping immigration in the early part of the century, the philosophy of eugenics was in full force at the institution during this decade. The eugenics approach was based upon Darwinist theories, that only those with good heredity and nobility of birth were worthy of procreation. In the 1920s the U.S. passed laws limiting immigrants from various countries or of various races for fear that the "unwanted" of those individuals would negatively affect the population. In the more severe cases, most states passed laws prohibiting marriage of individuals with various disorders (e.g., alcoholism, delinquency, mental deficiency). In some cases, these individuals were sterilized.

Most of this push for eugenics came through the work of the newly created social service department at the institution. In September 1929 Dr. Wylie created the Social Service Department. This department was headed by a social worker and given a number of major tasks and initiatives. These included home visits, community education, disposition of referrals, and the supervision of paroled and discharged residents. Partly as an outgrowth of his involvement with the North Dakota mental hygiene survey of the early 1920s (National Committee for Mental Hygiene, Inc., 1923), Dr. Wylie sought to establish a firm understanding of the nature of mental deficiency, and how that impacted the operation and growth of an institution.

The two heads of the social services departments in the 1930s, Henrietta Safley, and Evelyn Johnston, promoted a eugenics approach toward those with mental deficiency. In the early 1930s Safley conducted a number of quasi research studies to examine the heredity of individuals admitted to the institution. These studies examined the family history and outcomes of residents. One important study was a follow-up of 71 residents who had been sterilized. She concluded that most residents came from defective parents, and that, without sterilization, they were likely to produce others with mental deficiency.

Based on these results, Safley became an ardent promoter of sterilization in the institution. She was concerned that many people around the state misinterpreted sterilization. She reported, "*Eugenic sterilization to inhibit the fecundity of our mental defective implies neither a stigma or disgrace nor a punishment, but provides a protection to men and women seriously defective that they should not bear or rear children. The operation for eugenic sterilization merely involves the severing of the tubes through which germ-cells must pass if conception is to take place. No organs or tissues are removed, no physical changes result and the individual is not unsexed. Many opponents of sterilization use this last point as their principal argument against the act, saying that as long as the individual remains unsexed, and no longer fears conception, he is apt to become promiscuous. In our limited experience, we find only one of our sterilized patients taking advantage of her condition*" (Fifteenth and Sixteenth Annual Reports of the Board of Administration, 1934, p. 603).

Prior to 1932, only 16 residents had been sterilized, a procedure allowed by ND laws passed in 1913 and again in 1927. However, from March 1932 through June 1934 an additional 55 residents were sterilized. After publication of Safley's study and her comments in 1934, sterilization became a common procedure. By June 1940 Superintendent John Lamont reported that 478 residents had been sterilized, all in line with the justification of protection of the individual and protection of society. His 1940 report is relevant on this point. *"It should be evident that the lessening of the future load in Mental Deficiency may be promoted effectively by a common-sense control of propagation. The argument that Mongolism and other forms may be found in good families, and that successful men and women frequently come from obscure families, does not affect the law of averages. It is unalterably true that defective genes and chromosomes most often occur in defectives, and that nature compensates in number for defects in type. A farmer must prevent weed-propagation and low-grade stock or lose his farm. Sterilization is performed under the laws of most States"* (Nineteenth Biennial Report, 1940, p. 1221).

The social service department staff made numerous trips around the state promoting the institution. They held local clinics, offered community presentations, and met with physicians, nurses, and community leaders in an effort to teach them about the benefits of segregation and isolation at the institution. Their message was clear; *"Officials have been told conditions under which custodial cases should be removed from the home, and where it is not particularly beneficial. Again, the point has been stressed, that if a child is being committed to the Institution purely for educational purposes, he should be sent before he becomes too old; that earlier commitment gives him an opportunity to receive the amount of education he is capable of acquiring, and to develop a more desirable behavior pattern, thus making it more possible to later return him to the home."* Further they stated, *"Emphasis has been laid on the importance of the community officials learning to recognize the presence of the higher-grade feeble-minded person, who is all too frequently a problem to the parents, the community, and to himself, because he is not mentally capable of judging right from wrong, and thus unable to protect or control himself. This case generally has the mentality of an eight to twelve-year old child. Among them are found our discipline problems, bootleggers, children guilty of petty larceny, and, especially our sex delinquents and unmarried mothers."* (Fifteenth Biennial Report, 1932, p. 3996).

Other examples of eugenic activity at Grafton included numerous requests for additional space to facilitate segregation of the various classes of individuals, particularly those with epilepsy. The staff also provided a financial analysis of the impact of the feeble minded on the state. They calculated that from January 1, 1922 to January 1, 1934 the various state counties had paid over $1,000,000, and the state legislature had appropriated over $300,000 for the care and protection of residents at Grafton. However, many counties were arrears on their payments, especially those with large numbers of residents at the institution. They were concerned that, without proper understanding of the need for payment and support of Grafton, the county officials would soon be faced with more persons with mental deficiency. *"Counties that are paying out the least for the care of their feeble-minded are not yet alert to the seriousness of allowing certain mental defectives to procreate in the community. In future years, they are going to have offspring from these individuals to provide for instead of the one person they now have"* (Fifteenth and Sixteenth Annual Reports of the Board of Administration, 1934, p. 601).

In 1940 Dr. Lamont proposed a Central Registry of Mental Defectives and of the Insane. At the time he was frustrated that the law prohibiting marriage of persons who were mentally retarded were insufficiently enforced. The registry would be a card index of records on all those individuals in the state who had been identified as mentally deficient. Similar to other states with the registry and with marriage prohibition, North Dakota could then track those individuals once they left the institution, or once they had been identified in their home communities. He was certain that such an extreme measure was necessary, even as he considered something even more extreme. *"Until we approach our problems of Mental Deficiency and the psychoses upon a similar well-coordinated plan, the load of custodial patients will undoubtedly increase. Euthanasia is not a proper answer to human misfortune. Well-considered sterilization in the male and female of certain types may be a half-answer, and a tightening up of the laws governing marriage as applied to morons, epileptics and the mentally unstable would definitely help"* ((Nineteenth Biennial Report, 1940, p. 1217).

Hardships of the decade. The institution faced many difficulties during this ten-year period that mirrored those faced by the general population. The depression and drought had significant impacts on Grafton. The depression and the community recruiting efforts of the social service department brought about a large increase in referrals and admissions at the institution. Increasingly, families were having difficulty supporting children at home, especially those with learning and behavior problems. Thus, Grafton was a frequent option to relieve the family burden.

The depression made counties hard-pressed to pay their obligations to the institution for housing their residents. Although required to pay $15.00 per month for each institutional resident from their county, many county boards refused to pay the fee. By 1940 the total county indebtedness to the institution exceeded $70,000. Without an appropriate collection mechanism, the institution was unable to collect their fees.

The state government forced many cost-cutting measures on the institution. In the early 1930s the institution cut staff salaries by a full 20% across the board. These reductions were never recovered during this decade. Also, the governor's office asked all state agencies and institutions to cut other operational costs. Grafton State School cut some of its costs by using Works Progress Administration (WPA) funds and workers to complete several campus projects, including a laundry building extension.

The drought further stressed the institution. The farm operations significantly supported the welfare of the residents by providing some work, but more importantly a major source of food stuffs. When the rains ceased and production declined, the superintendent was forced to purchase many items previously produced on the farm. This, coupled with the generally reduced supply of quality food and higher prices, was a hardship for Grafton.

Education and training during the 30s. Even though several building and major initiatives were put on hold during this decade, education for the residents continued. In fact, many of the superintendents' reports during this era focused almost entirely on the education and training programs for the residents. The reports contain many pages describing the various grades and classes in great detail. Most of the instruction and training changed very little. In fact, one principal described the education program as "a period of plodding with no great progress".

However of great pride to the principals and the superintendents was the music program. Each Friday morning teachers would have one of their classes perform for the other teachers and students. Much was made of the choral and orchestra programs. Started in the mid 1920s the institution's orchestra became quite accomplished. About 20 residents received four to six hours of orchestra and instrumental lessons each week. These residents then performed at institutional gatherings and for various community groups. Apparently many of the residents were quite accomplished as evidenced by the following excerpt of lesson descriptions.

Class C

1. *Melvin – Clarinet*
    C Scale, 2 Octaves
    Exercises in Key of C, using whole, half and quarter notes
2. *Margaret – Cello*
    Memorize and Play C Scale
    Exercises in Key of C, using whole and half notes
3. *Bessie N. – Violin*
    C Scale
    Exercises in Key of C, using whole, half and quarter notes
    Slurs

(Fifteenth Biennial Report, 1932, p. 3987)

The staff felt some success in their work also, as many individuals were "paroled" throughout the decade. A paroled resident was one who, while still formally enrolled in the institution, was placed in the community with his/her parents, with a foster family, or in some cases on his own. Nearly all females who were paroled were sterilized prior to release. While on parole, the residents had to work or continue school, and had to live exemplary lives. If there were no problems after one year, the resident was officially discharged from the institution. From July 1930 to June 1940, 219 residents were paroled, and the majority were successfully discharged.

1940 – 1950: Decade of Maintenance
The decade from 1940 to 1950 was one of maintenance of effort for the Grafton State School. World War II had a profound effect on the country and the state, and this was passed on to the institution. Materials were difficult to obtain, worker turnover was high, and the prices of goods and services rapidly increased after the war.

Residents. The institutional population changed very little over these ten years. On July 1, 1940, the resident population was 970 and by 1950 had reached only 1,091. Figure 1 shows the stability of the population during this decade. This is in contrast to the rapid growth of the 1930s. While the institution still had the social service department, funds were more restricted, which resulted in fewer social worker trips to the counties, fewer presentations to the public, and subsequently fewer referrals for admission.

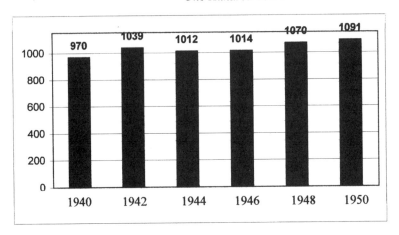

Figure 1: Resident Population in the 1940s

However, even though the referral rate had increased significantly, the institution had little space to house new residents. In fact, little construction occurred during the 1940s. Even when the state legislature did awarding funding for buildings, the war effort made access to most construction materials almost impossible, or put the expense so high that the building costs far exceeded available funds.

Staffing. Staff numbers remained nearly constant during this period. In 1940 there were 138 staff for the 970 residents, making a resident to staff ratio of about 7 to 1. In 1950 there were only 144 staff for the 1,091 residents, making the ratio about 7.6 to 1. (Actually the direct care staff to resident ratios were much higher, as the records show only 45 to 50 attendants, some day and some night staff, making the ratio closer to 25 or 30 to 1.) These high resident to staff ratios were a concern to the superintendent.

Staff turnover and staff pay were also major concerns. Qualified medical staff were difficult to obtain due to their need in the war. Frequently the institution hired physicians from Europe or from East Asia. Often these individuals were older, and as they neared retirement, resigned from the institution after less than one year of service. General staff turnover was high also. Many young men were inducted into the military and served overseas. Also several national employment programs were developed to support the war. On top of the difficulty in recruiting staff, the 20% salary reduction of the 1930s was still in effect. Dr. Lamont had this to say about staffing the institution: *"Larger salaries are offered under the Federal Government and among the rural farm population. During 1939 many people were entirely out of work and were glad to obtain institutional employment. In 1941 employees left, sometimes upon a moment's notice, to enter the army or accept increased salaries elsewhere. This situation can only be remedied by legislative action during the 1943 session. In the meantime it is difficult to say to what extent our institutions may be crippled..."* (Twentieth Biennial Report, 1942, p. 996).

At times institutional residents were paroled out to help on the local farms. In 1942 there were 20 residents working on farms. However, the care and supervision required by the farm families sometimes out-weighed the benefits derived from the extra help, and most residents were returned to the institution. During the 40s less than 20 individuals were paroled to farms for more than one year, upon which time they were discharged from Grafton.

Education and training. Educational programs were relatively stable during this period. Generally there were about 200 to 250 residents who attended educational or training programs each week. The school principal, Ms. Etta Hylden, frequently reported the general purpose of the Grafton education programs. She said, *"Our aims for happiness through education and industry, developing good living habits, a willing obedience and cooperation to the usual demands of the day, whether in the class room, ward or playground, are still uppermost in our endeavor."* (Twenty-Second Biennial Report, 1946, p. 1027).

Because of the large number of students and the few available teachers (usually about 8 teachers), some residents had half-day educational services throughout the week, while others had as little as 45 minutes for the entire week. Again, most of the training focused on basic academic skills, sense training, music, or manual (e.g., vocational) training. In 1949 the education department started a nursery school program, enrolling residents as young as two years old. Here they worked on stories and rhymes, finger plays, muscle coordination games, and puzzles and form boards.

On December 6, 1942 Boy Scout Troop number 23 was started at the institution. This was done partly in patriotic response to the war and partly in an effort for greater community contact. Reverend A.E. Smith served as the Scoutmaster of the 32 members, and Charles Tomson, the institution's pharmacist, F.T. Martell, the institution's horticulturist, and Dr. Lamont served as an advisory committee. The troop members attended club meetings in town, and were present for the opening of the Boy Scout cabin located on the Park River in Grafton.

Health. The health of the residents was fairly stable also. There were no major epidemics among the residents. Even so, the superintendent was concerned about an epidemic outbreak. The potential for large epidemics due to overcrowding of the wards and little space in the hospital loomed and a new hospital was needed. Superintendent Lamont stated *"Among building projects, the need for a new hospital becomes increasingly imperative. The presence of about 20 cases of open tuberculosis among the inmate population, the crowded condition of the side-rooms with new isolation cases, and our ever present lack of room for isolation of acute epidemic sickness, creates situations impossible to handle safely"* (Twentieth Biennial Report, 1942, pp. 1026-1027).

An institution-wide tuberculosis health survey was completed in 1941, and then repeated sporadically throughout the decade. This helped reduce a number of cases of contagious tuberculosis. Several residents were also transferred to San Haven in 1948. Still, 232 residents died during these ten years. The primary causes were upper respiratory infections like pneumonia or influenza, or tuberculosis. The medical staff completed 235 sterilizations, along with hundreds of other surgical procedures. By 1949, North Dakota was the second leading state in numbers of sterilizations per 100,000 citizens, second only to California.

The pharmacy department had a part time pharmacist who prepared not only the daily medications for the residents, but also the plant insecticides and bug sprays for the cattle. The part time dentist performed basic dental care for the residents, generally doing one to two thousand treatments each year. Some remodeling was done in the hospital building to provide for a mortuary in the basement.

Farming. The farming operations were hit hard with the high prices of machinery, the lack of good farm laborers, and the difficult growing conditions in the 1940s. There were several instances where low level flooding inundated gardens or cropland. Land rental costs doubled from $3.00 per acre in 1940 to $6.00 per acre in 1950. Although the institution owned 256 acres it still rented over 800 acres for crop and pasture land. By 1948 the institution was critically examining whether it should continue with the farming program. *"Potato raising has been unprofitable from water soaked land in later years. With a large state investment in farm machinery it seems best to continue farming for the main purpose of using surplus manpower furnished by older patients under the school training program"* (Twenty-Third Biennial Report, 1948, p. 1071).

Facilities. While there was little increase in population during the 1940s, the institution was still crowded. The superintendent lived in the Main building, and nearly one third of the staff lived on the upper floors of the ward buildings. Again, little construction occurred due to the war, although the WPA did assist with some remodeling, painting and general land work. An addition to the refectory was completed in 1949. The superintendent continually pressed for a new hospital, for separate superintendent quarters, and for a staff dormitory due to lack of housing in Grafton. After several plans and funding attempts, the state legislature approved funds for construction of the hospital that was completed in 1950.

1950 – 1960: Modernization

The 1950s was a time of modernization at Grafton State School. There were four superintendents during this period, and many new staff were added. New buildings were constructed, and old ones refurbished. New programs were developed such as the department of psychology and the recreation program. Newer medical procedures were used, and new drugs and medications were introduced. There was also increased attention to the education of the residents.

Residents. The institutional population grew from 1,091 in 1950 to 1,381 in 1960. This increase was accomplished by the construction of several dormitory buildings for residents. For short periods of time, the new buildings eliminated the long waiting lists. However, the reprieve was generally short-lived. For example on January 20, 1958 West Hall received its first residents, and by January 24th it was filled to capacity with 176 residents. Within the next three months there were 161 new admissions to the institution.

The residents enjoyed new freedoms during the 1950s. In 1954 two canteens were started, one for the males in Main, and one for the females in Pleasant View. Here the residents were allowed to use money provided by work or by their parents or guardians to buy sweets, small trinkets, soda or tobacco. In fact, Grafton State School applied for and received a tobacco sales license for many years, allowing it to sell tobacco on the campus.

The net proceeds from the canteens helped fund several recreation activities for the residents. They often went into downtown Grafton to attend movies or to use the community swimming pool. In 1959 the canteen funds were used to purchase a merry-go-round. Dr. Rand reported, *"In 1959 we were able to purchase a used merry-go-round through the combined efforts of Mr. Herman Joos, Chairman of the Board of Administration and Mr. William Collins of the William Collins Shows. This piece of equipment was paid for from the profits made in our School canteen and did not cost the tax payers any tax monies. It has been a source of much enjoyment for all of the children. The recreational department has made up a schedule that gives each child here two twenty minute rides each week, and to do this the machine is going quite a few hours each day*" (Twenty-Ninth Biennial Report, 1960, p. 2482).

The institution received its first televisions in November 1955. The Grafton Business and Professional Women's Club conducted a fundraiser and purchased 25 televisions, one for each resident ward. Mr. Harold Schaefer, President of the Gold Seal Company of Bismarck donated 13 of these televisions. He would later donate another four television sets in 1960 after Sunset Hall was completed. The impact of this donation was immediate. *"The children really enjoy them and the use of them has cut our sedative drug requirements almost in half. Besides that, the children are much more cooperative in other ways*" (Twenty-Seventh Biennial Report, 1956, p. 2018).

One major initiative was the Butternut Coffee Company Christmas program. The company would provide many toys and recreational games and equipment in return for strips from the coffee cans. The Grafton American Legion Auxiliary started this in 1956 and coordinated it for many years. Further, the residents were treated to hair and beauty care through the introduction of barber and beauty shops. The barbershop was located in North B in 1956, and the beauty shop was placed in West Hall in 1958. Dr. Rand reported that it took two barbers three weeks to cut hair on all the male residents.

By 1959 Dr. Rand was encouraging extended holiday and summer vacations by the residents. They were allowed to go home to their families during these times. Although the families were reviewed prior to allowing the vacations, Dr. Rand reported few problems. In fact, he stated that several residents requested shorter vacations to return to the structure of the institution, and to their friends.

Staffing. Along with the increases in residents, the staff more than doubled from 144 in 1950 to 312 in 1960. Most notable were the increases in direct attendant staff. Wages also increased. In 1950, the biennial expenditure for salaries and wages was $504,979.21 or about $3,506.80 per employee. In 1960 biennial salaries and wages totaled $1,705,259.15, or about $5,465.57 per employee, a gain of nearly $2,000 per employee.

This decade saw the introduction of psychologists to the institutional staff. These individuals were primarily psychometrists at first, simply administering tests to categorize and classify residents. However, they later became more involved in the mental health of both the residents and the employees. By the late 1950s psychological services were available to staff as well as residents. In addition, the psychology department began to conduct in-service training sessions for the direct care attendants so that they were more familiar with their jobs and with the characteristics of individuals with mental retardation.

There was significant change in leadership during the 1950s. After 24 years as superintendent, Dr. John Lamont retired on July 1, 1953. His replacement, Dr. James Marr from Iowa served only five months, dying from a heart attack on December 2, 1953. Faced with Dr. Marr's death and the need for a replacement, the Board of Administration met at Grafton on December 5, 1953 and appointed Mr. E.H. Intlehouse as Acting Superintendent. Mr. Intlehouse had served as the Executive Secretary of the institution since the late 1930s and was familiar with its operations. On May 1, 1954, Dr. Charles Rand began his duties as the ninth superintendent at Grafton State School.

Education and training. The 50s were a time of great progress in education at the institution. Crowded conditions still prohibited increased numbers of residents from participating in training, but newer programs were initiated. In the early 1950s the State Education and the State Public Health departments were requesting more education for children with mental retardation. Much of this came from a 1951 advisory meeting on the education of persons with mental retardation. Over 50 state and federal agencies were represented, along with parents, relatives, and professional workers. This committee's work served as the foundation for future legislation relating to institutional and public education of persons with mental retardation.

By 1954 the school program was using Scott Foresman Curriculum Series materials, along with Weekly Readers in its classes. Teachers were dropping the "non-academic" children, and increasingly pushing for earlier education of the youngest residents. By the fall of 1956, gender segregation in the school classes ended. Promoted by Dr. Rand, both boys and girls attended the same classes, particularly the academic based courses. Etta Hylden, school principal reported, "*We now have mixed classes in our school department instead of boys and girls alone. The first adjustment was quite exciting among the older children, but now, after two years, we have a minimum of trouble*" (Twenty-Eighth Biennial Report, 1958, p. 2491).

The children were exposed to psychological services at the institution. All were tested upon entry to the institution, and at various times to track their progress in education. Each biennial report of this decade contains tables showing the classifications of residents and students by mental age or IQ. Students were also allowed to visit the psychologists for general mental health services.

Gradually the curriculum evolved. While nursery school education and basic academic instruction were important, some of the curriculum was developed to prepare residents to leave the institution. This curriculum focused on the more practical, daily living skills necessary for successful transition into the community. These curricular issues would later push over into the public schools and the Division of Vocational Rehabilitation in North Dakota. By 1960 Dr. Rand was suggesting that communities might be well served by the operation of local sheltered workshops for persons with mental retardation.

Health. From July 1950 through June 1960 there were 230 residents who died at Grafton, nearly the same number as the previous decade. The institutional staff saw this as an improvement as there were more and more individuals with severe disabilities who were being admitted to the institution, and the population had increased dramatically. Thus even though the number of deaths was the same, the overall ratio or percentage of enrolled residents who died had decreased. Certainly the new hospital, opened in 1951, helped. Individuals with contagious illness were more easily quarantined and treated. Eugenic sterilizations continued in the early 1950s with 58 such surgeries completed in the 1950 – 1952 biennium, and 45 completed from 1953 to 1954. However, the biennial reports after 1950 no longer reported sterilizations, types surgical procedures, or reasons for death of the residents.

With the new hospital came new space for the pharmacy. The pharmacist also reported that newer drugs were being used with the residents. In 1956, Mr. Charles Thomson spoke of the transition from older medications to new formulas for the residents. "*You may be surprised to learn that several wonder drugs of today are actually centuries old. Rauwolfia, the recently developed treatment for certain mental disorders, was known in India hundreds of years ago as Sarpaganda. Veratrum, of recently proven value in hypertension, was known to the American Indians long before the Pilgrims came. These are recently re-discovered drugs. But many modern pharmaceuticals have been in consistent use since ancient times. Many of the new preparations including Thorazine, Sparine and Reserpine have provided to be of great value in many types of mental cases"* (Twenty-Seventh Biennial Report, 1956, p. 2037).

Two years later, Thomson reported on the progress of his discipline. *"Since the last issue of our Biennial Report when mention was made of the new preparations used in the treatment of mental cases, many more have been added to the growing list of tranquilizers, and some have been proven to be of value in many cases, while others have not. It will require much time and research as well as trial use to find out the most suitable to our varied type of patients. We are indebted to some of our Pharmaceutical Manufacturers, such as Smith, Kline & French Co., E.R. Squibb & Sons, Wyeths, Ciba, Schering Co. and others for their liberal supply of tranquilizer preparations for free trial on our patients. Among these are Thorazine, Compazine, Vesprin, Sparine, Equanil, Reserpine, Sandril amd Moderil. We have found that our budget allowance will have to be materially increased to take care of increased population and demand for modern drugs such as Tranquilizers and Antibiotics"* (Twenty-Eighth Biennial Report, 1958, p. 2494).

The medical staff also spent considerable time in preventative medicine during this decade. Upon admission, all residents were given the necessary inoculations. During the 1956 – 1958 biennium, the physicians worked with Dr. Margaret Candler from the US Public Health service in Atlanta, Georgia. Dr. Candler conducted a study of the effects of polio vaccine on the resident children. She also provided vaccine to inoculate 1,000 children for the Asiatic flu, averting a potential contagious outbreak at the institution.

Farming. By the 1950s the farming operations had become more sophisticated. The 1952 superintendent's report showed that the farm operations were somewhat divested, with budget categories for main farm income, dairy income, poultry income and garden income. The institution owned 113 head of purebred Holsteins, 128 hogs, and 840 laying hens. Horses had been replaced by machinery such as tractors, trucks with hydraulic hoists, and modern tilling equipment.

The farm became much more productive during this decade. For example, in the year from July 1, 1957 to June 30, 1958, the dairy produced over 105,000 gallons of milk for the institution, along with 18,000 pounds of meat, 35 tons of cabbage, and over 21,000 dozen eggs. Walfred Anderson estimated that the farm produce supplied to the institution was worth over $110,000 per year. By 1959, the farm production accounted for nearly $300,000 per biennium in foodstuffs to the institution. In addition, the farm supplied nearly $6,000 worth of meat and garden produce each biennium to other state schools such as the School for the Deaf in Devils Lake, and the Blind School in Bathgate.

Facilities. As the farm, medical services, and education and training were modernized at Grafton, so did the facilities improve. During these ten years, the institution constructed six employee cottages, completed the laundry addition, built a machine and repair shop, filled in the old river and well water storage reservoir, and completed a machine shed. In the early 1950s the institution received approval for the construction of employee cottages on the southeast edge of the central campus. Tight budgets and rising materials costs had made the earlier construction of the housing units too expensive. However, the institution found that by purchasing pre-fabricated homes, they could save considerable money. Thus, the first cottage was shipped by truck from Pagemaster Homes in Shakopee, Minnesota. Dr. Arvid Vitums, the medical assistant to Drs. Rand and Sulc, and his family moved into the first cottage in 1954.

Water service improved also, with the connection of the institution to the Grafton city water system. This greatly improved the quality of the water for washing and food preparation, and saved considerable money on water distillation from the artesian wells. The main building was no longer used for resident housing, but rather contained the school classrooms and had employee housing on the upper floors.

In 1955 the institution converted from direct current to alternating current (AC) electricity. While they still produced much of their heat and power through steam generation, the new AC power was more reliable and safer. A laundry addition was finished, and ground breaking for West Hall was held in 1956. However, Dr. Rand was predicting that even this new dormitory would do little to ease the over-crowding. In fact, he predicted the need for a new institution. He said, "*Another major thought to remember is that the Grafton State School is reaching a point where it can expand no more. In the past, when new buildings were added to the campus, they were built close to the existing buildings and no provision for future expansion was allowed. One more ward building of 175 population will utilize to full capacity our laundry, our bakery, our childrens kitchen, our warehouse storage facilities, and our employees dining room. There is no possible chance of enlarging any of these buildings due to the compactness of the campus. Even with one more ward building we will have to change our employees dining room to a cafeteria in order to accommodate the help. All in all this means that in the future, serious thought must be given to the starting of a new school for the care of mentally retarded and deficient. We should not wait too long to do this and should plan a school that can be enlarged and improved as time goes on*" (Twenty-Seventh Biennial Report, 1956, p. 2023). According to available records, this is the first instance where anyone mentions the need for a second institution for persons with mental retardation in North Dakota. According to his predictions, Dr. Rand converted the employee's dining room from family style into cafeteria style. The last meal at the separate officer's dining room was held on March 13, 1959. Dr. Rand continued to call for the construction of a new school building.

1960 – 1970: On the Cusp of Change

The 1960s were characterized by a period in which the institution reached record enrollment, and a time in which the services for individuals with mental retardation came under both national and state review. This decade served as the springboard for remarkable change in the 70s and 80s. In the late 1950s and early 1960s family organizations such as the Association for Retarded Children (later Citizens, and later yet just Arc) became more involved in the public movement toward services for persons with mental retardation. In addition public exposes of life within institutions came forward. Books such as Burton Blatt's *Christmas in Purgatory* (1965) spoke to the nation about the situation of persons with disabilities in institutions.

In 1962 the President's Panel on Mental Retardation recommended that states be funded to develop comprehensive plans related to services, professional development and training of professionals in the field of mental retardation (Presidents' Panel on Mental Retardation, 1962). In 1963 the ND Legislature created a Coordinating Committee on Mental Retardation. It had "*the duty and responsibility of making or providing for such studies and surveys of the needs of retarded persons n North Dakota as it may deem necessary, and shall coordinate the activities of all state departments, divisions, agencies, and institutions having responsibilities in the field of mental retardation*" (Chapter 219, North Dakota Laws, 1963).

This Coordinating Committee set up eight regional planning areas, along with regional committee chairs, to facilitate the planning process. During 1965 and 1966 these groups met and developed recommendations for a state plan that included actions for (a) prevention, diagnosis and clinical services, (b) children and youth, (c) adults, (d) aged, (e) the law, (f) manpower, training and research needs, (g) residential and institutional care, and (h) legislation and finance. Over 100 ND citizens participated in these groups, and the Coordinating Committee presented its final recommendations and plan in a report entitled, "*A Plan for North Dakota's Mentally Retarded: A Report to the Governor, Legislature, and Citizens of North Dakota*" (Division of Mental Health and Retardation Services, 1966).

Of particular interest was the more than 25 recommendations forwarded by the residential and institutional care task force. Several recommendations were directed toward Grafton State School and San Haven. Among them were calls for action regarding facilities, manpower, staffing, and sterilization. Regarding facilities, the task force recommended a more community-based program. They stated, "*The treatment and care program for the mentally retarded should be community oriented insofar as possible. Whenever possible, the mentally retarded child should be cared for in his own home*" (Division of Mental Health and Retardation Services, 1966, p. 72). In this vein, they also recommended small community facilities. "*The Residential and Institutional Care Task Force recommends small residential facilities to house 50 mentally retarded in four major cities of our State – those residential units shall be constructed so that additional dormitory and treatment areas might be constructed as the individual region indicates a need for these further services. The prime purpose of these residential units shall be to complement other community programs serving the mentally retarded, such as diagnostic, day care, and other treatment services developed in regions where residential care will be needed on a short-term basis to determine the long-range needs of the mentally retarded*" (Division of Mental Health and Retardation Services, 1966, p. 70).

Regarding Grafton and San Haven, they said, "*For future long-range projection, it is recommended that the Grafton State School be improved to care for the long-term residential care needs of the mentally retarded in North Dakota. After exhausting all efforts to provide special education, foster homes, day care services and other educational opportunities to relieve the need for residential care: If then a second institution is needed, it is recommended that Grafton State School be confined to serve the east secton of the State, while a second institution of adequate size be located in western North Dakota with a maximum capacity of 500. As to the future use of San Haven, the Task Force recommends that it be earmarked for purely custodial care of senile, geriatric patients needing a minimum of professional personnel*" (Division of Mental Health and Retardation Services, 1966, p. 70).

The Task Force suggested that professional staff be more focused on direct care staff supervision, and that direct care attendants receive ongoing in-service training. Gradually the training was to involve parents so they could assist their children in the home communities. The Task Force recommended salary increases to nationally competitive levels, along with improved staff to resident ratios as outlined by the American Association on Mental Deficiency. Finally, the Task Force suggested that the sterilization laws, previously revised to require parent or guardian consent, be left alone.

Residents. The 1960s saw the highest resident population ever at Grafton. By 1966 there were nearly 1,500 people at Grafton and nearly 150 people in San Haven. The state came under criticism for the large number of people at Grafton. Dr. Rand reported on some of this public comment, "*At a meeting held in Fargo, a speaker criticized the State of North Dakota for having too many of its retarded children in its institutions. A true look at the picture brings out the fact that North Dakota in 1960 was one of the few, if not the only state in the Union, that did not have a waiting list for admission to its School or Institution for the Retarded*" (Thirtieth Biennial Report, 1960, p. 2200). Starting with the transfer of 38 residents to San Haven in 1962, more and more residents were moved westward to accommodate the growing number of individuals at Grafton.

Overcrowding was severe, and many education and training programs were severely limited by the lack of funding and by the crowded facilities. However, many of these conditions resulted in some improvements of living conditions for the residents. One new ward building was constructed and new, more home-like living situations were devised.

By 1962, the institution was using a new classification system for describing the residents. Paul Witucki, hired as the school psychologist in 1961, stated, "*The former classifications of idiot, imbecile, and moron have become obsolete due to their adverse connotations and we are presently using the terminology of mildly retarded, moderately retarded, severely retarded, and profoundly retarded. This new classification is based strictly upon intelligent quotients. This new classification system was advocated by the American Psychiatric Association and the American Association of Mental Deficiency*" (Thirtieth Biennial Report, 1962, p. 2208). Thus, some of the more demeaning language was removed from daily practice at the institution.

In general the residents' health seemed to improve, and there were fewer deaths during this decade. A new facility, Prairie View, was built and opened in 1960 allowing for a small respite in crowding. However, new referrals and admissions still stretched available space for the residents.

Staffing. Staff changes were frequent during the 1960s, and staff increases were dramatic. The number of staff rose from 396 staff in 1960 to just over 700 by 1970. Nearly all of the biennial reports of this decade listed the names and annual wages of the staff.

Along with the rise in personnel came a series of staff and personnel issues that needed attention. In 1964 the state mandated that all institutional staff were eligible for a new employee retirement system and for a fringe benefit package. Dr. Rand was concerned about the availability of funds to support the institution's contributions (*The Ambassador*, December, 1965). While continually pressing the state legislature for additional staff, he had raised the Grafton State School budget a small degree, particularly in salaries. However the new employee retirement contribution effectively blocked some needed staff additions and resulted in little or no wage increases for existing staff (*The Ambassador*, December 1966).

The large number of employees also stretched the state government for reimbursements. In 1969, many staff did not receive their paychecks in a timely fashion. At one point the superintendent called for a legal interpretation through the Attorney General's office regarding deposits and reimbursements of employee pay. Later, there were allegations of "sloppy administration" of the institution, which were examined by the Anderson Company (*The Ambassador*, October, 1969). They examined the use of time clocks for staff, and later reported on the difficulties of the system in receiving, allocating, and disbursing both state and new federal funds received by the institution.

There was a renewed interest in staff development during the 1960s. The professional staff continued to attend regional and national conferences for their respective disciplines. The dentists attend the Association of Institutional Dentists conventions, while the superintendent and psychologists attended meetings of the American Association for Mental Deficiency.

There was a major emphasis on the development of direct care staff and in July of 1966 the first staff in-service classes were begun (*The Ambassador*, August, 1966). In-service trainers Agnes Kieley and E. Rosenau conducted basic classes in mental retardation for six to 15 staff at a time. Generally these programs lasted two to three months for a few hours each week, and were then repeated for new groups of staff. Four teachers took an eight week session of courses in special education at the University of North Dakota during the summer of 1962, and many teachers started attending the state meetings of the Council for Exceptional Children throughout the years. In addition, the institution began a staff and resident newspaper called *The Ambassador* in 1964. This paper was part staff information newsletter and part letter home to families of residents. New employees and programs were presented in the paper, along with general descriptions of resident activity by ward. In several cases, detailed listings of resident vacations, visitors, and accomplishments were presented.

Education and training. Educational services at Grafton begin to change in the 1960s. There is a marked shift from a purely medical model of services to a more education and community-centered approach. Again, this is likely a result of President Kennedy's initiatives in mental retardation. One marker of this shift was the increase in community job placements. In 1962 the Social Service department used state and local Vocational Rehabilitation services to assist in community placements. There was also interest in a new community program, sheltered workshops. Paul Dahl, the director of the Social Service department wrote, *"We are referring several of our children to Vocational Rehabilitation for special training and at the present time two boys are out-of-state receiving training in the fields of auto-mechanics and heavy equipment operation under this program. We are also quite enthusiastic about the development of two Sheltered Workshops for retarded children in Grand Forks and Fargo that expect to be in operation in the very near future. We understand that it will be possible to place several of our children in these workshops"* (Thirtieth Biennial Report, 1962, p. 2206).

Major changes occurred in the philosophy and approaches to resident education and training. For years, the school principal had presented the mission of education as a means to keep the residents busy and happy. However that changed dramatically with the publication of a new educational philosophy and goals. *"The philosophy of the education and training service can be summarized as: (a) The education and training program within the institution should be conceived and conducted as an integral part of the total institution community effort leading to the mental, emotional, physical, social and vocational growth of each resident. (b) The basic responsibility of the education service should provide education and training service to all residents deemed capable of benefiting from the program. The objectives of our school departments are (a) Intellectual development and academic proficiency in test subjects. (b) Development of emotional stability. (c) Development of personal and social adequacy. (d) Development of good health and personal hygiene. (e) Development of attitudes, interests and skills leading to the good citizens and community responsibility, and wholesome use of leisure time. (f) Learning to work for the purpose of earning a living."* (Thirty-First Biennial Report, 1964, p. 100-101).

This decade saw the introduction of new school programs for children in the institution. In 1964 the education staff took on the challenge of teaching five girls who were deaf. They used a tutorphone device to amplify sound for the girls. Their instruction focused on embroidery stitches and art. Also students with more significant disabilities (labeled as "trainable") were included in classes. Their instruction totaled only 7 ½ hours each week, but it focused on self-help skills, speech and language, and work habits. The third new school program was a home management class. This course had 12 girls who were targeted for community placement. These girls studied foods, sewing, and other home duties. On several occasions these students prepared luncheons for some of the staff.

On September 16, 1968 the institution formed Boy Scout Troop #322. Eight boys were initially enrolled, and were led by Paul Witucki. This was the second Boy Scout troop that had been formed at the institution, the first formed in 1942. This troop increased in enrollment and remained active through the 1970s.

A new school and auditorium was dedicated on July 26, 1967 opening the way for greater educational emphasis at the institution. Also four new federally funded programs made their impact on the residents. The Hospital Improvement Program funded pre-admission evaluations of prospective residents. This allowed for a more careful screening regarding the appropriateness of institutionalization, and allowed for some follow-up of residents already placed in the community. The second program, the In-Service Training Program, provided attendants with a consistent course of training related to work expectations on the wards. The Recreation Program project supported staff with degrees in physical education and recreation, thereby increasing the recreation and leisure programs in the school and in the wards. Finally, the Grandparents Program (later known as the Foster Grandparents Program) employed thirty grandparents who provided individual attention to many residents.

The Out-Patient, In-Patient program was another effort to improve outcomes for residents. This program provided comprehensive team-based evaluations of all individuals on the admissions waiting list, and provided follow-up services for people in the community. These evaluations and services supported a more efficient means for making institutional and community placement decisions.

One new program for the women was the Midway House project. Established in the fall of 1967, this program supported 48 women in a homelike atmosphere in the old hospital building. The objectives of the Midway House program were: *"A. Provide and Promote a home-like atmosphere. B. Maintain parent-attendant attitude among employees. C. Provide progressive training of residents for assuming increasing personal responsibility.""(The Ambassador*, June 1969, p. 1). The program was highly successful as several of the women were placed as domestic helpers in the community, and provided numerous support services across the campus.

Dr. Rand reported on one interesting measure of the success of the education and training programs. During the 1966 – 1968 biennium, the State Selective Service Board required Grafton State School to register nearly 250 men for military duty. Dr. Rand reported, *"I know of three residents that are discharged from the Grafton State School who are in the Armed Forces. One of them at present is over in Viet Nam and I received a very nice letter from him a short while ago thanking us for all that we have done for him while he was at our institution. I hope that he comes home safely and that we can see him and thank him for his letter"* (Thirty-Third Biennial Report, 1968, p. 75).

Health. As stated earlier, residents appeared to be healthier during this decade despite the crowded conditions and the potential for large contagious outbreaks. The resident screenings and inoculations that had begun in the 1950s were continued, and the medical staff had from three to five full-time physicians. One of the new screening mechanisms was the examination for a metabolic condition called Phenylketonuria (PKU). In 1961, Rene Pelletier, a medical student from the University of North Dakota, tested all residents for PKU, and found 27 cases. This information was provided to the North Dakota Department of Health, which further examined the relatives of these residents to prevent future cases of PKU. Additional medical services were often provided, as the medical staff roster from 1964 indicates. There were four physicians, two registered pharmacists, a dentist and a dental assistant, a medical x-ray technician, a hospital supervisor, and numerous nurses who provided medical supports for the residents.

The resident death rate also decreased dramatically to less than 2.5% of the population. This is an amazing situation as there was an increasing rise in the age of the residents, and increasing admissions of individuals with very significant disabilities and medical complications. Obviously the medical care was quality and appropriate for the majority of the residents.

The medical staff began using more drugs on the residents. After their testing of various medications during the late 1950s, the staff determined that pharmacological therapy was appropriate in many cases. However, they did not always solve all problems. Dr. Rand reported, *"At the School, considerable research has been underway in regard to the effect of tranquilizers on these children with improvement in their general condition. Our work shows that mentally they do not improve but that socially they do"* (Thirtieth Biennial Report, 1962, p. 2197). Even the dentists began using more medications for the residents. Dr. Cuthbert reports on his attendance at the Annual Conference of the Association of Institutional Dentists in Omaha, Nebraska, and the practice of using a "Lytic Cocktail" as pretreatment medication for dental patients. This cocktail was a combination of several tranquilizer drugs used to fully or partially sedate residents prior to various dental procedures (*The Ambassador*, July 21, 1965).

New therapeutic programs were also started in the 60s. The first occupational therapy program began in February of 1962. Jean Haugen, the new therapist, described some of her work as follows: "*This added service to the State School enables more children to take part in the school programs for some specific reason. Most of the treatment sessions are held in different buildings and wards while others are held in the Occupational Therapy Room. There are about ninety-five patients enrolled in these classes at the present time*" (Thirtieth Biennial Report, 1962, p. 2211).

By 1970 the shift from a more medically oriented facility to a more educational and community-based program was nearing completion. There was only one physician on staff, and many patients were being referred elsewhere for procedures. "*We have adopted a new procedure at the School, in that, we refer all of our surgical patients to a local surgeon and to a local Grafton Hospital for general surgery. We refer the special cases to specialists for surgery. We do not have the equipment to anesthetize a patient nor do we have an anesthetist on our staff. For the few surgical cases that we have each month, we do not deem it advisable to buy the expensive equipment necessary not to employ a registered anesthetist. The surgeons that take care of our patients keep them a relatively short while in the hospital of their choice, and then send them to the Grafton State School Hospital for post-operative care. We have performed some minor surgery at the Grafton State School Hospital for which personnel and facilities are deemed adequate*" (Thirty-Fourth Biennial Report, 1970, p. 12).

Farming. Little was written specifically about the farming operations during this decade. The available farm records do show that in 1960 the farm yielded 30,00 bushels of corn, 1,400 tons of silage, 1,000 tons of alfalfa, 20,000 bushels of potatoes and 50 tons of Sudan grass silage. There were 60 acres planted in garden produce.

In 1964 the Holstein herd produced nearly 120,000 gallons of milk for the institution. The butcher shop prepared 45,000 pounds of meat, 45,000 pounds of pork, and nearly 20,000 pounds of poultry. Staff and residents collected about 42,000 dozen eggs on the farm. Walfred Anderson was now overseeing over 650 acres that were owned by the institution, along with another 900 acres of rented property.

There was no report on the farm in the 1966 biennial report, but the 1968 report speaks to Mr. Anderson's retirement after 45 years at the institution. By this time, the farm was profitable enough to supply produce to the School for the Deaf at Devils Lake and the School for the Blind in Grand Forks, along with some potatoes to San Haven. A new milk house was built in August of 1966. A trade arrangement was made with the State Penitentiary where their beef was shipped to Grafton and butchered for resident consumption. In return, Grafton State School supplied oats for feed for the cattle.

The retirement of Mr. Anderson signaled the end of the farming operations at Grafton. By 1970 there were no longer any farm operations or production reports in the fiscal reports. Also, the institution began a gradual disposition of property and equipment from the farm.

Facilities. Several buildings were constructed or remodeled during the 1960s. Prairie View (later called Wylie) was finished in 1960. During this year the new greenhouse was completed on the west side of the campus, and a refrigerated potato house was built on the farm grounds. In 1961 the towers were removed from the Main building. Previously used as water storage towers, they had been struck by lightening several times, and the structure was cracked and weakening. These were removed as the brick buildings were being repointed and mortared. In 1963 a new carpenter shop was built, and a new barn was built on the farm site. This new barn was built to replace the one that burned in 1962. In 1966 the new milk house was built, as was a new bus garage. This garage was funded by canteen profits.

In February 1967 the new laundry was finished. However it was not opened until March 1968 as the receipt of the new equipment was delayed several times. Also, the laundry machinery broke down several times as the staff perfected the operating cycles. Building #8, the paint shop, was also constructed during 1967. The tunnel from main was rebuilt, as it was deteriorating from the elements and years of use.

Perhaps the most significant construction of this period was the Collette Auditorium and the Education Center. These facilities were a vast improvement over the classrooms that had been housed in main and in various ward buildings. The recreation program no longer needed to use space in the refectory, and there was sufficient space for resident dances, graduation ceremonies, and other public events.

Dr. Rand ended the decade by calling for additional construction to modernize the campus, and to alleviate some of the overcrowding. He requested funds for the modification of the new laundry building, as it was insufficient to handle the new laundry equipment. He also spoke about the preliminary plans for a food service center. He stated, "*This request is thoroughly supported and justified through the report and recommendations of the Food Service Facility Committee, which encompassed a study of food handling practices at all state institutions. The deficiencies within the present food handling and services areas of the state school were of such magnitude that proper correction of these deficiencies could be accomplished only through the construction of a new facility*" (Thirty-Fourth Biennial Report, 1970, p. 13). Rand also requested funds for the construction of a new administration building citing the age and poor condition of the Main structure. Finally, Division of Vocational Rehabilitation funds were requested to remodel Midway even further so that a more natural family-style setting could be replicated.

1970 – 1980: Changes

The 1970s were a decade of major changes in the institution. For the first time in its history, the resident population began declining. In contrast, while the resident numbers declined, the staff numbers increased significantly. With the increase in staff came the new challenges of staff development, wages, and benefits. Education and training programs became an important focus at the institution. On campus and community-based programs were developed. By the end of the decade nearly every resident had some type of programming.

Several new facilities were built, including the food service center and the professional services building. The farming program, long a staple part of the institution, was discontinued. Finally, the medical services were changed. No longer were major surgical and medical procedures handled at the hospital. Instead these cases were referred to community facilities.

Residents. The resident population changed dramatically during this decade. On June 30, 1970 there were 1,351 residents on the roll at Grafton State School. In addition, there were approximately 225 residents with mental retardation in the San Haven facility at Dunseith, ND. By June 30, 1980 there were 988 residents at Grafton and 248 at San

Haven. For the first time in its history, the population trend at the institution was declining.

Part of the reason for the decline was the introduction of legislation at the state level, and some national recognition of the situation of persons with mental retardation in state faculties. In the late 1960s and early 1970s, North Dakota passed laws establishing community programs for persons with mental retardation (Division of Mental Retardation Programs, 1970; Kolstoe, Gearheart, & Hoffelt, 1970). Also, lawmakers required special more stringent admission procedures for the institutional placement of children less than six years old.

State and national parent organizations become more involved also. For example in 1972 the ARC in North Dakota filed a lawsuit against the state and against Grafton State School for denial of public education for students with mental retardation. This legal action was based on similar action in other states. Dr. Archer explained the rationale of the North Dakota lawsuit this way, *"The principle guiding the lawsuit recently filed in North Dakota follows along the same lines. The suit seeks to have declared unconstitutional a North Dakota law which provides that a child may be excused from attendance if 'the child is in such physical or mental condition as to render attendance or participation in the regular special education program inexpedient or impractical.'* ...*What the people are really saying is that the Constitution of North Dakota guarantees a free and public education to every youngster, but that we have laws which nullify or prevent this. It is those laws that they are attempting to have repealed or removed and place the burden of education and training for each handicapped youngster upon the school district in which he resides"* (*The Ambassador*, December, 1972). Thus, as laws and lawsuits shaped our state practice, as community programs were developed, and as families became increasingly involved in advocacy, the numbers of residents at Grafton declined.

Of those that did remain, Dr. Archer felt that many were capable of moving to community programs. *"...more residents are ready for placement and could be placed if appropriate community facilities were available"* (Thirty-Seventh Biennial Report, 1977, p. 10). Further, the institutional population demographics were changing. The average resident age was increasing, and the degree of disability of these individuals was more significant. Of the 895 residents at Grafton in 1977, many had significant service needs. *"The levels of retardation within the residential population are 362 profound, 234 severe, 158 moderate, and 141 mild. Those residents requiring complete self-help care number 207, partial self-help care 575, and 113 residents are able to function completely independently in self-help care"* (Thirty-Seventh Biennial Report, 1977, p. 12).

While the population patterns changed, the resident life changed as well. In 1971, the resident mail was no longer censored (*The Ambassador*, July/August, 1971). Previously, all resident mail was routed through either the Superintendent's office, or the institution's Department of Social Services. Here money that had been given to residents was taken and deposited into residents' accounts, and information about families screened. Then, the information was conveyed to the residents, either verbally or through the actual letters. Now, the residents received their mail directly and unopened. However, this raised some new issues, and the administration now had to somehow manage resident funds in methods other than through central accounting.

Residents were also allowed more latitude in movement, both within campus and within the community. Those who completed their daily programming had increased access to the institutional canteens. In some cases residents were allowed to go to downtown Grafton on their own, perhaps for coffee, shopping, or to the movies. Certainly these new freedoms were refreshing to the residents but raised some issues for staff.

Staffing. As a result of legislative action and because of changing population demographics, the staffing patterns at Grafton had to change. Early in the 70s, the staff to resident ratio was about 1 to 20. The recommended American Association on Mental Deficiency standards at that time were far lower, and were frequently used to request additional staff. Administrators used these standards, and then used newer sources of state and federal funding, such as the Comprehensive Employment and Training Act (CETA) and Hospital Improvement Program (HIP) funds, to hire new staff.

Increasingly these new staff and the legislative changes surrounding the new employees caused considerable stress on institution administrators. While the superintendent and the institution secretary had generally handled all personnel and business matters, the legislature now required that the institution have an Office of Business Administration. This office adopted a cost-center system of accounting, encouraged by consultants from the Arthur Anderson Company. With these business office changes, the administration began developing job descriptions and adopted salary and wage scales based on categories of jobs.

However, wages at the institution were still much lower than other employment opportunities. Male staff were difficult to hire and retain. Frequently the institution had to request emergency funds to complete a biennium, using most of the funds for staff salaries. But the staff were not always satisfied. They threatened massive staff walkouts, which were averted by superintendent and even governor action (*The Ambassador*, August, 1974). By 1979, the state legislature had passed two significant bills, House Bill 1301 and House Bill 1639, to support staff. HB 1301 provided for payment of full family medical insurance for state employees, while HB 1639 required a $50 per month salary increase to employees earning less than $9,2000 per year.

The foster grandparent (FGP) program and the large cadre of volunteers were a great help at Grafton. Supported by external grants, the FGP program allowed retired citizens to provide one-on-one attention to persons needing more individualized attention. Both the staff and residents expressed their appreciation for FGP (*The Ambassador*, September, 1975).

While the FGP staff were paid, there were numerous other volunteers at Grafton State School. Often the Grafton High School students would volunteer for various events. One important volunteer program was the Youth Service Corps. This program allowed high school and college students to volunteer up to ten weeks at Grafton and San Haven. These Corps volunteers worked for short periods on the institution grounds, and then supervised residents at camping events at Lake Metigoshe. These events were beneficial both for the residents and for the volunteers. *"An experience like this has changed their outlook on life. From these girls emits an attitude of growing, maturing human personalities. As Patti Priebe put it, 'I came to San Haven thinking I would teach them, and I will leave knowing they have taught me'* "(The Ambassador, August, 1974, p.1).

Among the major personnel changes at the institution during this decade were the three different superintendents. On June 30, 1972 Dr. Rand retired after 18 years as head of Grafton State School. On July 1, 1972 Dr. Ronald Archer became the new superintendent. He was the first non-medical doctor to head the institution. In fact, due to his hiring the state legislature passed Senate Bill 2178, which amended the qualifications for the superintendent at Grafton. The medical responsibilities were shifted from the superintendent to a new medical director, and the superintendent was the overall director of the institution. Dr. Archer ran the institution until August 1979 when he resigned to return to higher education at Minot State College. Dr. Milton Wisland, formerly a director of special education in Washington state, became the eleventh superintendent of the institution at Grafton on August 15, 1979.

Education and training. The education and training services for residents at Grafton State School made astounding advances in the 1970s. In previous years, only a portion of the residents received educational programming or training, often due to lack of funds, lack of staff, or both. However that changed in 1971 when a full-time education principal, Don Watson, was hired to serve under Paul Witucki, the director of the Resident Program Department. Mr. Watson had a master's degree in mental retardation, and with Witucki, developed a staff of 15 teachers, 11 of whom had bachelor degrees in special education. These staff immediately began changing the structure of school services, ensuring that all students with mild mental retardation received a full day of education, and those students with moderate mental retardation received at least a half day of education. The relatively new facilities at the Collette Auditorium and Education Center soon became filled with over 200 resident children each day.

While most children attending school were from the institution, the Education Department began accepting local children for classes. In October 1972 the first six local children began attending school. They were driven to the campus either by parents or by staff from the recreation department. These children then went home each day to be with their families.

In 1974, Dr. Dennis Follman became the school principal, a position he held for numerous years. Under his direction the education program continued to grow, with some changes. Staff were continually upgraded, both in numbers and skills. Teachers frequently took part in state CEC workshops and conventions. Also, many in-service sessions were brought to the campus.

In August 1975 eight children from the institution's deaf-blind unit were transferred to Grand Forks and the School for the Blind. The state legislature had passed SB 2021 allowing children with blindness and other associated disabilities access to the services of the School for the Blind. The fall of 1975 also saw the passage of landmark national legislation related to the education of children with disabilities. In November President Ford signed PL 94-142, the Education for All Handicapped Children Act. This required that all children, regardless of disability, were entitled to appropriate special educational services as outlined by an individualized education plan (IEP). Over the next several years the Grafton State School teachers developed IEPs for all school aged children between the ages of six and 22. This law significantly changed the way services were designed and provided to children with mental retardation.

As the school's education services changed, so did the adult education and training programs. Records show that a limited number of adult residents received training in the early 1970s. The most critical factor here was staff. There was insufficient staff to conduct the training, and few staff had any training to work with persons with mental retardation. However by 1980 nearly all residents had some active programming during each day, and some individuals were being served in the community. By 1977 residents were receiving an average of 4 to 5 hours of programming per day.

Two programs started in 1970 that supported the increase in adult services. The out-patient program, previously funded by federal grant dollars, was now state funded. This program supported individuals who were requesting admission, or who had been placed in community settings. Federal Title I funds were used to start another program. A summer training program for individuals with the most severe disabilities was begun. These individuals had not previously received any training. While it was only offered in the summer, it was a vast improvement over previous circumstances.

In 1971 Grafton State School started the Midway Project. The Midway building, formerly the old hospital, was refurbished to house 48 female residents. These women were provided instruction in basic domestic skills, cooking, and daily living skills. By January 1972 several women were placed in the community in both work and residential settings. Later this program would be modified when Vocational Rehabilitation funds were used to further remodel Midway, and the program curriculum changed for a greater emphasis on community living. The lessons learned at Midway about teaching daily living skills as means for transitioning to community living would prove valuable through the 70s and 80s.

Title I funds were also used to start another training effort, the Behavior Management program, later called Behavior Modification. New staff were added and 44 residents received services. "*The Behavior Management Program has a two-fold purpose: 1) To ensure the continuity of services to those residents who represent special program needs in addition to mental retardation; and 2) To provide a segment of staff with training and experience which enhance the possibility of meeting their special needs*" (*The Ambassador*, January, 1974, p. 1). Staff used token economy systems to reward appropriate behavior while teaching basic living skills, arts, crafts, and community access.

The biggest focus of adult resident education during this decade was on community transition. While the Midway program flourished, more and more residents found themselves living in communities throughout the state. The precursors to today's group homes, then called hostels, sprang up in Bismarck, Dickinson, Grand Forks, Fargo and Minot. Further, sheltered workshops were developed in several communities, allowing persons with mental retardation to receive sheltered work training or community-based instruction. Community placements of institution residents grew from about 65 per year in 1970 to nearly 200 per year by 1980.

Health. Resident health was generally good during the 1970s. Even as the resident population was older and had more significant and complex disabilities, the institutional death rate declined from about 3.1% in 1970 to about 1.8% in 1979. The institution continued to take residents to community hospitals for surgery or other more complicated medical procedures.

As Grafton State School attempted to comply with Joint Commission Standards, and Title XIX procedures, corrective and preventative medical care became even more important. By 1977 many residents were receiving corrective orthopedic surgery in preparation for community placement.

Medical staffing patterns changed at Grafton during the decade. While the superintendent was no longer required to be a physician, there was to be a physician medical director. However hiring qualified medical staff was difficult. In 1973, Dr. Arvid Vitums, a Grafton State School physician for 21 years, retired. For the next three years, the institution searched for a new medical director, and eventually hired Dr. Harry Butler in January 1976.

Previously an administrator for the Rehabilitation Hospital in Grand Forks, Dr. Butler began working to improve the physician care at Grafton. The three physicians on staff at the time were non-resident doctors and were not licensed for private practice in North Dakota. Thus, Butler had these doctors attending weekly physician in-service meetings in Grand Forks. In addition, he brought consultants and medical students to the institution. Butler saw this as a benefit to his staff and to others as well. *"The environment here is remarkable for teaching...there are a number of symptoms prevalent at the State School that a physician might encounter very infrequently during his life's practice, yet he must be able to recognize them. And this recognition, he said, simply cannot be learned from textbooks"* (*The Ambassador*, August, 1976, p. 1).

Dental and pharmaceutical services continued to be provided, as did occupational therapy for the residents. In 1972 a physical therapy program was added to provide movement and motor therapy to residents. Services continued to be integrated during the decade and staff began using a teaming model. By the late 1970s nearly every resident had received a full team assessment that included a medical examination.

Farming. After the retirement of Walfred Anderson in 1967 the farming operations declined at the institution. In 1971 the North Dakota legislature required that the institution phase out farming at Grafton. Over the years the farmland was sold to the Grafton Park District (1971), the Grafton American Legion (1973) or leased to the city of Grafton or private farmers. Clifford Bender, the business administrator, reported *"Farmland owned by the School is under lease to private parties and is the only farm asset remaining under control of the school. All other assets have been disposed of through either slaughter, public sale, or gifted to other state institutions"* (Thirty-Fifth Biennial Report, 1972, p. 17).

Facilities. After nearly seventy years of use, many of the buildings and grounds were showing signs of age. While the new tunnel from Main was completed in the late 1960s, Dr. Rand called for continued upgrading of other tunnels and buildings, *"The state of deterioration within the tunnel area which was reconstructed, would seem to indicate that a program of systematic replacement of these areas is extremely desirable and quite necessary"* (Thirty-Fourth Biennial Report, p. 12). During this report, Dr. Rand reported on the completion of the new boiler installation in the summer of 1970 and the awarding of the bids for the All Faiths Chapel in March 1970. He had additional construction requests including a new food service center, further modifications of the laundry building due to the installation of new machinery, an additional classroom for the Collette Educational Center, construction of a new administration building, and further remodeling of Midway Hall (the old hospital). Nearly all of these projects, along with extensive upgrading of the older buildings, occurred during the 1970s.

Midway was remodeled by early 1971 with federal Vocational Rehabilitation funds. This facility allowed female residents to reside in more family style units, and thus practice more community-oriented living skills. A number of these women would go on to permanent community placements.

In June 1972 the campus celebrated the dedication of the All Faiths Chapel on the west side of the institutional grounds. Constructed with donations from the community, the Chapel was dedicated by many state and national dignitaries, including Mrs. Eunice Kennedy Shriver. Pastor Victor Tegtmeier became the first full time Protestant chaplain at the institution, with his services funded by the Missouri Synod Lutheran Church organization. Father Anthony Milne also provided Catholic services to the residents on a part time basis at the chapel.

The year 1973 saw major changes in facilities and use on the campus. During the summer the new Food Service Center was completed and put into operation. This building allowed the closing of the refectory for meals and dining. The Food Service Center was touted as a major improvement in meal preparation and dining for the staff and residents, partly as a response to state health department concerns of the older refectory facility. It was also seen as a way to promote a more normalized meal experience for many of the residents. Wayne Haley, Director of Social Services at the campus wrote, *"With the opening of this center the residents who eat there will have the advantage of congregating in one central place and will also enjoy the benefit of leaving their wards and having a change of environment. The residents will also have the advantage of eating in a coeducational setting which is, of course, a more normal setting. Normalization is one of the chief goals of Grafton State School and the food service center will help us in achieving that goal. With the choice of foods and the coeducational setting we expect to find that the residents will learn more appropriate table manners"* (*The Ambassador*, March 1973, p. 1).

On July 1, 1973 the San Haven facility was put under control of the Grafton State School. Although persons with mental retardation had been placed at San Haven since the 1950s (and perhaps even some individuals with mental retardation and tuberculosis were placed there in the 1930s), the 1973 legislature officially designated San Haven as a facility for persons with mental retardation. Most of the residents at San Haven had significant physical and medical conditions. Dr. Archer wrote, *"After extensive remodeling the first group of mentally retarded residents was transferred from the Grafton State School in 1959. By 1972 there were 260 mentally retarded residents and five or six TB patients residing at the San Haven State Hospital. With the closing of the TB wing there will be room for approximately 25 additional mentally retarded residents. Of the residents at San Haven, approximately 140 are bed-ridden and require total nursing care. The remainder are older ambulatory residents who enjoy this restful and serene location"* (*The Ambassador*, July, 1973, p. 1). With the addition of the San Haven facility, Archer appointed Paul Witucki as Assistant Superintendent at Grafton and Richard Charrier as Assistant Superintendent at San Haven.

A new swimming pool was completed during the summer of 1973. Located behind Collette Auditorium, the pool was constructed with federal funds from the U.S. Department of Education through the Elementary and Secondary Education Act. The pool was designed to be accessible to persons with disabilities and to allow formal swimming and rehabilitation services.

During the fall of 1973 the staff dormitory rooms and apartments in Pleasant View, North B and North A were remodeled for resident housing. Federal guidelines for resident space, along with the still overcrowded situation at the institution promoted this move. For the first time in nearly 70 years, staff were not living side by side with the residents.

The mid 1970s saw several remodeling and construction projects on the campus. Buildings needed rewiring, new windows, updated bathrooms, new roofing, new ventilation, fire escapes, and other general repairs. Many of these projects were long overdue. In addition, the national energy crisis pushed utility costs exceedingly high, forcing the staff to develop most energy efficient buildings with new insulation and energy efficient windows and lighting. During the winter of 1976-77 the director of administration, Mr. Gary Lorinser, estimated that the institution spent nearly $1,980 per day in heating the Grafton buildings. In 1977 the swimming pool was enclosed. This allowed for swimming and therapy use year round, and ultimately saved on heating costs.

The late 1970s saw another major change, the construction of a new professional services building. The Main building had served as the primary administration and office building on the campus for 75 years. Governor Art Link dedicated the Professional Services Building on July 18, 1978. This building had over 21,000 square feet of office and meeting space, providing room for administration, professional, and some therapy services. Within a short time after the Professional Services Building was completed and occupied, the Main building was torn down. The keystone building of the institution was now gone.

1980 – 1990: Scrutiny and Change

The decade of the 1980s saw perhaps the most significant changes in the history of the institution. In less than 15 years from the late 1960s to the early 1980s, the institution changed from a farming, agrarian facility for housing residents with mental retardation, to a compliance-directed facility focused on preparing residents for community living.

Much of the change was a result of the ARC lawsuit, filed against the institution and the state in 1980. This lawsuit required considerable scrutiny and focus on the manner of treatment and habilitation of persons with developmental disabilities, both at Grafton and throughout the state. While some argued that the state would have made the necessary changes at the institution without the lawsuit (Strinden, *North Dakota Weekly*, January 23, 1995), others argued that the lawsuit was both necessary and timely in bringing about needed changes for services for individuals with disabilities (Clemens, *North Dakota Weekly*, January 23, 1995). As it stood, the lawsuit and Judge van Sickle's implementation orders clearly drove the changes in Grafton during the 1980s. Staffing patterns changed, residents received new freedoms and responsibilities, and facilities changed. Grafton State School eventually became the Developmental Center, and forever the institution was changed.

Residents. There were significant changes in the population of Grafton State School during the 1980s. From a census of 980 individuals in 1981, the resident population declined to 437 in 1989, a decrease of over 50%. This decline was a direct result of the ARC lawsuit. Judge Van Sickle's orders set specific targets for population decreases in both Grafton and San Haven. And while the state had difficulty meeting the targets in some years, the orders had tremendous impact.

The largest impact was the closure of San Haven. On December 31, 1987 the San Haven doors were closed forever. At the start of the decade there were 249 individuals with mental retardation housed at San Haven, most with profound mental retardation and physical disabilities, or who were aged. At the end of 1987 there were approximately 50 people in San Haven. Most of these people were transferred to Grafton for services.

A major development during the 1980s was the change in guardianship. The ARC lawsuit charged that the superintendent of Grafton State School should not be the primary guardian of individuals enrolled at the institution. This practice of superintendent as guardian had been around for many years, the direct result of ND legislative action.

While the lawsuit required the change, the implementation was somewhat problematic. ND Catholic Family Services was charged with finding suitable proxies and guardians for residents of Grafton, but the process was slow. Dr. Henry Meece reported, "*During this biennium we began the court proceedings whereby the superintendent divests himself of the statutory assumed guardianship of residents, and parents/relatives or other interested parties are appointed guardians. The law enabling this went into effect at the start of this biennium. Thus far, 253 guardianships have been appointed. We have about 269 left to do. The deadline to accomplish this was extended from July 1, 1985 to July 1, 1987, and we do not anticipate a problem meeting that timeline. This process has gone very well with a Grafton judge and the Walsh County State's Attorney handling the proceedings. Grafton State School social workers petition the court to initiate the guardianship hearing.*" (Biennial Report to the Governor of North Dakota, 1985, p. 74).

Other services were greatly improved for the residents, including habilitative medical and therapeutic care, as well as additional staff, and more active daily programming. The daily per diem cost of service in 1980 at Grafton State School was $30.33. By 1989 the cost of care was $235.83 per day, a significant increase.

As residents left Grafton they entered a variety of residential and programming centers throughout the state. From the early hostels and halfway homes of the 1970s, the state had developed regional centers for disability services that included group homes and vocational workshops. Several residents were discharged on their own, and sought homes, jobs and friends in their new-found freedom.

Staffing. Many staff changes resulted from the ARC lawsuit. Most notable was the huge increase and then decrease in staff, both supervisory and direct care. In 1981 there were 601 state-supported staff and 67 federally funded positions. By 1985 there were 1,072 staff positions of which 14 were federally funded. Then with the decrease in resident population, there was a decrease in staff. During the 1987-1989 biennium Dr. Meece reported a decrease of 144 temporary positions and 147 full-time staff, nearly a 28% loss. Meece stated that most losses were the result of attrition rather than layoffs.

The institution continued to struggle with staff turnover during the 1980s. By the end of the decade the turnover rate was less than 20%, a dramatic decrease from the over 50% biennial turnover rates of the late 1970s. Part of the reason for the high turnover rates was the staff wage. Frequently the Grafton State School personnel director commented on the low wage and benefit packages offered to employees.

In January of 1981, staff were given the overall 4% salary increases allocated by the state legislature, and then institutional staff were given a 10% catch-up raise. In 1985 all staff were given an additional $60 per month catch-up pay raise. The personnel director also worked on several pay grade and salary plans. By 1983, staff were given raises based on merit and performance rather than simple tenure.

The records also reflect several organizational changes in the institution. Flowcharts from the biennial reports show departmental shifts, program staff and supervision changes, and even the development of new program areas. For example, in 1983 the institution hired a standards compliance coordinator to help meet Title XIX program standards as mandated by the Van Sickle order. The institution also hired a full-time personnel officer and recruiter to assure an adequate supply of staff.

The new staff also required training to help meet the needs of residents. By 1983 the institution had an in-service system of 60 courses and workshops on various program policy and practices. All new staff were required to take part in a new employee orientation. A new employee newsletter, the *Insider*, was published to keep staff abreast of training and program changes at the institution.

Along with the many staff changes at Grafton State School, there were leadership changes too. Dr. Wisland resigned in 1983 to pursue university teaching and a special education director's position. Paul Witucki, a Grafton employee for over 20 years at that time, served as interim superintendent from the Fall of 1983 until March 1, 1984 when Dr. Henry Meece assumed the superintendent position. Also the Grafton State School oversight moved from the Department of Institutions to the Department of Human Services in the late 1980s. This reflected the new state system of services and coordination brought about by the ARC lawsuit.

Education and training. The early 1980s saw a continuation of the education and training advances of the 1970s. The school's programs continued to improve as staff responded to the policies and regulations of Public Law 94-142, the Education for All Handicapped Children's Act. Nearly all children between the ages of 6 and 22 were receiving educational school services at the institution, most for a full six-hour day.

Training programs for adults continued to improve also, as more and more individuals were prepared for transition for life outside the institution. The Midway Program continued to train women in daily living and work skills, and the adult vocational programs, supported by federal and state vocational rehabilitation funds, helped many people with part to full day services.

However, the ARC lawsuit was the primary impetus for most changes during the 1980s. One of the original charges in the lawsuit was that individuals with mental retardation were being denied appropriate treatment and training at the institution. When Judge Van Sickle's orders came through, this was addressed. In his March 6, 1984 implementation order he said, *"Defendants must provide members of the plaintiff class with an individualized program of treatment and habilitation that affords each member a reasonable chance a) to acquire and maintain those life skills that will enable each member to cope with the demands of person and environment as effectively as the class member's capacities permit, and b) to raise the level of each class member's physical, mental and social functioning"* (Van Sickle implementation order, 1984, p. 10). Van Sickle also directed that the institution provide *"an environment that represents the most normal living condition possible. The principle of normalization includes providing a normal rhythm of life; normal rhythm of the day, with respect to getting up, getting dressed, participating in play and work activities, including differentiation of daily activities and schedules,; and normal rhythm of the year, including observing holidays, days with personal significance, and vacations* " (Van Sickle implementation order, 1984, pp. 10-11).

The institution made several program changes to address these orders. First, the residents were given comprehensive assessments to assist in planning individualized programs. Then, staff teams, which included family members and the individuals themselves at times, developed individualized habilitation plans (IHP). These IHPs included *"individualized and measurable goals and objectives; identification of least restrictive alternatives in programs and residence; plans that are developmentally appropriate and address the individual's greatest priorities in treatment and programming"* (Biennial Report to the Governor of North Dakota, 1989, p. 202). The development of IHPs for all residents was not an easy or quick task. Often those persons slated for community placement were first addressed, leaving those with more significant disabilities the last to receive plans. Also, the variability in staffing made the task difficult. Few staff were trained in writing appropriate IHPs, and they were often more needed on the ward than in meetings. However, by the mid to late 1980s nearly all residents had IHPs on record.

In the early and mid 1980s North A became the center for a new adult education program. Headed by Charlie Robinson, Assistant Director of Resident Education, the program focused on increasing resident involvement in meaningful daily activities. By 1984 over 60 residents were receiving six hours of programming each weekday, and an additional 30 residents were receiving about three hours of programming per day. The adult education program was divided into four learning centers, Vocational Skills I, Vocational Skills II, Activities of Daily Living, and Leisure and Craft Skills Center. *"The activities in Vocational Skills I are designed to promote skill development in the work areas such as sorting, packaging and assembling. The Vocational Skills II is designed to promote skill development in the areas of sorting, packing and assembling. In Vocational Skills II the students work in small groups, learning to cooperate and work together. Activities of Daily Living teaches those skills necessary for a more independent and self-sufficient lifestyle. The Leisure Crafts Skill Center provides training in leisure time arts and crafts activities, basic art skills and in fine motor skills"* (*The Ambassador*, November-December, 1984, pp. 4-5). For many residents this was a marked departure from days of solitude and inactivity.

This shift to proactive programming for citizens with mental retardation was evident in the new mission statement of Grafton State School. Completed during the 1985-87 biennium, the mission statement sought to define Grafton's role in the developing human service system in the state. The statement included comments about quality services, and defined services to include *"1. individual-centered program development; 2. training in which the skills of autonomy and of community appropriate behavior are fostered and maintained; 3. the removal of arbitrary barriers to individual choice making and individual risk-taking; 4. the provision of opportunities to acquire involvement in community settings; and 5. the provision of health care, leisure and fitness services"* (Biennial Report to the Governor of North Dakota, 1987, pp. 55-56).

Superintendent Meece described how these services furthered the lives of persons with mental retardation and were in line with the implementation order from the ARC lawsuit.

In line with the mission and built on the foundation of the adult education program, Grafton State School started an entrepreneurial vocational program in the late 1980s. Dakota Enterprises was a work experience program that employed over 200 residents to provide services or contract work to the community. Residents operated an aluminum recycling center, did cleaning, yard work and maintenance with mobile work crews, and operated a store where various resident-made products (e.g., fishing tackle, ceramic ware, woodwork) were sold. The Dakota Enterprises program served as a good transitional program for many adults with developmental disabilities.

By the late 1980s Grafton State School was providing training services using the unit model of service delivery. Meece described the model as follows. *"In each of the residential living units there is an interdisciplinary team, whose foremost responsibility is to formulate an IHP for each individual. An interdisciplinary team is comprised of staff members of a variety of professional disciplines and direct care staff who plan, carry out and maintain programs provided for each individual based on their needs. Team members are responsible for integrating services and programs into a balanced vocational and residential plan"* (Biennial Report to the Governor of North Dakota, 1989, p. 202). This unit concept was considerably different from the centralized services approach previously used at the institution. Meece felt that the model allowed for more staff-resident interaction, and a closer understanding of resident needs. This model has been used extensively since that time, both at the institution and in various community facilities throughout the state.

Residents continued to benefit from the foster grandparents program and local community volunteers. In addition, an on-campus office was established for the Protection and Advocacy (P & A) Project. The P & A program staff assisted residents in assuring that their rights were met, both under the auspices of the ARC lawsuit, and as a transitional measure to community placement.

Health. Health services were still a major component of services for residents at Grafton State School during the 1980s. The medical and health related team members were much more diverse than in previous decades. While there was often a physician on the campus, most major medical procedures continued to be conducted in local or regional hospital facilities. Other medical staff included physician assistants, nurses and nurse practitioners, laboratory personnel, a dentist, dental assistant and dental hygienist, a pharmacist and dietitians.

As more residents transferred to community placements, a larger percentage of the remaining residents had significant and multiple disabilities. Thus, it is no surprise that while the population decreased during the decade and the constellation of medical services expanded, the death rates increased. In 1981, the resident population was 970 and there were nine deaths. In 1988 and 1989 the resident population was respectively 549 and 437. There were 11 deaths at Grafton State School during each of these years. During the 1980s decade, there were a total of 83 resident deaths. There is no available record as to the cause or nature of those deaths.

The institution continued to provide habilitative surgeries for residents prior to moving to the community. Also the adaptive equipment program provided hundreds of assessments, fittings and devices for residents in preparation for more independent living.

While expensive, the adaptive equipment made huge differences in mobility, communication and productivity for persons with developmental disabilities.

Facilities. Many changes were made in the facilities at Grafton State School during the 1980s. In 1982 Maplewood and Cedar Grove were constructed. These new facilities were placed on the south side of the campus. Built around a central commons area, these buildings were seen as state-of-the-art facilities for persons with mental retardation. Individual rooms were built around common kitchen, dining and living areas, much like small efficiency apartments. Staff facilities and offices were nearby, with unit teams of support staff including psychologists, speech-language pathologists, and direct care staff. Residents also had access to laundry facilities and classroom space for both group and individualized training.

In 1983 the Physical and Occupational Therapy wing was added to the health services building. These new areas allowed for more sophisticated therapeutic techniques, including warm water therapy for residents with severe physical disabilities. During this same year Wylie and West Halls were renovated, providing long needed updates to resident living quarters. A coal fired boiler and building was added to the campus in 1983.

In 1985 West Hall was renamed New Horizons. A new vehicle maintenance and carpentry shop was built on the west/central side of the institution. Also new utility distribution tunnels were built around campus. These tunnels allowed the main service systems of heating, water and electrical pipes to be removed from the staff and resident tunnels, providing greater safety for residents and staff.

During the 1983-85 biennium there was a plan to raze North A. It had fallen into great disrepair, and was no longer used for resident housing or services. However, the plans were shelved when the institution decided to remodel the building for the adult education program. It served as a vocational training program site for several more years until it was remodeled for community housing in the 1990s.

During the 1985-87 biennium a new tunnel was constructed to link the health services building, Sunset Hall and the refectory. Sunset Hall was remodeled to serve as an additional vocational training center, and the Food Services Center was connected above ground to Sunset Hall. Also space was added to house a canteen and the foster grandparent program.

By the late 1980s there were four residential facilities, Cedar Grove, Maplewood, New Horizons, and the Health Services Center. All four units contained nearly 300 Title XIX certified beds, which were required for meeting the intent of the ARC lawsuit. These certified units met standards for privacy, facilities and resident space. On December 31, 1987 San Haven closed and the remaining 50 residents were transferred to Grafton State School.

1990 – 2000: Establishing a New Mission

The decade of the 1990s was a period of transformation for the institution at Grafton. The ARC lawsuit had a huge impact on the institutional population, such that by 1991 there were only 211 residents on the campus. While the staff numbers had risen substantially from the early 1980s, these dropped quickly during the 1990s. The state found itself with a large campus, with 37 buildings and few immediate uses. These changes forced the staff of the institution, state leaders and the community of Grafton to rally around a new mission, in effect re-inventing the institution for the new millennium.

Residents. After the rapid decreases of the 1980s, the institution population hovered at about 200 residents during the early 1990s. The 1989 – 1991 Biennial Report of the ND Department of Human Services shows that on June 30, 1991, there were 211 residents at the Developmental Center. Staff had admitted 41 residents during this biennium; however, only three were for regular admission. The remaining 38 were for evaluation. Forty-seven residents were placed in the community during this period, and only one resident returned to the institution from a community placement.

The resident population decreased slightly throughout the decade. In 1995 there were 144 residents, and in 1999 there were 137 on the Grafton campus. All residents had individual habilitation plans, and most were employed in some form of work or work experience. Residents lived in one of four residential units, all of which had received Tittle XIX certification. This allowed the institution to access federal Medicaid funds for supporting the residents. Along with the on-campus support systems, staff also supported residents who had been placed in the community, often serving as consultants to the community providers. By the end of the decade, the resident population at Grafton had reached the resident population level of the 1908 – 1910 biennium.

Staffing. Along with the resident population decline, the staff numbers decreased over the decade. In 1991 there were over 800 staff at Grafton. In July of 1993 there were sizable staff reductions that resulted in great controversy. In fact several employees contested their dismissals, and appealed to the State Personnel Board for redress. Staff were concerned that the reductions would place residents at risk for inappropriate care, further exacerbating the ARC lawsuit requirements. The Board upheld nearly all of the staff reductions, citing both reduced resident population and the reorganization of services at the institution as supporting reasons. Budget cuts and reorganization again reduced staff levels in the mid and late 1990s, such that by 1997 there were fewer than 500 staff at the institution.

Leadership changes occurred several times during the 1990s. Henry Meece, superintendent since 1984, resigned in April of 1993. With Dr. Meece's departure, Ms. Wanda Kratchovil was tabbed as the interim superintendent. Ms. Kratchovil had been at the institution since 1983, serving at one point as the unit director for the health services programs, and later as the residential director. By May 1994 Kratchovil resigned to serve as director of nursing for a Park River nursing home.

There was considerable posturing during this time in deciding how to operate the institution. ND Department of Human Services director, H.C. "Bud" Wessman was concerned about the viability of the institution with such a low resident population. The Grand Forks Herald stated, *"Wessman said the population may fall from 150 to 120 within a year. 'You get much below that number and it starts no longer to become a cost-effective operation,' said Wessman. 'You hope within the next six to 12 months, you have a much clearer focus, a clearer goal as to where you might be going with the facility.'* (*Grand Forks Herald*, March 30, 1994, p. 1A).

Kratchovil's resignation allowed Wessman to propose a new arrangement where Friendship, Inc., a residential service provider organization, would manage Grafton. The proposal included a $6,000 per month fee to Friendship, Inc. The Friendship management staff were also charged with examining other options for making the institutional grounds a viable economic contributor to the community.

While Friendship, Inc. was named to manage the facilities, another institution staff member, Brian Lunski, was put in charge of daily program operations. By May of 1995 Wessman appointed Lunski as the permanent superintendent of Grafton. While Lunski saw the appointment as a bit of a surprise and an honor, Wessman had very specific expectations of the new appointee. His appointment letter stated, *"You are aware of the duties for the position that you have agreed to assume, and you will be evaluated based on your performance of those duties... In addition, you're cognizant of my desire to diversify the use of our very fine facility at Grafton, and you are hereby charged with doing everything in your power to facilitate the diversification and expanded use of that facility"* (*Grand Forks Herald,* May 16, 1995, p. 1). Obviously Lunski had a large task before him in his new appointment.

Facilities. With the exodus of large numbers of residents during the 1990s, there was little need to construct new facilities. However, some existing buildings needed updates to meet certification codes for accessing state and federal Medicaid funds. These renovations were conducted without huge disruption to the campus.

In 1990, the Collette Educational school services were closed, and all school-aged residents of the institution were provided educational services in the Grafton community schools. In late 1990, the building was re-dedicated as the Collette Community Fitness Center, a combination institutional and community center for health and wellness. Community members were afforded access to the aquatic facilities, the gymnasium, and the new fitness equipment.

In 1993 Grafton applied for and received a $100,000 grant from the ND Department of Economic Development and Finance. This grant supported a local committee charged with determining the future use of the institutional facilities. An Indianapolis, Indiana company, Municipal Consultants, was hired in December 1993 to assist the committee in fielding and evaluating proposals for facility use.

There was considerable discussion and many proposals submitted over the next six years. One particularly contentious debate was over the placement of a veteran's home at the institution. During the 1995 legislative session, there were two proposals for veteran's homes, one in Stanley and one at Grafton. The local community was extremely supportive of the Grafton proposal, even suggesting that they could add up to $50,000 to the proposal from community funds. However, the legislative assembly denied both proposals, apparently ending the drive for a northeastern ND center for veterans.

But community leaders were not dissuaded, and invited Senators Dorgan and Conrad to tour the facilities. There was some talk with them about the use of the institutional buildings and services to support community services in the area. This discussion proved fruitful, as in February 1996, Senators Dorgan and Conrad, and Representative Pomeroy announced the award of federal funding for a Veterans Satellite Clinic at the Developmental Center.

The public proved to be quite a force to be reckoned with when the state proposed demolition of North A, North B and the Annex in 1994. At about this time, there had been talk of converting the former resident halls into community housing for the elderly. However, the state posted a request for bids for demolition in the Grand Forks Herald, catching many citizens by surprise. The community Historic Preservation District quickly listed the buildings on the historic registry, making demolition extremely difficult. The group also organized a cleanup crew in October 1994 to clean and organize the once abandoned facilities.

This community support drew the attention of a development corporation, Retirement Housing Foundation of Long Beach, CA. In June of 1995 the Foundation proposed the development of an elderly housing facility, encompassing North A, and much of North B and the Annex. While development plans were still in the works, the Foundation stepped aside and Metro Plains Development Inc. took over in October of 1997. They broke ground in October 1998, and residents moved into the facility in 1999.

During the late 1990s, other programs took root at the campus, including a Head Start program, a Domestic Violence center, and a local group home provider. A traumatic brain injury unit was added to the hospital/residential area in July of 1999. Although they were primarily human services oriented programs, the face of the institution and the mission for community service had expanded beyond those with developmental disabilities.

Education and training. During the 90s, the institution continued its focus on improving the quality of services for the residents. In 1991, Dakota East Vocational Services, a vocational and transition program of the institution, provided training and work supports to a significant number of the residents. These individuals were employed at the gift shop, in various community retail establishments, in the institution recycling center, and on mobile work crews. The ND Human Services Department Report shows that residents received over $12,000 in salary and wages during the biennium from Dakota East.

The institution diversified its set of services to accommodate the needs of those individuals both on campus and those heading to or already placed in ND communities. Along with the typical residential and vocational training services, the Developmental Center also provided adaptive equipment fitting and maintenance, medical, dental, physical therapy, occupational therapy, psychology, audiology, speech/language therapy, recreation, nutrition, and social services for the residents. In addition, the foster grandparent program continued to provide companionship and support for younger residents, and local volunteers added over 4,000 hours of service to the campus.

In 1996 the Developmental Center entered into an agreement with the UND Family Practice Clinic in Grand Forks for medical services. Two or three times each week, a staff physician and a resident physician provided medical care to the campus. At about the same time, Unity Therapy services moved its therapeutic program from the Grafton hospital to the institution, making use of the state-of-the-art therapeutic facilities for community residents. Finally, by 1999 the institution established a sexual offenders program for individuals with developmental disabilities. The STOP (Specialized Treatment of Sexual Offenders) program was designed specifically in response to statewide need and the request of community providers. STOP staff were able to provided 24 hour supervised care and educational treatment programming to individuals deemed to be sexual predators, or to have a pre-disposition for such actions.

During this decade the institutional staff focused on meeting national standards for service for residents. Partly as an outcome of the ARC lawsuit and partly as a strategic effort for improving services, the institution entered into multiple accreditation reviews during the 1990s. The Accreditation Council reviewed institutional programs at least four times (1991, 1993, 1995, and 1998). Council examiners reviewed both the number and the quality of available programs for individuals on the Grafton campus. While the standards changed during this period (outcomes-based standards were added in the late 1990s), the Developmental Center received passing marks each time. It was apparent that the mission and services of the institution had changed, and the standard of quality was met.

Today

Today, the institutional grounds combine some of the old with some of the new. There are approximately 150 residents on campus. Most have been placed for specific rehabilitation or support reasons, such as specialized medical care, sexual offender or predator treatment, or intensive behavioral issues. The institution shares a director with the ND State Hospital in Jamestown. Mr. Alex Schweitzer was appointed as the director of both the Developmental Center and the State Hospital. He splits his administrative time between Jamestown and Grafton. In additional, the Developmental Center has a full time, on-site administrator in Sue Foerster, the assistant superintendent of the Developmental Center.

There are several service and support programs operating at the institution today. Two major residential units, Maplewood and Cedar Grove, continue to house residents with developmental disabilities who need specialized and consistent supports not typically available in our communities. The Developmental Center houses a state of the art adaptive equipment center. Here staff can design, construct and fit specialized adaptive equipment for residents. Also, the staff have a mobile clinic which allows them to travel throughout the state to assist others who need their services.

One unique program at the Developmental Center is the sexual offender program. Here staff train and support individuals with disabilities who have problems related to sexual offenses in the community. The specialized training is presently not available in other areas of the state, and the centralized facility in Grafton allows for a more controlled and directed treatment program.

Several local, regional and state agencies lease space at the institution. These include a day care center, an outreach office for the North East Human Services Center, the Upper Valley Special Education unit, and a Veterans services center. North A and B have become community housing facilities, privately operated and serving many of the elderly in the community.

Summary

The institution originally designed for "the feebleminded, epileptic and idiotic of our state" has undergone dramatic changes in its 100 year history. The buildings and grounds have expanded and retreated, the resident population has grown and waned, tens of thousands of staff have lived and worked on the campus, and over 5,000 residents have lived, worked, and died there.

There is likely as much to mourn as there is to celebrate about the institution. For all of the problems and defects of the system of institutions throughout the last 100 years, I am convinced that nearly every staff worker, supervisor, and administrator was truly doing the best that he or she knew how to do. The literature shows that the institutional services in North Dakota were really not much different from those of other states (Trent,

1994). The patterns of farm production and provincialism, changes in the care and treatment of residents, over-crowding, staffing, and overall provision of services were typical of institutions throughout the United States during these last 100 years. It is clear we were all struggling along as best we could.

And while there might be much to condemn, there is still much to celebrate. The institution at Grafton has caused North Dakota to learn much about people with disabilities and about our overall societal responsibilities. As a state we have learned to change and grow as we assumed these responsibilities. I expect we will continue to learn and change even more in the next 100 years.

Chapter Three

The People

Literally tens of thousands of people have passed through the doors of the North Dakota Developmental Center in the past 100 years. This has included residents, superintendents, staff, governors, legislators, family members, and other assorted visitors. This chapter will describe some of the people and their daily lives in the institution, beginning with the superintendents and ending with the residents.

Superintendents

Job Description and Duties
Over the past 100 years, there have been 16 superintendents. These individuals were responsible for the overall operation and supervision of the institution. Originally, North Dakota law stated that the superintendent had to be a physician *"skilled in caring for, and in instructing the class of unfortunates to be provided for by this act"* (Laws of North Dakota, 1903, p. 142). However, as the institution changed and the duties became more administrative, the position description changed. Early on, the superintendents served as the institutional physician, treating the residents as necessary. These individuals also were responsible for all personnel, programs and facilities management. Eventually, the superintendent came to govern both the institution at Grafton and the San Haven facility, and later the Developmental Center in Grafton and the State Hospital in Jamestown.

One primary duty of the superintendents was to interact with and promote legislation with the various boards, agencies, and legislators. This was important in the early days of the institution, as the idea of the institution was so new. Most typical North Dakota residents had little knowledge of the purpose or operations of the facility. Thus the superintendent was a visible spokesperson who kept the public informed. The superintendents' reports are filled with photographs, stories, budget requests, and legislative initiatives designed to make the institution a viable and economically feasible operation.

The following is a listing of the superintendents at Grafton and their terms of office. This information was drawn from the superintendent reports, state agency reports, and newspaper articles. When possible, the year and the month of employment and termination are provided.

Superintendents of the North Dakota Developmental Center
1. Louis B. Baldwin, M.D., December 1903 – April 1907
2. H. A. LaMoure, M.D., April 1907 – December 1910
3. A. R. T. Wylie, Ph.D., M.D., December 1910 – July 1933
4. James P. Aylen, M.D., F.A.C.S., July 1933 – 1938
5. Frank W. Deason, M.D., 1938 - 1939
6. John G. Lamont, M.D., 1939- June 1953

| 7. James Marr, M.D., July 1953 – December 1953 |
| 8. E. H. Intlehouse, Acting Superintendent, December 1953 – May 1954 |
| 9. Charles C. Rand, M.D., May 1954 – June 1972 |
| 10. Ronald E. Archer, Ed. D., July, 1972- – August, 1979 |
| 11. Milton Wisland, Ed.D. August 1979 - September 1983 |
| 12. Paul Witucki, September 1983 – March 1984 Acting Superintendent |
| 13. Henry C. Meece, Jr., Ph.D., March 1984 – April 1993 |
| 14. Wanda Kratochvil, June 1993 – May 1994   Interim Superintendent |
| 15. Brian Lunski, May 1994 – April 2000 |
| 16. Alex Schweitzer, April 2000 – present |

Most of the superintendents lived on the institutional grounds. From Dr. Louis B. Baldwin to Dr. Charles Rand, these superintendents and their families lived in family quarters in the Main building. Over the years several superintendents commented on the need for new residencies for the staff, particularly the superintendent. For example, in 1938 Dr. Frank Deason said *"Eight years ago (in the 1930 report) a cottage was requested by the Superintendent because of the crowded condition in the Administration Building. It was said then that such a cottage 'would contribute to the rest and peace of mind of the Superintendent and consequently to his efficiency.' The enrollment of 669 at that time has grown to 936, and the statement is proportionally apt. Such a cottage is an urgent need."* (Eighteenth Biennial Report, 1938, p. 919).

Deason and other superintendents worked endlessly to obtain suitable housing for themselves and for other staff. Finally, in 1953, 1954 and 1955 several staff cottages were built. The superintendent's home was built in 1959, with Dr. Charles Rand being the first superintendent living in the quarters. Later superintendents would live in the superintendent home. While still on the campus grounds, they were somewhat removed from the daily activity of the institution and afforded some privacy.

Major Accomplishments

The superintendents at Grafton had various philosophies in running the institution. The following section provides some description of the major challenges and accomplishments of the superintendents. In the case of the earlier superintendents, these descriptions are generated from their reports and the summary of events that occurred during their tenure. Descriptions of events of the more recent superintendents include an analysis of the state legislation and the numerous institutional and local newspaper articles.

Dr. Louis B. Baldwin. Dr. Baldwin was the first superintendent of the ND Institution for the Feebleminded. Formerly the assistant superintendent at the State Hospital for the Insane in Jamestown, Dr. Baldwin came to the institution with some experience with individuals who were mentally retarded. Prior to the construction of the institution at Grafton those individuals who were classified as feeble minded were often placed at the Jamestown facility.

Dr. Baldwin had the daunting task of furnishing, staffing, and opening the institution. Hired on December 16, 1903 by the Governor's appointed Board of Trustees for the institution, he faced an enormous task. Early in 1904 he and two of the board members traveled by train to Minnesota. There they visited the Fairbault State Hospital, Minnesota's institution for the feeble minded. Continuing on to St. Paul, they met with several suppliers to purchase office goods, beds and other furniture necessary to outfit the over 26,000 square foot building.

Baldwin's first report to the Board of Trustees and the Governor details the tremendous amount of work done to open the facility. In this report he also calls for the purchase of additional land, buildings and structures (root cellar, porches on the west side of Main, and a barn), and equipment for the institution. Baldwin opened the institution on May 2, 1904, admitting six residents that day. By November 1, 1904 there were 75 residents at the institution. He also hired the first teacher and organized formal classes for the residents. His description of the purpose of the training at the institution served as the primary goal for many years after his departure. He said *"the aim is to so train and develop him, that his life in the institution may be useful and that the greatest amount of happiness and comfort my be realized by him. The training therefor is of the most practical nature and is largely individual, being adapted to the possibilities of each case"* (First Biennial Report, 1904, p. 10). Baldwin served only four years, resigning in 1907.

H. A. LaMoure, M.D. Dr. LaMoure was the second superintendent of the Institution for Feeble Minded, and served from 1907 to 1910. He was the first superintendent to use his biennial reports to market the viability of the institution, and to press for legislative support for the institution's mission. LaMoure's 1908 report presents some of the first photographs of the institution. The main building, powerhouse and laundry facilities are displayed on the front cover of the report. Additional photographs show the farm buildings, the interior of the powerhouse, dormitory wings in Main, and both the men's and women's handwork classes.

LaMoure used his reports to push for the restriction of rights and movement of the residents. He had provided the Board of Trustees with numerous reports from other states' institutions. Their analysis of these reports prompted the Board and LaMoure to ask for legislation regarding commitment and movement of residents. *"Under the existing laws, we have no legal right to hold any child if its parents wish to remove it. I cannot but feel that this is wrong and that it would be best for the welfare of the state and for the children themselves if all cases were regularly committed to the institution, and their discharge depend upon the approval of yourselves (the Board) and the advice of your superintendent."* Thus, LaMoure proposed *"that legislation be enacted making the board of trustees the legal guardians of all cases admitted to this institution"* (Third Biennial Report, 1908, pp. 9-10).

LaMoure saw the development and construction of the hospital building in 1910. He hired the first nurse, Miss Anna Emge, to run the daily operations of the hospital. But even with this facility, LaMoure was concerned about overcrowding in the institution. In his 1920 report he states, *"Our institution has now very nearly reached its capacity and within a very short time we will be unable to take more cases. It seems to me to be absolutely imperative that accommodations be furnished for the increase that is sure to come. I would, therefore, recommend the erection of a building with a capacity for at least one hundred cases as well as more rooms for employees and officers*" (Fourth Biennial Report, 1910, p. 15).

A. R. T. Wylie, Ph.D., M.D. Arthur Rufus Trego Wylie was a physician and a scholar having earned both medical and academic degrees. He served as the third superintendent at the institution for 23 years, from 1910 to 1933. Dr. Wylie had a prominent professional and academic career prior to coming to North Dakota. Vyzralek provides a telling description of this gentleman. "*Wylie began his professional career as pharmacist at the Minnesota State School for Idiots and Imbeciles at Faribault, after which he completed a doctorate in psychology at the College of Wooster in Ohio. He published his research on 'mental pathology' during the early years of the twentieth century, exploring the senses, reaction time and other phenomena of developmentally disabled people. Wylie later pursued medical training and took over at Grafton after serving as the first assistant physician at Faribault, thereby having the distinction of being both a Ph.D. and an M.D. While has been credited as being 'the first clinical psychology to be employed in a mental retardation institution in the United States'*" (Vyzralek, 1996, p. 14).

Wylie had previously been the president of the American Association for the Study of the Feeble Minded in 1909-10. He was the first such president who, at the time of election, was not a superintendent of an institution. During his tenure as president of the organization he laid out a theme that he used extensively during his years at Grafton; the general public had little knowledge of the purpose and operations of institutions for the feeble minded. He therefore pushed for a large public awareness campaign, something he used extensively during his time at Grafton. This was especially evident in his use of case studies and stories in his biennial reports.

At Grafton Wylie saw the population of the facility rise from 165 to over 700 residents. This population increase was also matched by numerous construction projects at the institution. No less than 10 structures were built during this period, most notably the North A, the east and west sections of North B, and the Pleasant View dormitories.

Dr. Wylie also started the social service department. Based on his work in 1922 and 1923 with the national mental hygiene survey of North Dakota, he envisioned a department that would conduct research on the residents and their circumstances regarding admission, and then educate the public about the perceived dangers of individuals with mental deficiency in the communities. To this end Wylie used his biennial reports to educate the public about mental retardation. His most notable method was to use long narrative case studies to illustrate the benefits of institutionalization. In his 1914 report, Wylie provided the first written history of the institution, a sort of 10 year perspective of the work toward combating feeble mindedness. He also used a portion of this report to urge for greater societal control of feeble minded persons, describing the results of his reading and research on the subject, along with providing some genetic charts which suggested that mental deficiency was a hereditary characteristic that must be controlled. Other reports continued to push his philosophy of social control, using example stories such as *The Improvement of Metro* (1922), *The Story of Ottne* (1922), and *The Story of Barbara and Her Family* (1928). Each story related how, without proper institutional control and care, the feeble minded of the state might continue to procreate and inflict ill upon the communities.

Wylie continued to use photographs in his biennial reports to show the progress of construction and training at the institution. In June of 1933 Wylie resigned having served the longest of any of his previous colleagues, and eventually serving the longest term of any of the institution's superintendents. *"Never again would a single superintendent remain for as long at Grafton or exert so much influence, both locally and nationally"* (Vyzralek, 1996, p. 17).

James P. Aylen, M.D. Dr. Aylen was the fourth superintendent at Grafton serving from 1933 to 1938. He was an accomplished surgeon, holding the prestigious Fellow of American College of Surgeons (FACS). Aylen led Grafton during the central time period of social control of citizens with mental retardation. In many ways, Aylen's work continued where Wylie had left off. By 1933 the institution had just begun to regularly implement procedures for the sterilization of women of childbearing age, and men under 60 years of age. State law permitting sterilization had been available since 1913, with a revision occurring in 1927. Wylie had used the law very little, especially early in his career.

Aylen, however, had two pressures points that pushed the institution toward large-scale sterilizations. First, Henrietta Safely's Social Service Department studies suggested that sterilization was an effect way to control the spread of mental deficiency. Second, the depression caused the institution to become more accountable for itself, and thus come under greater public scrutiny and public examination. Citizens were skeptical that persons with mental retardation could or should be allowed in society for fear of perpetuating the moral degeneration of the state. One alternative was to use and promote sterilization. This decision suited Aylen, since his surgical skills could be put to use for the benefit of society. Thus the institution went from a handful of sterilizations in its first thirty years, to more than 200 per year for the next 15 years.

Frank W. Deason, M.D. Dr. Deason was superintendent at Grafton for only one year. He submitted only one biennial report, and no records exist in the state archives that provide much detail to his time at Grafton. The 1940 report by Dr. Lamont shows that Deason did initiate a major Works Project Administration (WPA) effort that resulted in painting the wards and halls of both the North A and North B men's dormitories. In addition one WPA crew constructed a new machine shed for the farm in early 1939. Deason's report suggests that he simply carried on the work of his predecessors, continuing the sterilizations, asking for more ward space for the residents, requesting a separate superintendent's quarters, and maintaining the daily activities of the institution.

John G. Lamont, M.D. Dr. Lamont was the sixth superintendent at the Grafton institution, serving from 1939 to 1953. Lamont served the state of North Dakota for 30 years, first as superintendent of the San Haven Institution (the Tuberculosis Sanatorium), and then as superintendent at Grafton for 14 years. He had oversight of Grafton State School as it transitioned from an era of social control to the beginning of a growth period. Perhaps Lamont's greatest challenge was taking the institution through the World War II and post-war situations. During this time public support shifted from concerns at home to concerns for the war abroad. Male staff were difficult to find, the cost of building materials and products rose dramatically, and financial support from the state was sparse.

However, Lamont persevered and Grafton maintained its facilities and purpose for serving ND citizens with mental retardation. The 1958 biennial report shows that Dr. Lamont passed away in January 1958 in retirement at his home in Oklahoma City, Oklahoma.

James Marr, M.D. Dr. James Marr served the shortest time of any of the superintendents, working from July 1953 until his passing in December 1953. Dr. Marr came to Grafton from Glenwood, Iowa. He was hired as Lamont's replacement and started work during the summer of 1953. At that time the institution had over 1,200 residents and a biennial budget of over $3 million. His unexpected death (a heart attack) created an emergency in finding a new superintendent during the winter of 1953-54.

E. H. Intlehouse, Mr. Intlehouse served as acting superintendent upon Dr. Marr's death. Mr. Intlehouse had served as the secretary for the institution for quite some time. Having done an admirable job in organizing the administrative offices of the facility, Intlehouse was appointed as acting superintendent. This appointment occurred as the Board of Administration members attended Marr's funeral. On December 5, 1953 Intlehouse began his new job serving from December 1953 until June 1954 when Dr. Charles Rand was appointed permanent superintendent.

Charles C. Rand, M.D. Dr. Rand had the second longest tenure of superintendents at Grafton, serving from 1954 until his retirement in June 1972. Rand received bachelor and master's degrees from UND in 1929 and 1930, then completed his medical training at Temple University in Philadelphia. He had practiced medicine in Walsh County from 1933 until taking over Grafton in 1954.

Dr. Rand was the first superintendent to live away from the Main building, moving into the separate superintendent's quarters in 1960. He had a dramatic impact on the shape and future of the institution, moving it from a custodial, protective institution to one focused on community transition of persons with mental retardation.

As the leader of Grafton State School, Dr. Rand implemented many new initiatives. The first was an initiative of greater choice and independence of the more capable residents. He carried out this initiative on several fronts. First, he organized several institutional stores called 'canteens'. These resident and staff stores carried some basic daily necessities like combs, toothbrushes, and hairbrushes, along with candy and snacks. One item that quickly became popular with many residents was tobacco. Residents were allowed to use their money (from family donations or their work on campus) to buy individual items. The canteens were so popular that Rand was later able to use canteen profits to purchase a merry-go-round that became a huge source of pleasure and entertainment for the residents.

Another innovation in resident choice and independence was the increased ability of residents to have extended summer and holiday vacations. Previously, few if any residents were allowed to leave the institution. However, Dr. Rand thought it was important to provide residents with some continued contact with family. Although all vacations required Social Service Department approval, including family background checks, dozens and then later hundreds of residents took vacations each year, many who enjoyed their new connections with their home communities.

Rand, originally an East Grand Forks resident, retired from Grafton in July 1972 and returned to medical practice in Grafton, retiring from medicine in 1979. He passed away in Grafton on February 28, 1996 at the age of 88.

Ronald E. Archer, Ed. D. Dr. Ronald Archer was the first institutional superintendent who did not possess a medical degree. He served from July 1972 until August 1979. Trained in speech language pathology at Minot State College, and later receiving his doctoral degree in Colorado, Dr. Archer had started the mental retardation teacher training program at Minot State College in the mid 1960s. He had also served on several state and local boards that developed planning documents for services for ND residents with mental retardation. Thus he was both familiar with the circumstances of individuals with mental retardation and aware of their service needs in the state.

Archer's appointment forced the state legislature to re-examine the superintendent qualifications. Upon his initial appointment the state had to award him an 'interim' status, as he did not meet the physician qualifications of the state position. However, the 1973 legislature changed the superintendent qualifications, allowing for a non-physician to run the institution as long as there was a qualified doctor appointed as institutional medical director.

Coming from a non-medical field, Dr. Archer had a different view of the institution's purpose. His studies in mental retardation at Greeley, Colorado led him back to the initial reasons for the institution, that residents should be trained to become productive members of society. Thus he implemented a variety of initiatives that drew upon his work with the state mental retardation planning councils. He believed in the concepts of community housing and vocational workshops, and pushed for institutional programs to further those causes. His ideas became realities in programs such as Midway House and the adult education program.

The shift from medical to functional programming was not without its trials. Archer suffered at least two heart attacks and had open-heart surgery during his tenure at Grafton. There was nearly a staff walkout in the mid 1970s primarily as the result of wage disputes with the state. The Governor and several state department officials had to step in, stop the walkout, and calm staff fears about rumors of wage cuts. The shift of San Haven to the Grafton State School in 1973 also brought about some stress. Now the superintendent had two diverse staffs and facilities separated by several hundred miles. Archer quickly appointed Dr. Richard Charrier as Assistant Superintendent at Grafton and Mr. Paul Witucki as Assistant Superintendent at Grafton to deal with some of the more pressing issues.

Under Archer's direction the institution opened the Food Services Center, the Aquatic Center at Collette Education Building, and the new Professional Services Building. This last building replaced the old Main building that was razed during Archer's last year at Grafton.

In March of 1979 Dr. Archer announced his resignation. In his resignation letter to Edward Klecker, Director of Institutions, Archer said, "*I personally feel that I have given the institutions, their residents, parents and employees, as well as the citizens of North Dakota the maximum of my abilities, talents, skills and humanness, often times at the expense of my wife and my personal health. Bringing the functions of the institutions, including their personnel, closer to a contemporary level has been extremely challenging and exciting, however, the long hours, lost weekends, the drudgery of travel and the work load has taken its toll and as you know, many of the daily tasks associated with and required by this office can be much less than pleasant.*

I feel that during my tenure the record of progress, solving of may problems and redirecting the missions of the institutions has been very satisfying and rewarding and that it heralds a definite beginning of a greatly enhanced way of life for our residents that just a few years ago was an impossible dream or an unthinkable thought. The best of efforts is the least that all the residents deserve, therefore, the time for me to leave has come, before I too become a government administrator who 'burns out' and becomes guilty of underserving his charges who do hot have the ability or opportunity to speak for themselves" (*The Ambassador*, April, 1979, p. 1). Dr. Archer returned to Minot State University where he again directed the teacher training programs in mental retardation. He taught undergraduate and graduate special education courses until his death by heart attack in May 1982.

Milton Wisland, Ed.D. Dr. Wisland was the second non-medical superintendent of Grafton running the institution from1979 to 1983. He had earned a doctorate from Greeley, Colorado also, and had published several articles and books, most notably on assessing individuals with disabilities. Previously a regional director of special education in Washington state, Dr. Wisland arrived at Grafton during a particularly contentious time. While some deinstitutionalization occurred during Rand and Archer's reign, the resident population was high and San Haven was under the control of the institution. Also, there was large staff turnover that was gradually being improved. Most difficult for the new superintendent, however, was the filing of the ARC lawsuit against the institution and the state claiming inappropriate services.

Dr. Wisland's philosophy sometimes clashed with the principals in the ARC lawsuit. This was evident by his statements shortly after he was hired. Institutional staff were concerned about their jobs as the plaintiff's lawyers argued whether there should even be an institution. An article by John Strand presented Wisland's ideas on deinstitutionalization. *"Federal law states that developmentally handicapped individuals should be placed in the least restrictive learning environment possible. Dr. Wisland agrees with that concept, however, 'in the event that we feel the community services are not there, we would be doing them a disservice. The people need to know there will always be an institution'"* (*The Ambassador*, October, 1979, p. 1).

After struggling with the ARC lawsuit and initial base order, Wisland retired in September 1983, going to Minot State College for a brief period. He later returned to his first love, directing a rural special education cooperative unit in southwestern North Dakota.

Paul Witucki. Mr. Witucki served as acting superintendent from Dr. Wisland's departure in 1983 to the hiring of Dr. Meece in 1984. Witucki was a longtime fixture at the institution, having been hired as a staff psychologist in 1961. He knew the institution and the people, as well as the issues related to operating the facility. He was an excellent acting superintendent until Dr. Henry Meece was hired on a permanent basis.

Henry C. Meece, Jr., Ph.D. Dr. Henry "Bud" Meece was the thirteenth superintendent of Grafton from 1984 to1993. Meece received his Ph.D. in administration and special education from Ohio State University and held an undergraduate degree from East Tennessee State University and a master's degree from the University of Virginia. Prior to working at Grafton, he had been a teacher, an administrator of mental retardation programs, and was the chief executive officer for Southern Nevada Retardation Services in Las Vegas.

During his tenure he oversaw many changes resulting from the ARC lawsuit. Most notably the population of the institution dropped from over 900 residents to less than 200 in his nine years on the job. His major task was to ensure that the basic components of Judge Van Sickle's orders were implemented while ensuring a quality management system for the institution. Meece adopted a Total Quality Improvement (TQI) system that led the staff through a self-analysis of their operations and led to many state and national accreditations. In many ways, Dr. Meece was the chief engineer for ensuring the smooth and successful transition of residents from the institution to community living. This was complicated by the continual scrutiny of the court and the reorganization necessary to make the transition complete.

Dr. Meece resigned from the ND Developmental Center in 1993 after the majority of the ARC implementation orders had been met. He moved back to Tennessee to lead another state institution and eventually became the Chair of the Board of Directors of the Council, the primary accreditation body of mental retardation facilities in the United States.

Wanda Kratochvil. Ms. Kratochvil served as the interim superintendent from June 1993 to May 1994. Originally hired at Grafton in 1983 as a unit nurse, she moved to assistant director of nursing and later took over as unit director for health services. Kratochvil, a nurse, became the supervisor of all residential units.

Human Services Director H.C. Wessman appointed Kratochvil as director in 1993 to serve a three to six month appointment after Meece's resignation. Wessman wanted Kratochvil to focus her efforts on successful completion of upcoming accreditation visits. Kratochvil left the Developmental Center to work as director of nursing at the Good Samaritan Nursing home in Park River, her hometown.

Brian Lunski. Mr. Lunski was a former institutional employee at Grafton who became superintendent in 1995 and served until 2000. During the interim from Kratochvil's departure in May 1994 until Lunski's appointment as superintendent in May 1995, the center had been run by Friendship, Inc., a private non-profit provider of services for adults with developmental disabilities. During this time, Lunski was a key liaison between Friendship Inc. and the institution. When Friendship's contract expired, Dr. Wessman formally appointed Lunski as the superintendent. In his appointment letter Wessman had very specific directions for Lunski. *"You are aware of the duties for the position that you have agreed to assume, and you will be evaluated based on your performance of those duties. In addition, you're cognizant of my desire to diversify the use of our very fine facility at Grafton, and you are hereby charged with doing everything in your power to facilitate the diversification and expanded use of that facility"* (Walsh County Record, May 16 1995, p. 1, 8).

Lunski oversaw the transition and reformation of the Developmental Center from a primary care institution to a larger, more multi-formed set of programs. During his tenure North A and B were developed into community housing, the Veteran's clinic was established, and various community, regional and state agencies and programs.

Alex Schweitzer. In a somewhat historic twist of fate, the superintendent of the ND Developmental Center at the one hundred year mark is from Jamestown, the origin of the very first superintendent, Dr. Louis Baldwin, who had been the assistant superintendent of the ND Hospital for the Insane in Jamestown. On April 10, 2000 Human Services Director Carol Olson appointed Alex Schweitzer as the Superintendent of Institutions with responsibility for both the Jamestown and Grafton facilities.

This decision was not a complete surprise. For several years prior to 2000, the state legislature actually considered combining the Grafton and Jamestown programs, housing both sets of residents at one facility. However, Lunski and Schweitzer had both argued against such a merger. Schweitzer put it this way; *"Brian (Lunski) and I have been busy providing information to the committee in terms of population, type of clients, cost data, revenue expenses and employees. The recommendation of the committee was not to co-locate because it wasn't practical because of the different clients involved within the two institutions. Plus the drastic impact a move like that would have on employees. How do you fill the void left by closing an institution?"* (Grand Forks Herald, May 24, 2000, pp. A-1, A-9). One week after Schweitzer's appointment as head of both institutions, the ND Legislative Interim Budget Committee on Institutional Service voted on a resolution to operate the institutions as separate facilities and programs.

Over the last four years, Schweitzer has had the responsibility of managing the legislative actions, public perceptions, and organizational behavior of the two programs. His management style has been to delegate programmatic responsibilities to his assistant superintendents and other administrative staff. Schweitzer says, *"I have basically an assistant at both facilities. Sue Forester, residential services unit director, is the person in Grafton. She has a strong understanding of the needs of the clients, which is real important. We have good management staff and supervisors in both institutions to deal with those day to day things. ...It works well because their primary orientation is in the direct care of clients and all participate in the daily decision making and direction on how we provide care for clients..."* (Grand Forks Herald, May 24, 2000, pp. A-1, A-9). As of May 2004 this process has worked, and both institutions are viable and in capable hands.

Institutional Staff

Along with the superintendent, the institution employed thousands of staff throughout the years. The majority of the staff were from the surrounding Walsh County area and were charged with the direct care and instruction of the residents. Initially there were few staff other than the superintendent. Along with some direct care staff, there was a matron, a school principal and a farm hand. For example the following figure shows the primary staff reported for the 1910 through 1912 biennium.

Medical staff. Medical care of the residents was important to early institution operation. While the institution was built as a training school for persons with mental retardation, it was operated on a hospital model. The superintendent was a physician, much in line with the practice in institutions all across the country. In some circles, feeble mindedness was approached as a medical or genetic defect. Additionally, many institution residents presented multiple health and medical issues such as epilepsy, physical deformities or tuberculosis. Thus good medical care was necessary for resident survival.

Superintendent	A.R.T. Wylie, Ph.D., M.D.
Stenographer	Miss Hilma Anderson
Bookkeeper and Storekeeper	F.S. Oberman
Matron	Mrs. Eugenia Wylie
Supt. Nurses and Hosp. Matron	Miss Harriet Cook
Principal of School	Miss Alice B. Scott
Chief Engineer	Martin Scharwark
Farmer	T.C. Johnson

Figure 2. Principal Staff at the Institution for Feebleminded, 1912.

Although most of the staff in the first ten years were selected to run the school, the superintendent soon realized the necessity of additional physicians. Part of this was a direct result of the construction of the hospital. Nurse Harriet Cook was put in charge of the hospital operations, and Dr. Wylie tended the hospital patients throughout the day. However, as the institutional population grew, and the demands of running the facilities grew, the superintendent had less time to devote to medicine. Thus by 1916, the first surgeon, Dr. Countryman, and the first dentist, Dr. Crydermann, were hired.

Over the years dozens of physicians, dentists, nurses, and pharmacists were hired to provide medical care to the residents and employees at Grafton. Their facilities were quite modern for the times, although the large numbers of residents made for sometimes less than the best care. With the large number of medical staff, the superintendents increasingly provided data on the services they provided. For example, in 1920 Dr. Wylie reported that the institutional medical staff treated nearly 150 residents for a variety of ailments, including arthritis, boils, fallen arches, gastritis, influenza, laryngitis, pneumonia, rheumatism, and tonsillitis. They also delivered on child, set three fractures, and performed one vasectomy.

By 1950 the medical staff was performing nearly 600 operations each biennium, and treating over 1,000 other medical cases. Also, the medical facilities had expanded to areas outside the hospital and to newer procedures. *"Dispensary stations are maintained in hospital and in North Building for female and male patients. Ultra-violet, infra-red and other physical therapy methods are used daily at the hospital. All patients on admission are isolated for two weeks and given the necessary immunizations for small pox, whooping cough, diphtheria and also Tuberculin and Schick tests"* (Tweinty-Fourth Biennial Report, 1950, p. 1697).

Direct care staff. Some of the most important people in the institution were the direct care staff. These individuals were responsible for 24 hour care, training, and supervision of the residents. This occurred in the residential halls, on the farm, and in the community. Most direct care staff in the first 75 years of operation had little training or prior experience in working with individuals with mental retardation. Rarely did this dissuade them from their work, and most frequently they did their work for low pay but with passion and conviction. As Dr. Wylie said in nearly every report, "...*employees have been loyal and faithful*" (Fifth Biennial Report, 1912, p. 165.)

Other support staff. The number and type of positions staffed at the institution would rival any small or medium sized community in North Dakota. The institution had farm hands, accountants, electricians, plumbers, carpenters, power plant attendants, lawn crews, staff trainers, psychologists, nurses, and food service personnel among its numerous employees. The other support staff also worked with conviction and passion, making the operation of the institution often one of the most efficient and productive businesses in the state year after year.

Residents

The first residents began arriving at Grafton on May 2, 1904. Upon admission a variety of data were collected on the residents. For the first 850 residents, their admission was logged into an admissions ledger. This ledger was a Peerless Toplock Section Post Binder. Made of heavy cardboard, metal and burlap with red leather corners, this ledger was the official record of admission and diagnosis for the residents. The ledger contained the name of the resident, an admission number, and general family data including address, ethnicity, and responsible paying party. Other data included previous education of the resident, a presenting or past diagnosis, and presenting condition upon admission.

The records indicate that six individuals were enrolled on that day. However the specific records of these individuals have not been found. However, we do have data on several other young boys and girls who were enrolled in May 1904. These included John, age 8, admitted on May 4, and was feeble minded by result of measles; Aaron, age 6, admitted on May 5, with congenital feeble mindedness; John, age 19, admitted on May 6, with a sickness resulting in feeble mindedness; Ruth, age 5, admitted May 11, whose meningitis caused feeble mindedness; Earl, age 9, admitted May 17, also with feeble mindedness from meningitis; and Richard, age 6, admitted May 23, with hydrocephaly resulting in feeble mindedness.

On May 28, 1904, Governor John Burke signed an order transferring 27 patients from the Hospital for the Insane in Jamestown to the Institution at Grafton. Some of these residents included Samuel, age 24; Milbert, age unknown; Margaret, age 51; Marion, age 32; Isabel, age 53; Mary, age 43; and Zilla, age 26. All had unspecified congenital causes resulting in feeble mindedness. It is interesting to note that Zilla, who had already spent several of her 26 years in Jamestown, lived at the institution at Grafton until April 1961, when she passed away at 83 years old. She had spent well over 60 years in institutions in North Dakota.

By November 1, 1904, Superintendent Baldwin reported a resident population of 75 people. In six short months the institution was nearing its stated capacity of 100 residents and 25 supporting staff. This pattern was to continue for the next 75 years.

Resident Population Trends

From nearly the beginning, the institution was crowded. Originally designed to house 100 residents and the accompanying staff, Superintendent Baldwin found the institution at its limit in only two years after opening. Quickly he called for additional buildings to house the residents. Figure 3 shows the recorded resident populations from

the various institutional reports. The highest reported population was 1,456 people in 1967.

Admission trends varied throughout Grafton's history. Some times the limits were self-imposed by institutional staff when space was not available to take individuals referred for placement. At other times there were rapid population increases, such as the late 1920s and the 1930s, when the social service department made 'recruiting' visits to various North Dakota communities.

Table 1 shows the general population trends by decade. One can see that in the first 15 years there was a rather modest yet continual growth of about 14.5 residents per year. However, from 1920 to 1950, the resident growth rate had nearly doubled to 26.7 residents per year. Note that this does not include deaths or discharges, during these same periods. If included, these factors would raise the 1920 – 1950 rate considerably, as the death and discharge rates were generally higher during this time period. There was a gradual and continued increase in population until the late 1960s when community programs were beginning to be developed across the state.

Table 1: *Resident Institutional Population by Decade*

Year	Resident Population
1904	75
1910	165
1920	292
1930	625
1940	970
1950	1091
1960	1381
1970	1351
1980	980
1991	211
2001	150

Resident Support

When one considers the tremendous complexities of running an institution, it is difficult to present a metric that adequately shows how residents were supported. However, state departmental heads and various legislative bodies were always concerned about the amount of support given to the institution, and ultimately to the residents. One method of measuring this support was the use of a per capita daily rate. This figure was a calculation of the total expenditures of the facility, staff, and programs divided by the number of resident days of service per year. These figures were often presented as per capita per diem costs of maintenance of residents or as daily cost per resident. From 1940 through 1989, these figures were reported in the biennial reports. Table 2 shows the rates presented in various reports on a biennial basis.

Figure 3. Resident Population Trend at Grafton 1904 – 2001

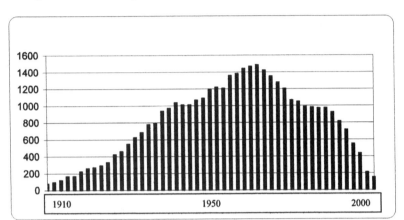

Table 2. *Biennial Per Capita Per Diem Costs for Grafton*

Biennium	Per Capita Cost
1940	$0.6543
1942	$0.646
1944	$0.794
1946	$0.98
1948	$1.20
1950	$1.30
1952	$1.4253
1954	$1.6215
1956	$1.8075
1958	$2.0488
1960	$2.8478
1962	$2.8478
1964	$3.81
1966	$4.32
1968	$4.73
1970	$6.20
1972	$7.40
1974	$12.59
1976	$18.44
1978	*Not Available*

1980	$30.33
1982	$49.29
1984	$76.16
1986	$197.40
1988	$207.67
1989	$235.83

These data show a marked increase during the 1980s, primarily as a result of the ARC lawsuit and Judge Van Sickle's implementation orders. Currently the per capita daily rate is over $300, with exact figures depending upon the set of supports needed by an individual.

Resident Life in the Institution

It is difficult to describe a typical day for a resident at the institution. Their situations varied depending upon the time period, the classification of the resident, and the particular set of circumstances of the individual. Dr. Wylie presented one of the first descriptions in his case story of Metro, a young boy enrolled in the institution in the early 1920s. *"During the third and fourth years he has improved steadily. He is now doing third grade work. He reads quite well in the third reader and recognizes more words, but it is hard for him to get expression. He talks a great deal. His speech is much improved and his voice is clearer and more musical. The "th" sounds are still difficult for him. He writes very well and can compose and write a fairly good letter. Now he knows the value of numbers and can do easy work in addition, subtraction, and multiplication. Last year he went to the physical culture, basketry, net and manual training classes. In the manual training class he at first did brush work. He learned to make polishing, vegetable and scrub brushes and now makes a perfect brush. The brush work became monotonous for him and he wanted to make things in wood. So he was taught the use and care of tools. He can now lay out his own work having learned measurements very quickly. He has also learned how to square up wood. He made ten toys, several kites, and a birdhouse. As Metro grows older, he will make a good wood worker because he is accurate and careful. He improved a great deal in basketry, learned the "figure eight" stitch, keeps a design straight now and shapes a basket very well. He has a real boys aversion to sewing carpet rags, but sewed faithfully as his teacher urged him one afternoon each week. He has learned to tell time, is active, has a good sense of rhythm and dances nicely. For one year he has had fifteen minutes in class practice with the band teacher. He showed some much skill and application that he was given work on a cornet. His tones are quite pure. His range for both reading and playing is from middle C to high F. He knows the value of every kind of note and promises to become a good cornet player.*

Metro has an enormous appetite, especially for potatoes and we have not been able to teach him even a semblance of table manners. He is so anxious to satisfy his appetite that he simply forgets everybody else and crams. He makes a good bed, can polish and scrub floors, sew on buttons, and helps take care of the crippled children in his class. At times he becomes boisterous but is easily disciplined. He is truthful, generally obedient and usually kind and thoughtful with new boys" (Tenth Biennial Report, 1922, p. 2493-2494).

During the 40s through the 60s many residents worked on the farm and held support positions, known as details, across the campus. Dr. Rand gave the residents much more freedom, and when they were not working or in education or training classes, might often be seen in downtown Grafton at the park, the swimming pool, the movie theater, or out for coffee.

Metro's case story shows an active young man with simple yet seemingly fulfilling tasks presented each day and likely acceptable for many citizens of North Dakota. Contrast this with several descriptions of San Haven and Grafton residents as presented by the ARC lawsuit.

"Many of the residents at San Haven are forced to sleep in cribs rather than beds. Some cribs and beds are crowded into rooms with a nursing desk in the middle. Some of the cribs contain a wire canopy which is designed to transform the crib into a cage. Toilet facilities are inadequate for the number of residents. Both toilet and bathing facilities are open and do not provide for the privacy of all residents."

"The walls of the day room areas at Grafton are bare cinder block or concrete, without acoustical materials. The resulting noise level can be intolerable. There are too few lamps, sofas, rugs, chairs, pictures, magazines, books or other home-like furnishings or equipment. A home-like environment is not provided for residents."

"The incessant boredom and lack of programming have caused many residents to lose skills they had when they cam to the institution. Many who could speak no longer speak; many who could walk no longer walk. Lack of adequate habilitative services deprives the plaintiffs of appropriate programs suited to the individual's needs and subjects them to intellectual, emotional, social and physical stagnation and to the loss of developmental potential." (ARC Complaint, 1980, pp. 23-26).

Some residents were paroled or discharged from Grafton, even going on to serve in World War II or the Vietnam War. Programs such as the Midway program or the adult education program were designed specifically to prepare residents for successful community transitions. As early as the late 1960s more able residents were placed in community hostels (the predecessors to community group homes) and vocational workshops that sprang up throughout the state. In the mid 1970s all school aged children attended classes for at least part of the day, with their education directed by individualized education plans (IEPs) as mandated by federal law. To characterize any one individual's day as typical for most or all of the residents is incorrect and misleading. Some individuals had active pleasurable daily activities while others had more mundane or outright boring days. Some spent their entire lives in hospital or infirm-patient wards, while others spent as little as one month a Grafton before re-entering the community.

Summary

The records are rather sparse about the lives of individuals at Grafton. In some cases we can piece together what life might have been for the superintendents, the staff and the residents. It is more likely that interviews with these individuals would provide a rich picture of activities and interactions throughout the years. However, that was not the purpose of this book, nor a method employed for gathering data. We do know that the lives of the residents in the institution were as varied as the staff who lived and worked there. And we might guess that each life in some way was profoundly affected by others, and so too profoundly impacted someone else.

Chapter Four

The Institutional Landscape:
Buildings and Facilities

The institution at Grafton has taken on a varying complexion over the last 100 years. The institution site was purchased in 1893 with funds set aside by the U.S. Congress through the Department of the Interior for the development of a penitentiary for the new state. The site was originally about one half mile from the downtown business district of Grafton. Over the years several buildings have been constructed, renovated, torn down, replaced, repaired, and moved. More than 30 central structures were located on the institution grounds at one point or another.

The first structures were the main building with a boiler house, and a laundry building, both finished in 1903. Ten of the institutional buildings housed residents at some point. These included the old main building, Midway (the original hospital), North A, Sunset, Annex, Pleasant View, North B, Prairie View, Maplewood, and Cedar Grove. The two hospital structures also were temporary or permanent residences for some residents. Of course, the first building was the main building, completed in 1903. The last building constructed was the vehicle maintenance and carpenter shop in 1984.

The following table is based on a listing obtained from the Developmental Center staff in January 2003, and updated with information from the superintendent documents and the historical archives. In some cases supplementary information was obtained from the State Historical Society records, which show insurance documents with listings of buildings, site locations, building purpose, square footage, material of construction, and potential value. Where possible this list provides the actual or estimated square footage of the buildings.

Table 3
Construction and Facility Changes at the ND Developmental Center

Building	Date Built	Square Footage
Main	1903	approx. 26,000
Laundry	1908	unknown
Boiler House	1908	960
West Wing of Main	1908	unknown
Powerhouse & Smokestack	1908	15,456
Hospital (Midway)	1910	6,912
North A	1911	24,800
Cottage #7 (Farm House)	1916	unknown
Refectory	1921	18,480
North B (east section)	1923	33,600
Root Cellar for Refectory	1923	unknown
Spiral fire slides on Main	1924	not applicable
Pleasant View	1926	21,070
Laundry Addition	1928	1,120

North B (west section)	1928	28,356	
New Cattle Barn	1930	3,600	
2nd Story to Shop	1930	unknown	
Smoke Stack (powerhouse)	1932	not applicable	
Utility Building (farm)	1936	unknown	
Sunset	1937	34,898	
Annex to North B	1938	14,144	
Refectory Addition	1949	unknown	
Health Service Center	1950	32,352	(opened in 1951)
Central Receiving/Shops	1950	16,263	
Cottage #1	1953	unknown	
Cottage #2	1954	unknown	
Cottage #3	1954	unknown	
Cottage #5	1955	unknown	
Laundry Addition	1955	unknown	
New Horizons (West Hall)	1957	28,096	(opened in 1958)
New Shop	1957	unknown	(included carpenter shop)
Machine and Repair Shop	1958	unknown	(built on farm land)
Filled in old reservoir	1958	(original had 30,000 gal. capacity)	
Cottage #6 (superintendent)	1959	unknown	(occupied January 1960)
Building #4 (machine shed)	1959	1,600	
Greenhouse	1960	2,448	
Prairie View (Wylie Hall)	1960	33,108	
Refrigerated Potato House	1960	5,390	
Main Towers Removed	1961	not applicable	
Carpenter Shop	1963	1,920	
New Barn	1963	unknown	(old barn burned in 1962)
New Milk House	1966	unknown	
Garage	1966	1,972	(used canteen proceeds)
Laundry	1967	12,780	(opened in 1968)
Building #8 (Paint Shop)	1967	1,536	
Collette Auditorium	1967	30,791	(and education center)
Chapel	1971	11,136	
Food Service Center	1973	48,000	
Aquatic Center	1977	unknown	
Professional Services Bldg	1978	31,680	
Maplewood	1982	40,713	
Cedar Grove	1982	40,713	
PT/OT Center	1983	21,742	
Vehicle Maintenance	1984	15,020	

Buildings
First structures. The original buildings of the institution consisted of the main building and a separate laundry. Designed by the Hancock Brothers Company of Fargo, the main building was constructed by Nollman and Lewis contractors. It was a two and one half story brick building with a full basement. Measuring 174 feet long total , the building had a central portion of 34 x 37 feet, wings on each end measuring 30 x 54 feet, and connecting sections of 37 x 41 feet. A rear (west) addition of the institution was 32 x 40 feet. There was over 26,000 square feet of space in the main building, which was intended to house 125 residents, staff, and the superintendent and his family. Two large towers faced the east. These towers held large 3,000-gallon water tanks and furnished pressurized water to the building, mainly for fire protection. On each floor were 75-foot lengths of fire hose, connected to pipes leading from the towers. These towers were removed in 1961 as the exterior of the building was being redone. The water tanks were no longer in use and lightening had struck each tower, creating large cracks and threatening their fall.

The laundry building was an unplanned addition to the campus. Originally the laundry was to be housed in the basement of the main building. However, the originally power plant took up considerable space, leaving little room for the laundry. Also, Baldwin had purchased state of the art washing machines, which would never fit in the main basement. Thus the laundry building was constructed about 75 feet to the southwest of the main building.

The boiler house, built in 1908, measured 30 x 32 feet and was located approximately 200 feet to the west of the main building. Although the original power plant was placed in the west basement area of main, there were several problems with that location. First, there was little room for coal storage, making the operation of the plant more problematic that needed. Second, the smoke stack was of insufficient height. Thus the furnace did not have sufficient draw for fresh air, nor did the smoke stack provide adequate venting for the soot and coal dust. Thus the new boiler house/power plant was constructed several hundred feet to the west of the main building, and a large metal water tower constructed next to the plant. Several minor additions were made over the years, including a coal storage area to protect the coal from the weather elements.

For the first several years, there were several smaller buildings around the Main building. For example, prior to the rental and subsequent purchase of the 100 acres of land north of the original site, the institution had a hog barn to the west between main and the boiler house. Other smaller storage sheds were built and either moved to the farm site or dismantled over the years.

Hospital quarters. The original hospital (now known as Midway) was built in 1910. This was quite an accomplishment for superintendents Baldwin and LaMoure, as state funds were tight. However, they had made an excellent presentation to the state legislature, pointing out the benefits of the hospital. It had two purposes. First, it was a necessary feature of most institutions, and particularly for the ND institution in housing and caring for the sick. There were many times during the first 30 years where disease spread quickly through the over-crowded facilities. Pulmonary tuberculosis and pneumonia were particularly problematic for this population. The hospital allowed the staff to segregate those with contagious illness. Second, the hospital also provided room for the care and treatment of a variety of other conditions such as broken bones, general surgery, and dentistry. Space was also provided in the basement for a pharmacy, which was a widely used program in the 40s and 50s. Later, a mortuary was added to the basement of the hospital.

The Health Services Center was built in 1950, opened for service in early 1951, and was dedicated by Congressman and former governor Fred Aandahl on October 23, 1951. The building had space for over 130 bed patients, a new surgery and medical ward, X-ray laboratory, a dentist's office, and a new pharmacy. This facility was state of the art for its time, and was a major improvement for the institutional medical program. Shortly after the construction of the Health Services center, the institution added physical and occupational therapy programs, and began receiving more residents with significant physical and medical conditions.

Residential Buildings

North A. The North A building was the fourth major structure built on the institution campus. Early on, superintendents Baldwin and LaMoure decided that segregation of males and females was necessary for a safe and efficient operation of the institution. Thus, males were housed in the north wing of Main while the females were housed in the south wing. However the male population quickly grew and outstripped the building's ability to keep the sexes segregated. The new North A dormitory, designed for the male residents, facilitated this segregation. Dr. Wylie was pleased with the result, noting "*the intention to use this building for the boys, leaving the Main Building for the use of the girls. In thus separating the sexes we can not only add much to their comfort, but also add much to the ease of caring for them*" (*Fifth Biennial Report*, 1912, p. 159).

Designed by the Hancock Brothers of Fargo and constructed by C.H. Johnson and Company, also of Fargo, North A was quite a facility. Made of reinforced concrete floors and roof, along with iron stairways, the building was virtually fire proof. The brick and concrete exterior added to the safety of the building. Early on North A was linked to the other campus buildings by a tunnel system, connecting the basement dining room in the southwest corner directly to the basement hall of Main.

Over the years North A remained a male dormitory. In 1969 Melvin Maxwell, North A supervisor, wrote a short description of the building and its history, pointing out that even 50 years later, it was a men's dorm. "*North A is the building for male residents who have the most freedom around the institution, thus we have to be careful that the men placed here are trustworthy and can cope with this flexibility. We are always proud of our group of residents in North A for their fine behavior and willingness to do their share in keeping the building a pleasant one in which to live*" (*The Ambassador*, December 1969, p. 2). Today, the building is used as a community residence known as Hancock Place.

North B. The next resident facility built was North B. Again built as a male dormitory to ease the overcrowding occurring in North A, the east section of the North B building was built in 1923, the west wing built in 1928, and an Annex added later in 1938. "*Grand Forks architect Joseph Bell DeRemer was hired to draw the plans and in July 1922 a construction contract was awarded to Redlinger & Hansen of Wahpeton, a contracting firm operated by Jacob Redlinger of Breckenridge, Minn., and Wahpeton resident Peter C. Hansen. The three-story, 110-by-84-foot 'Dormitory B' was completed in June 1923 and initially consisted of the central section and east wing of the present*

---

structure. *It was occupied in September of that year after a new appropriation allowed completion of the interior, including terrazzo floors. Designed to house 78 patients, the building soon sheltered 110 male residents, divided into three wards, with staff quarters provided on the top floor. When the 1927 Legislature set aside $125,000 for another 'Boys Dormitory', DeRemer simply added a new wing west of the entrance which essentially duplicated the earlier building as a mirror image. The enlarged facility could handle 200 males in sex separate wards. In addition a dining room was erected in a one-story brick structure located behind (to the south of) North B, which was connected to the dorm by a semi-subterranean tunnel. This became the basis for what was later known as North B Annex"* (Vyzralek, 1996, p. 2). Presently the building contains a community housing facility known as Villa DeRemer.

Pleasant View. Built in 1926 Pleasant View was the first dormitory exclusively for female residents. Dr. Wylie, superintendent during the construction and initial occupation of the building, was especially concerned about the growing number of North Dakota women who were feeble minded. He requested funding for the building with the following words: *"We have been able to care for the boys on account of our increased accommodations, but not for the girls. We have thirty-seven girls on the waiting list now – nearly all low grade cases. Some of these have been waiting as long as five years for admission. Many of them are of a most urgent character, and although we have kept our girls' side crowded we have been unable to furnish relief. Feeble-minded women out in the world are the source of illegitimacy, delinquency and mental defect. The urgency of our needs should be recognized and additional room should be made for them"* (*Eleventh Biennial Report*, 1924, p. 2121).

Pleasant View was designed to house about 100 residents, but soon after opening it held over 150 women. The upper floor contained staff housing, while the basement was the dining room. The tunnel system also connected this structure to the other institution buildings, and was especially useful in moving food from the Refectory to the dining room.

It is interesting to note that Pleasant View was the first institutional structure given a more pleasing, non-institutional name. From the mid 1920s through 1930 Dr. Wylie was cognizant of public perceptions of the institution. He thought that the names of places conveyed certain meanings to citizens, and thus wanted Pleasant View to be an expression of warmer, more acceptable considerations. (He carried this idea forward to 1930 when he proposed changing the institution's name to Grafton State Village.) However, Pleasant View was placed on the southern-most edge of campus, overlooking a flat, rather barren landscape. There was anything but a 'pleasant view' from this building.

Sunset Hall. Built during the tenure of Dr. Aylen, Sunset Hall was developed as a second women's dormitory. Opened in 1937 the new dorm quickly filled the six wards, being two per floor. The original tenants were women deemed 'custodial', or those with rather intensive care needs. As a new facility Sunset helped relieve the long waiting list for admission to Grafton. However, this building was soon filled to overflow capacity, housing upwards of 250 residents in a very short time.

In 1969 Joan Swanson, Sunset Hall supervisor, provided a description of some of the residents and conditions in the dormitory. *"Ward I has a population of 44 women, many of whom are physically handicapped and are either confined to wheelchairs or have difficulty walking. As one might surmise intensive physical and nursing care is required on this ward. In spite of their handicaps these women seem happy and content and constantly try to help themselves as much as they can.*" Swanson describes the other five wards in a like manner, and summarizes the staff and resident situation as follows: "*Our attendants in this building are all females and they serve our residents as mothers and nurses. Their duties are many and varied, depending upon the care needed by the residents on their ward. Every day there is bedmaking, cleaning on the ward, serving of meals, helping each resident with her personal hygiene, caring for the ill (when there is illness, this of course takes priority over all other work and is very time consuming and because of the limited staff, deprives the well children of the usual attention.)*" (*The Ambassador*, July 1969, pp. 2-3).

Today, Sunset Hall serves as a center for resident work and vocational training. In 1989, Sunset Hall was reorganized and a commercial venture, Dakota Enterprises was developed. This organization was arranged to "*provide productive and meaningful work and training for all individuals*" (*Biennial Report to the Governor*, 1989, p. 211). The staff developed work contracts for the residents including yard and maintenance crews, small novelty item manufacturing, greenhouse work, a recycling center, and operation of a gift shop. By June 1989 215 residents were served by Dakota Enterprises paid either through the production payroll, state payroll, or vocational payroll.

West Hall (New Horizons). Built in 1957 and opened in January of 1958, West Hall was constructed on the southwestern most corner of the Grafton campus. The 1950s saw a large increase in residents and an even larger increase in the waiting list. Dr. Charles Rand convinced the state legislature that another women's dormitory was needed. And the building filled quickly. Rand stated, "*West Hall has been constructed and on January 20, 1958, the first children were moved into it. By the 24th of January, it was filled with 176 and in full operation. Over the next few months the School had admitted 163. There are still a few vacancies in some of the female wards, but there is again a waiting list of over 50 males for the School. This list is increasing rapidly...*" (*Twenty Eighth Biennial Report*, p. 2474).

West Hall was a three-story structure, built on a smaller first floor surrounded by exterior piers that appear to support the upper floors. The upper floors provided a sheltered lower level on the outside of the building that served as a sitting or recreation area for some residents. In later years, this area was enclosed, enlarging the first floor by some 30 percent. Shortly after opening, Mr. Harold Shaefer of the Gold Seal Company of Bismarck provided four television sets, one for each ward.

Frances Kowalski, West Hall supervisor, wrote a short historical and present day perspective on West Hall in 1969. She stated, "*There is a serving room on each floor. The food is sent up cooked. However, the meat must be ground and vegetables mashed before it is served. This is done by the attendants.*" ..."*Ward 1 has 11 girls, Ward 2 has 21 girls, Ward 3 has 15 girls, and Ward 4 has 16 girls who have to be fed by the attendants. Twelve moderately retarded girls who live and work in West Hall, eat their meals at the Pleasant View dining room. One attendant goes with them*" (*The Ambassador*, September 1969, p. 1).

After serving as a women's dormitory for nearly four decades, West Hall was renamed New Horizons, and became a residence for men with behavioral difficulties, and later housed a sexual offenders program for adults with disabilities.

Wylie Hall (Prairie View). Built in 1960, Wylie Hall was the northwestern most dormitory and building on the institution grounds. This two-story building was built of steel and concrete with a glass and steel exterior. Presently the blue window panels make it one of the most colorful buildings at the Developmental Center. Named after Dr. A.R.T. Wylie, the dormitory was built to house male residents, keeping with the pattern of male residents on the north edge of the campus and female residents on the south. It was designed to house those male residents with the most significant disabilities, especially those with severe or profound mental retardation and others with extensive behavioral support needs. Wylie Hall supervisor Harold Peterson wrote, *"Each ward consists of a rather large dayroom, dormitory, clothes room, linen room, bathroom, and there is also a locker room and bathroom for the attendants. Right off the tunnel in Wylie Hall is where our barber shop is housed."* He also wrote, *"Since most of the residents in this building are severely or profoundly retarded, the required supervision is intense and many of them have to be helped in taking care of their personal needs. There are about 15 to 20 residents on each ward that have to be fed. The attendants also do the shaving of the residents as well as the tooth brushing each day"* (*The Ambassador*, February, 1970, p. 1).

As Grafton went about the deinstitutionalization process brought about by the ARC lawsuit, many of the residents were moved from Wylie Hall. It was later renamed Prairie View (a much more correct and appropriate name than that given to Pleasant View), and remodeling done. During the 1987 – 1989 biennium, Prairie View was closed for residential services. The institutional population had declined sufficiently that the space was no longer needed. Grafton State School then began renting space to various local and state agencies. Presently there are several community programs in Prairie View, including a daycare, Head Start and preschool programs, and the Upper Valley Special Education unit offices.

Maple Wood and Cedar Grove. The newest residential facilities on the institution campus grounds are Maple Wood and Cedar Grove. Built in the early 1980s these buildings are significantly different from the other dormitory residential areas at the Developmental Center. Constructed on the southern most edge of the campus and connected by the tunnel system, each one is built around a central office and services center. Much like a hotel, one enters into a large common area with a receiving desk. From this central area of support staff offices are several residential areas. Each has a dining and commons area, with individualized apartment style rooms for the residents. Television viewing rooms and laundry facilities are available as well, allowing for staff to provide daily living skills training in cooking, washing, and leisure skills. The setting has a family-style about it, and meets national accreditation standards for facilities for persons with developmental disabilities.

Maple Wood and Cedar Grove were built to house about 90 residents each. Presently the majority of the existing residents live in these two units, with about 60 residents in each one. A general supervisor with qualified mental retardation professional (QMRP) status oversees the staff and residents in each facility, reporting directly to the assistant superintendent of the Developmental Center.

Staff Housing

From its inception in 1904 until the 1960s many of the staff actually lived on campus. Seen as one of the perks of the job, staff received essentially free housing with a very minimum price for meals obtained as the various dining halls on campus. As most residence halls were built, the upper floors were designed for staff. Their spaces were generally larger and more private than those afforded the residents. However, as institutional space became a premium commodity when overcrowding of residents occurred, staff quarters began to be limited. By the 1960s very few staff were living on the institution grounds. Usually only the medical staff, the superintendent and other higher ranking institution officials and their families took residence on campus, with most being housed in the cottages built for the official staff.

The transition from housing most staff on campus (and housing the superintendent in the Main building) was a long awaited move. For over 50 years, the superintendent of the institution lived in the Main building. There were separate superintendent's quarters in the building, along with kitchens, classrooms, dormitory space and offices. Starting in 1930, the superintendents continually asked for separate housing. However it was not until the mid 1950s that this housing was constructed. Six cottages were constructed for institutional staff to the south and east of the main building, near the Grafton cemetery. These buildings were laid out in a half circle around a looping, dead-end street.

The cottages were pre-fabricated homes, purchased from a company in Shakopee, Minnesota. These pre-fab homes were relatively cheap, of generally good quality, and were quickly assembled on site. Dr. Arvid Vitums, chief of medical staff and his family occupied the first cottage in 1953, with the other cottages completed between 1954 and 1959. Staff were excited for these new homes and eagerly moved in. While still on the institutional grounds, they now had some individual space and at least a modicum of leave from work.

One particularly arduous task in the early 1900s was securing appropriate quarters for the farm staff. The institution purchased about 100 acres of land immediately to the north of the main campus. On this land were several buildings, including a house. This house was in rather bad shape, and early on the superintendents pressed for better living arrangements. Dr. LaMoure wrote, "*As regards the present farm house, I can only repeat what my predecessor has said in the last report, that it is in exceedingly poor condition. It is absolutely essential that a new house be built. In its present condition, it is scarcely fit for habitation*" (*Third Biennial Report*, 1908, p. 15). It was not until eight years later that Dr. Wylie reported on the construction of a new house for the farm. "*A comfortable but modest seven room farm house has been erected. While we were not able to do all that was desirable with the appropriation available yet it has given us a long needed improvement and the farmer at last has comfortable quarters*" (*Seventh Biennial Report*, 1916, p. 1195).

School Buildings

For over 60 years, most school and training programs were housed either in Main, in the Refectory, or in various areas in some of the residential buildings. At its inception, Baldwin saw the larger north and south wings as ideal places for classroom training areas. As the resident population increased, more of these areas were taken for sleeping quarters, generally shrinking the classroom space, and overall reducing the number of residents who received school services.

In 1967 Grafton opened the Collette Education center. The building was quite remarkable, having an auditorium/gymnasium, and classroom space. This allowed many of the recreation programs to move either from the large meeting hall in Main or the Refectory building, the only indoor spaces large enough for resident physical activity. This new structure became the focus for a renewed education effort, especially for school age residents. By 1971 Grafton had hired a new principal, Don Watson who had a master's degree with training in mental retardation education. Later, Dennis Follman was hired as principal. He also held a mental retardation degree. These two principals made good use of Collette, carving out classroom space and developing programs taught by qualified special education teachers. By the end of the 70s children at the institution were receiving individualized instruction based on the requirements of federal special education law.

In 1977 the institution added an aquatic center to Collette. This indoor swimming and therapy pool allowed residents to participate in therapy and recreation activities 12 months a year. They no longer had to go into Grafton during the summer to the community swimming pool. About this same time, North A was remolded slightly to provide space for an adult education program. Under the direction of Charlie Robinson, this four stage vocational and preparation program allowed many adult male residents opportunities to learn necessary work and life skills in preparation for later community placement.

Further Midway (the old hospital) was remodeled at least twice to provide women with community and life skills preparation. Using federal and state vocational rehabilitation funds, the Midway interior was reshaped into family style areas. Instruction focused on community work skills, social skills, and activities of daily living. Gradually, many of the residents transferred into permanent community placements. Similar remodeling occurred in the 1980s and 1990s in Sunset Hall so that vocational training could occur. Today, there are no school age services conducted on campus. The Collette Education center is now a community center with facilities to support community recreation and fitness.

General Institution Grounds

Building and maintaining an institution on the Red River Valley plains in North Dakota was not an easy task. While the soil was rich for farming, there were few trees or hills to break the incessant wind. Often staff and residents would be faced with blinding windstorms accompanied by snow or dirt, or even a mixture of the two, called 'snirt'. Dr. Baldwin was the first to recognized the need to improve the grounds and asked for funds to complete the landscaping around main, and to plant trees. He also ensured for proper sanitation by redirecting the institution sewage from the original plan of dumping it directly on top of the ground near a slough east of the campus, instead to a cesspool.

Once institution farm staff were hired, the superintendents had better resources and direction toward the proper presentation of the grounds. More trees were added, land leveled, playgrounds and picnic areas established, and hedges built around buildings. Later, fencing was placed around most of the campus, not so much for appearance but rather for control of residents. Horticulturists were added to the staff, primarily for the farming operations. However, these individuals raised a number of flowers in the greenhouses, and upgraded the institution appearance with floor beds. Later, vines were added to the exteriors of buildings and some of the fences.

Floods. In April and again in May 1950 spring floods affected the institution. Rapidly melting snow and large amounts of rain flooded the nearby Park River and the low lands around the institution. The lower levels of many buildings were inundated with water, and required some residents to be moved to already crowded upper floors. Staff built dikes around the institutional grounds, and for nearly three weeks the staff and most supplies had to be ferried by boat from town to the institution. Floods occurred again in the late 1970s. This time the waters did not reach the levels of the 1950s, with sandbags and dikes able to hold much of the water back from the institution. However, staff had some difficulty getting to work and general staff and resident movement on campus was limited due to the potential for quick flooding of the tunnel system.

Another Institution?

Throughout its history, the institution has continually been overcrowded. Dr. LaMoure first noted this in 1910 when he reported a population of 165 residents in a facility built for 125 people. By 1956, the campus was extremely overcrowded even with 12 major buildings on the main campus, and several more on the farmland north of the institution site. Superintendent Rand presented several photographs of the campus in his biennial report, making the point that the campus was limited in it ability to grow. In fact, he even urged the state to build another institution. He said, "*Another major thought to remember is that the Grafton State School is reaching a point where it can expand no more. ...All in all this means that in the future, serious thought must be given to the starting of a new school for the care of the mentally retarded and deficient. We can not wait too long to do this and should plan a school that can be enlarged and improved as time goes on*" (*Twenty-Seventh Biennial Report*, 1956, p. 2023).

During the 1960s, a state commission on mental retardation, funded by President Kennedy's Commission on Mental Retardation, examined the situation at Grafton and made several recommendations. One was to limit the population to around 1,000 residents on the Grafton campus. By the later 1960s the population had reached nearly 1,500 residents, far exceeding the industry standard of about 500 to 1,000 residents per state institution. The commission, in reviewing the Grafton situation, proposed the construction of a new 500 bed facility in the western half of North Dakota. In the late 1960s the state legislature considered a bill to create another facility for person with mental retardation, considering locating it in Minot. Although the bill was defeated, the issue was debate for many more years until the population was decreased through community placement efforts and later by the ARC lawsuit.

San Haven

The San Haven institution was built in 1911 as a tuberculosis sanatorium. Throughout the years, thousands of North Dakota residents were admitted to this facility located in the wooded hills just north of Dunseith. The facility was constructed as a typical medical facility with hospital and nursing care along with residential housing in dormitory areas. In 1959, as the general medical health of North Dakota citizens improved, and the population of the San Haven facility declined, several residents from

Grafton were sent there. These residents were generally those who were non-ambulatory and needed greater medical care and nursing supervision than most residents at Grafton. In 1973 San Haven was officially designated as a satellite facility of Grafton State School under North Dakota Century Code Section 25-04-02. By 1980 nearly 250 individuals with mental retardation were housed at San Haven. Later, all residents were placed in community facilities or transferred back to Grafton. The facility was officially closed in December 1987.

Summary

The buildings and grounds at the Developmental Center have a rich history. Several have been remodeled extensively, some serving as community housing facilities, others serving various community agencies, and still others housing residents with developmental disabilities. Today at least four of the buildings are on the national historic registry, thus preserving a value piece of the institution, and the state's legacy in serving people with mental retardation.

Today, a walk across the campus will lead one to old, stately buildings like North A or Midway. Other more modern buildings like the Professional Services Building or Maple Wood and Cedar Grove speak to the progress of the institution, both in terms of the new construction, but also the new vision for supporting the state's citizens with developmental disabilities. The walk will also take one past the old Refectory building, now closed with boarded windows. One can see parts of the tunnel system still above the ground level. The new tunnel system is now wider and brighter, with staff and resident movement separated from the service tunnels. There is even a tunnel walkers group that uses the underground system for recreation and fitness during the long North Dakota winters. One wonders if the state leaders one hundred years ago envisioned such a diverse place.

Chapter Five

Education and Training

The Institution for Feeble Minded was established in 1904 *"for the relief and instruction of the feeble minded and for the care and custody of the epileptic and idiotic of the state, and they may introduce and establish such trades and manual industries as in their judgment will best train their pupils for future self-support"* (Senate Bill 4, 1903). Thus, the initial purpose of the facility was to educate and train persons with mental retardation.

This was similar to the purpose of nearly every U.S. institution in the late 1800s and early 1900s. Scheerenberger states *"...institutions were educational, intended to serve school-age (CA 6 – 16 or 18) mentally retarded youngsters and adolescents. Most of the facilities started during the 1850s and early 1860s had a single, simple admission criterion: 'by deficient intellect is rendered unable to acquire an education in the common schools'"* (1983, pp. 123-124). However, that focus changed over time. As these young residents reached the age of maturity, institutional staff were uncertain as to the residents' futures. *"Left with little choice other than sending older residents to county homes, almshouses, and other such less dedicated operations, administrators requested permission to retain residents into their adult years"* (Scheerenberger, 1983, p. 124).

Since education (at that time thought of as schooling in the traditional academic subjects) was no longer relevant for these older individuals, institutions devised a variety of work and training programs. Soon residents were practicing various manual trades, often for the production of marketable goods that helped support the institution. Older residents worked on institution farms, did woodwork, made baskets and nets and completed various other tasks necessary to run an efficient institution.

The Beginning of Education at Grafton

Although Dr. Louis Baldwin, the first superintendent of the institution, faced many organizational challenges in opening the institution, he knew that he would soon need to develop a viable instructional program for his future wards. On his early trips to Faribault Institution in Minnesota, he spent time with staff there, watching and learning about their education systems. He also spent time corresponding with other institution administrators, seeking their advice on good educational systems.

Baldwin had very clear goals as to the purpose of the institution's education programs. In his first biennial report he wrote, *"The educational aim in the training of a normal child is to develop him for any occupation in life he may choose to take up, while in the case of the feeble minded child, the aim is to so train and develop him, that his life in the institution may be useful and that the greatest amount of happiness and comfort may be realized by him. The training therefor is of the most practical nature and is largely individual, being adapted to the possibilities of each case"* (First Biennial Report, 1904, p. 10). Shortly after opening the institution, he hired the institution's first teacher, Miss Alice B. Scott.

Miss Scott was a former teacher and principal for the Indiana School for Feebleminded Youth. Although the specifics of the hiring are not available, it is likely that Baldwin's correspondence allowed him to make the necessary connections with Miss Scott and convince her to come to North Dakota. Scott began the first classes at the institution on September 1, 1904, just four months after the opening day. She began with 26 students, and by November 1, 1904 had 30 students in classes.

Her report on the initial progress of the school echoes Baldwin's ideas about institutional education. *"Every exercise given has some meaning and encouragement and praise is freely given. We have to deal with the sluggish and indolent, the perverse and obstinate, the nervous and excitable. Discipline of the right kind is important. Firmness tempered with kindness brings order where it would seem impossible. Happiness, as a result of discipline and the fact of being able to do something, pervades the school room"* (First Biennial Report, 1904, p. 11).

The Basis of the Early Education Programs

The early education programs at Grafton were based on the methods of Edouard Sequin. As a young French physician, Sequin worked with several prominent researchers in studying the conditions now known as mental retardation. It was during this early period of his life that he dedicated his work to people with retardation. Often called the "Father of Special Education" Sequin is best known for his demonstration of instructional techniques that allowed persons with mental retardation to actually learn new tasks.

Sequin's techniques were called the physiological methods, and encompassed five major steps; 1) muscular system training; 2) nervous system training; 3) education of the senses; 4) acquisition of general ideas; and 5) acquisition of abstract thinking and moral reasoning. Scheerenberger (1983) stated *"Sequin's theory of education and its application was encompassing, ranging from passive exercises for the nonambulatory child through academic training and vocational placement for the more capable individual. His curriculum was quite contemporary in nature: learning involved perception, imitation, coordination, memory, and generalization"* (p. 79). His methods, known as 'sense training', became the prominent focus of most institutions, including Grafton. A core belief was that nearly any person with mental retardation could learn at least some task, and most could learn appropriate moral behaviors.

A second focus of the instruction at Grafton capitalized on the hands on vocational nature of Sequin's methods. Within the first four years at the institution, Scott and Baldwin introduced the Sloyd method of instruction. Developed in Sweden as a winter manual arts pastime, Sloyd consisted of basket weaving, small woodwork, net work, and sewing to produce marketable goods. Like the rural Swedish people, the Sloyd-work products of the institution not only kept the residents busy, they resulted in income for the institution. Thus the work became valuable not only to the care, education and control of the residents, but to the viability of the institution.

Two reports illustrate just how the institution's educational approach fit Sequin's philosophy, and how Sloyd work was integrated. In 1906 Scott wrote, *"Pleasing and encouraging results are evident. The method of teaching in the class is direct and simple. The child is made to do, to see, to think and to remember. The material used in this class furnishes varied sense training. Handwork which is conceded to be such an important feature in the education of this class of children, begins here. The practical value is*

evident to an interested visitor and much more so to those engaged in the actual work"
(Second Biennial Report, 1906, p. 14). Grafton's second teacher, Mary Louise Hays,
later wrote, "*The basket class has increased in size and some of the boys and girls have
become very proficient. A number of very beautiful baskets have found a ready sale.....On
June 3rd this year an exhibit of the school work was held. The classes were in session and
all the children's work was displayed in the hall. The purpose of this was to bring before
the public the fact that this is a training school for feeble-minded children. It also showed
what can be accomplished by proper training*" (Fourth Biennial Report, 1910, p. 17).

While Sequin's methods continued to be the foundation for all educational work
at the institution, the teachers gradually expanded the learning activities. The Montessori
method was employed with some of the younger children, manual training programs
were expanded to include brush and furniture making as well as farm work, and a chorus
was added. In fact, music was employed in many activities in the institution. "*The feeble
minded of all ages are extraordinarily fond of music. Children who may not speak words
distinctly will often hum songs in our Chapel and Sunday School exercises in fairly good
time and tune. So we use music everywhere, in work and play, in all grades and classes.
There is a chorus class of some thirty members which receives special vocal training
every day.... Instruments have been procured and a band is included in our plans for the
coming year*" (Seventh Biennial Report, 1916, p. 1194).

By 1918, the school program had expanded to include the following classes;
Kindergarten, English, Manual Training, Sewing, Basketry and Lace, Physical Training,
and Music. Miss Maud Stewart, the head teacher, wrote a description of the education
efforts. "*The aim of the school is first of all to make the child happy; second, to teach him
to become helpful to himself and useful to others. In order to keep a child happy,
occupation and recreation in proper proportion must be provided for every hour in the
day. A busy boy is generally a happy one. So in addition to the school program, some
regular daily work is assigned the children according to their age, size or capacity; and
this is often changed*" (Eighth Biennial Report, 1918, p. 2938). This philosophical
approach to education was repeated in most biennial reports for the next 20 years.

Gradual Development of Programs

During the 1920s the number of residents receiving an education increased, and
so did the number of teachers. From the single teacher and principal, Miss Scott who had
two classed in 1904, the 1922 school program had grown to five teachers, eight classes,
and 148 students. Many of the training department reports of the 1920s talk about the use
of music in classes, and the importance of various related programs such as Sunday
School religion classes, special season and holiday programs, choral performances, and
dances. The school orchestra even supported two operettas, *In India*, and *The Pied Piper*.

Dr. Wylie used many case stories to describe the success of the education
program and the institution. *The Improvement of Metro*, published in his 1922 biennial
report, speaks to the success of the training department in raising a young man's overall
functioning level from 3 years, 1 month to 8 year, 3 months in four years at Grafton.
Continuing with his focus on public instruction of the actions and purpose of the
institution, Wylie also published a daily schedule for a female resident. He said, "*The
following is not the record of a 'Perfect Day' but it shows in detail an average day for an
average girl in our Institution family:*

6:00 – Rise, bathe, dress.
7:00 – Set Superintendent's table and get ready to serve breakfast.
8:00 – Serve breakfast, wash silver and tidy dining room.
9:00 – Attend Chapel.
9:15 – In Sewing Class.
10:00 – In Literary Class – doing fifth grade work.
10:15 – Violin practice with teacher.
10:30 – Literary Class.
11:00 – Orchestra practice.
11:30 – Play time – out doors if pleasant.
12:00 – Set table in Superintendents' dining room.
12:30 – Serve lunch.
1:00 – Free time to read, play or sew.
2:00 – Gymnasium class in Hall.
2:30 – Lace class.
3:30 – chorus class.
4:00 – Walk or organized play with attendant.
5:00 – Set table and other dining room work.
6:00 – Serve dinner.
7:00 – Outdoors.
8:00 – Read, play cards, fancy work.
9:00 – To bed.
(Tenth Biennial Report, 1922, pp. 2492-2493).

By the late 1920s the number of children in school classes had risen to 162, but now there were eight teachers and 11 different instructional programs. In some cases the programs were split into two or more sections. For example, there were two kindergarten classes and two intermediate classes in 1928. The classes were always divided by gender, and they were just beginning to be separated by the results of intelligence tests. *"We have tried to organize the school to meet the needs of all grades of intelligence. To train both minds and bodies so that happy, useful lives will result. The mental test has helped us very much in classifying our children. The test is given to all who are admitted to the Institution. If a child has a mental age of six he can be taught the work of the first grade, if he has a seven year mental age he can do the second grade work and so on"* (Thirteenth Biennial Report, 1928, p. 1321).

The orchestra and chorus groups progressed remarkably so that by the end of the 1920s the students were playing complicated pieces such as Schubert's Serenade, Ave Maria by Bach-Gunod, Traumerei, by Schumann, and Humoresque by Dvorak. There were weekly Tuesday parties in the Main assembly hall, Thursday night dances, and movies were shown one each month.

Education in the 30s and 40s

School enrollment increased dramatically by 1930. From the 162 students in 1928, the enrollment in 1930 was 201. The school now had nine teachers, and a class for lower functioning boys, called custodial cases, was started. While the number of teachers was increasing, finding them was difficult. Soon the institution began a program to develop their own teaching staff. *"Teachers of these classes need special training as the work necessarily is different from the regular grade work. The best location for training schools for teachers of special classes has been found to be in cities where the State Institution is located. It provides the laboratory, model school, clinics, and material for the study of types. The summer of 1929 saw the beginning of such a summer school here in our Institution. It was started in connection with the University summer work. Credits were given by the University as for any summer course. In addition to our own superintendent, principal and staff, two teachers from outside were employed"* (Fourteenth Biennial Report, 1930, p. 2945). Courses taught included methods of organization and management, practice teaching and observation, industrial arts, mental testing theory and practice, abnormal psychology, and history of work for feeble minded.

The 1930 report also contained the first actual lesson plans for activities in the institutional classes. There were seven pages of lesson plans that included a goal for each lesson, seat work activities, memory work, handwork, and games. Most lessons followed what is now known as the unit approach, where several activities are used with a unifying theme, each activity incorporating multiple academic skills. For example, the January and February 1930 unit on clothing contained geography lessons on wool-producing states, writing and telling stories such as *My Pet Sheep* and *My Visit to a Sheep Ranch*, and writing letters to children who lived on a sheep ranch.

In 1934 the school implemented a home economics course for the girls. The course served a dual purpose, preparation for those girls likely to leave the institution, and skills training for those who would probably never leave. *"Practically all scheduled to the course this year were those who may be paroled soon. We do not feel, however, that the course should serve this group only. Many of the girls who may never leave, would become happier and more useful institution citizens as a result of this practical training. Any girl capable of learning to make her own clothes and to prepare, plan and properly serve a wholesome meal is justly proud of the accomplishment. This knowledge increases her self-respect and her helpfulness wherever she may be"* (Fifteenth Biennial Report, 1934, pp. 598-599).

The school enrollment increased to 246 students by 1938. The biennial report has very little narrative about the school programs. However, numerous charts show the enrollment of the various school groups by course and gender, displaying the number of students in each group and the number of hours of instruction each week. Because of the large number of students and the cramped instructional quarters at the institution, most students received only one hour of classes each day, with some having as little as 15 minutes each week.

The records show a small increase in student enrollment in training department classes in the 1940s. The lesson plans and class descriptions were much the same as those presented in the late 1920s and throughout the 30s. However, it appears that the teachers were somewhat despondent about their work. The goal of the instruction had not changed *"aims for happiness through education and industry"* (Twenty Third Biennial Report, 1948, p. 1040), and student progress was slow *"they won't all reach the top, nor will they all be paroled"* (Twenty First Biennial Report, 1944, p. 959). And apparently the community was questioning the value of the education program. *"I believe that the majority of people think that we have only custodial patients here –those who need only physical care and who have never been able to learn anything or even take care of their simplest needs....There is very little personal glory in this type of work. A teacher who devotes her patience and energy, finding this work very interesting and absorbing, receives very little praise or credit for her accomplishments except from her immediate supervisor or co-workers. In place of encouragement we often her detrimental remarks such as this: 'Since the pupils are slow in learning, teachers don't need to know very much at the State School'''* (Twenty First Biennial Report, 1944, pp. 959-960).

Because of the depression and World War II, much of the institution had reached a stagnated point. Few buildings were constructed, and those that were built were done so to house new residents, not to expand educational programs. Public scrutiny combined with and the lack of new methods of instruction and little student progress had a depressing impact on teacher attitude. It is truly amazing that there was actually little teacher turnover during this time. But while they stayed, they were not particularly happy.

The First Fifty Years of Education

During the early 1950s there were some changes in the educational curriculum, most notably that the school followed a general curriculum prescribed by the state Department of Public Instruction. At first, this curriculum was not specifically designed for children with mental retardation, but rather for the general school population. However, the state department began a program in 1954 to support special education for these children with mental retardation, and the institution adopted it. Along with the curriculum came more classrooms for these children in the state's public schools. The institution teachers were certain that these classes would result in lower ability students coming to the institution, thus making the institution's school programs even more basic and custodial in nature.

Another change was the decrease in students attending school classes. From an average of nearly 250 school students per year, the enrollment dropped to about 200 per year in the late 1950s. This was a result of the continuing crowded conditions, and the lack of classroom space. The principal and the superintendent constantly asked for a new school building.

Perhaps the biggest change in institution education in the 1950s came from Dr. Rand's edict to combine males and females in the school classes. Beginning in 1957 boys and girls attended classes together. Long-time principal Etta Hylden described this move. *"We now have mixed classes in our school department instead of boys and girls alone. The first adjustment was quite exciting among the older children, but now, after two years, we have a minimum amount of trouble"* (Twenty Eighth Biennial Report, 1958, p. 2491).

In 50 years the institution had grown from one teacher and 30 students to ten teachers and 200 students. Early classroom instruction focused on sense training and manual work, while the later curriculum focused on academic instruction for the more capable students, and some vocational skills training for those with more significant cognitive disabilities. The foundation for education in 1904 was Sequin's physiological methods, while the standard institutional curriculum of the 1950s was one promoted by the state special education program personnel. The common factor in all of this was that nearly all of the instruction was still occurring in the Main building. While children in

1904 might attend classes for 20 – 30 hours per week, students in the 1950s might only receive classroom instruction for 2 to 10 hours per week.

The Next Fifty Years of Education and Training

Dr. Charles Rand had a profound influence on the education and training of Grafton State School residents. His early decision to integrate boys and girls into the same classes was just the beginning. From the beginning of his tenure until the 1967 opening of the Collette Education Center, Rand pleaded for a new school building and better instructional support.

In 1962 Rand supported four teachers in continuing education to upgrade their skills in special education. These teachers took an eight-week summer course at the University of North Dakota, focusing on special education and psychology work. Principal Margaret Ashenbrenner explained the reason for the additional teacher education. "*Due to the fact that many of our public schools are establishing opportunity rooms, we are receiving children of much lower mentality for academic training. This is very much in evidence and individual work is more and more necessary.*" She also stated, "*...it seems very important that our instructors should enroll in classes for special education so that they may better prepare themselves for teaching boys and girls of lower mentality, those with speech defects or those who are physically handicapped. Our academic classes will necessarily have to be held to a minimum of ten because work in many cases must be individual rather than group participation*" (Thirtieth Biennial Report, 1962, pp.2201-2202).

Because of this new training and because of the type of students enrolling in their classes, the teachers began to emphasize more functional and work-based instruction. One of the teachers was spending time on the residential wards, teaching women handwork (e.g., sewing, lace work, and knitting). Several boys did woodwork, seed craft, painting and bead work.

By 1964 the school department had devised a new philosophy and objectives. "*The philosophy of the education and training services can be summarized as:*

(a) The education and training programs within the institution should be conceived and conducted as an integral part of the total institution community effort leading to the mental, emotional, physical, social and vocational growth of each resident.

(b) The basic philosophy of the education service should provide education and training service to all residents deemed capable of benefiting from the program.
The objectives of our school department are:

(a) Intellectual developmental and academic proficiency in test subjects.

(b) Development of emotional stability.

(c) Development of personal and social adequacy.

(d) Development of good health and personal hygiene.

(e) Development of attitudes, interests and skills leading to the good citizens and community responsibility, and wholesome use of leisure time.

(f) Learning to work for the purpose of earning a living.
(Thirty First Biennial Report, 1964, pp. 100-101).

Note how different this philosophy is from that of the early 1900s, where the teachers were interested in keeping the children happy and productive in support of the institution. Here, Rand and his educational staff made major changes in the view of institutional education. First, there is a marked shift toward a goal of productive citizenry outside the institution. Second, the education and training programs are directed toward all residents, not just those 18 and under. Third, the skill sets are broader and more life focused. No longer is academic instruction the primary focus.

The teachers began experimenting with instruction with more diverse populations. The 1964 report shows that a new nursery school program was begun. Also, the teachers began working with more 'trainable' children, those with moderate mental retardation. Finally, the teachers began a new project in working with three deaf girls. The instruction was facilitated by a tutorphone, a pre-cursor to current sound amplification systems for deaf or hard-of-hearing children. The deaf girls learned simple embroidery and art in these classes.

The vocationally oriented instruction apparently paid off, as residents were frequently successfully placed in community settings. The October 1966 institutional newsletter, *The Ambassador*, shows that nine individuals were placed on community jobs. In 1967, the Midway House project opened as a transitional living and training unit for higher functioning women. These residents received community living training, along with supports for community inclusion. Dozens of women were successfully placed and discharged from Grafton.

Many of the residential buildings now had vocational or daily living skills training occurring on a daily basis. For example, 25 men in North B worked on the farm, in the bakery, laundry, kitchen, shops, canteen and the hospital. Residents were also taught personal hygiene and social skills. Individuals in North A worked on the farm, in the greenhouse, in the storeroom, and in the children's kitchen. Some were taught basic daily living skills, while others went to religion classes or to shop instruction (*The Ambassador*, December 1969, p. 2).

Changes in the 70s.

The construction of the Collette Education Center was a major improvement for the education program at Grafton State School. Unfortunately the classroom sections of the building were still insufficient for all the residents requiring education, and some classes were still held on the top floor of Main. In his 1970 biennial report Rand asked for more funds to increase the number of classrooms at Collette.

In 1971 the Education Department was combined with resident services to become the Resident Program Department. Paul Witucki was appointed program director, and the education and training programs developed a new focus. Dr. Ron Archer, the new superintendent, stated *"Previously the educational program ha been one of arts and crafts with a limited education curricula not necessarily designed to return residents to the community. The educational component is now staffed with a principal, who holds a masters degree in special education of the mentally retarded, and 15 teachers (including a music therapist), 11 of whom hold baccalaureate degrees in special education. With the increased staff we are now able to provide the educable, or mildly retarded, students with a full day of educational programming. The trainable, or moderately retarded youngsters, are receiving a one-half day program. The educational component currently works with 188 students in the classroom setting with another 18 students in programs which have been inaugerated (sic) on the ward in which they live. We also have four teacher aides and, for the first time since last school term, we had student teachers from both the University of North Dakota and Minot State College*" (Thirty Fifth Biennial Report, 1972, p. 12).

Along with this new commitment to the school age students came further developments for older residents. The Midway Project, which provided 'pre-vocational' programming for women, was funded with federal and state funds on a long term basis, lending stability to Archer's community integration focus. Grafton also began the Behavior Modification Program with federal Title I funds. This program emphasized the development of appropriate behavior, self-help and social skills of residents with more significant disabilities. Much of this training occurred directly on the residential wards. Finally, Archer initiated the deaf-blind education program. This program was also supported by federal funds and promoted intensive instructional efforts for those individuals with dual sensory impairments.

In 1972 Grafton State School became a defendant in a lawsuit focused on the educational programs at Grafton. ARC vs. Grafton State School et al. was "*brought on grounds of constitutionality which follows a trend in our nation which was begun in September of 1971 when a group of parents in Pennsylvania brought suit against the Commonwealth declaring that although the Constitution declared that children shall receive a free and public education, that there was in fact discrimination against mentally retarded children.... The parents of the one resident of the Grafton State School named in the suit are in essence saying that 'our youngster has not received any educational opportunity and that he has regressed or deteriorated in intellectual development.' They feel that this is due to possibly the lack of facility and staff and those in charge of running the School should secure more legislative support and funding to rectify that situation*" (*The Ambassador*, December, 1972, p. 1).

This lawsuit brought about a renewed focus to Archer's plan. In 1973 the institution developed a new three-part mission. One aspect of the mission was the provision of long-term care, another covered evaluation services, and the third was focused on education and training for inclusion into the community. Specifically it said, "*Education and training for possible return to society. This mission deals primarily with the upper moderate or trainable, and mildly or educable range of mental retardation. These are the people who possess intellectual limitations which do not need to interfere with social and vocational functioning provided that they are given a learning environment in which to achieve these goals. It is possible that in the future these individuals will be trained in a community*" (Annual Report of the Grafton State School, 1973, p. 10). With this mission in place most residents with mild or moderate mental retardation received 6 to 8 hours of education or training (Archer used the word programming) each day. Archer's vision was to assure that these individuals, especially those with mild mental retardation, obtained social skills instruction as part of the movement to the community. He said, "*..most of the mildly retarded who are placed in an institution today usually have many social and emotional problems in addition to retardation. Therefore, more social training for this groups is needed if they are going to be as successful as we want them to be once they are placed back in the community*" (Annual Report of the Grafton State School, 1973, p. 10).

With the passage of Public Law 94-142, the Education for All Handicapped Children's Act, in 1975, and the national implementation of the law, Grafton State School began providing individualized education programs (IEPs) for all school age students. These plans outlined a set of annual goals and objectives, specific to the needs of each child. By now Dennis Follman was the principal of the school and the additional classrooms had been built at Collette. The teaching staff consisted entirely of teachers with special education degrees. Most students received a full day compliment of instruction in the school building, or at the residential hall if health or physical limitations prohibited participation at the school building. Within a short time, many area residents were sending their children with special needs to the institution during the day, solely for the school program.

The remainder of Archer's 1970s reports emphasize the commitment to community preparation of residents and support of the school program. His reports list a full compliment of support services including speech therapy, hearing services, physical therapy, occupational therapy, music therapy, behavior modification, psychology services, and multi-disciplinary evaluation. Clearly the education and training programs at Grafton had reached a new point in serving residents of the institution.

Institutional Scrutiny and Another Shift

The 1980 lawsuit, ARC vs. State of North Dakota, caused the institution to take another look at the training and education services it was providing. While Archer's idea of training for community placement was forward thinking, it was insufficiently funded. And although many residents received some level of programming, some residents received only a few hours of instruction per week. In addition, the lawsuit charged that the instructional programming, called habilitation, was not active nor was it appropriate to the needs of the individuals. In other words, the residents were often passive recipients of instruction which was of short duration and not directly applicable to their needs.

Throughout the process of the lawsuit and judge's orders, the staff at Grafton developed new programming approaches. First staff began to implement a unit-based approach to services. Rather than using a centralized support service model, therapy and direct supports were brought into the residential units. This placed the therapists and staff workers directly on the wards where much of the instruction occurred. Second, all residents received individual habilitation plans (IHPs). Like the IEPs for school-age children, IHPs listed individualized goals and services for the residents. These plans clearly identified the supports necessary for each resident, and were useful in examining progress and making needed changes throughout the year.

During the 1980s and 1990s, many residents were placed community programs throughout the state. As residents moved from Grafton, the staff numbers were reduced. By the 1990s the resident numbers were at the 1910 level, about 150. With the development of community programs and better special education services in the public schools, the Collette Education Center closed. Also, the resident population had changed significantly, requiring a different set of habilitative programs. Several citizens with mental retardation who had been labeled as actual or potential sexual offenders were transferred to the institution. These individuals participated in the Sexual Treatment Offender Program (STOP). Also, individuals with significant behavioral problems that were not successful in community programs were transferred to Grafton. These individuals received intensive behavior programming with an emphasis on a return to the community.

Throughout the 80s and 90s, vocational and adult educational services have also flourished. The Dakota East vocational program brought significant supports to individuals as they learned pre-vocational and direct vocational skills. Individuals were placed in both paid and volunteer work experiences on the institution grounds and in the community. In many cases individuals work full days all week, and earn wages at or near the minimum wage.

Summary
Throughout its one hundred year history, resident education has been a major part of the operation of the institution. Starting from a one teacher, two-class system in 1904, the ND Developmental Center has transformed its educational practices, often influenced by changes in philosophy and approaches in the field, and the availability of recourses and supports at the state level. While the levels of education stagnated somewhat in the mid century, a renewed interest in school programming for younger residents and community preparation for older residents was evident in the 60s and 70s. The ARC lawsuit brought about a completely new level of training accountability for the institution, requiring new ways of documenting services and new models of service delivery. Finally, the last 10 years has seen the molding of different supports for individuals with more specialized and intense training needs. Throughout the history of educational services, one can see the commitment that the staff has had, always striving to support residents the best that they could.

Chapter Six

Laws and Legislation of the Institution

During the infancy of the institution the superintendents and the members of the Board of Trustees saw the wisdom and power of the law in furthering the mission and operation of the facility. The laws of North Dakota, and even the Constitution of the state, shaped the development of the institution. This chapter reviews some of the more important laws that established, developed, and later refined the work of the institution in serving persons with mental retardation in North Dakota.

Early Legal Efforts

As discussed in the general history chapter of this book, Grafton was originally designated as a spot for a federal penitentiary. In fact, the 1889 North Dakota Constitution specifically designated land and funds to establish this prison. Further, on September 30, 1890 the U.S. Congress passed an appropriations act to grant of thirty thousand dollars *"for the construction of a penitentiary building, to be expended under the superintendency of the secretary of the interior, in the state of North Dakota, upon a tract of land at or near the city of Grafton, in the county of Walsh, to be designated by the secretary of the interior, a portion of which sum has been expended in the purchase of a site for said building, consisting of forty acres of land near said city of Grafton"* (*Laws of North Dakota*, 1901, pp. 78-79).

By 1897 the state realized that the land thus purchased by the secretary of the interior need not be used as a federal penitentiary but rather as a state penitentiary, since North Dakota was no longer a federal territory. Thus, the North Dakota legislature passed Chapter 81, *"An Act Providing That the Means Derived From the Fund Known as the School for the Feeble-Minded at Grafton Shall be Credited to Such Fund. Be it enacted by the Legislative Assembly of the State of North Dakota: 1. How Funds Shall be Credited. All interest and means derived from the appropriate made by Congress and now carried on the books of the State Treasurer as a fund for the 'School for the Feeble-Minded at Grafton' shall be credited to such fund and reinstated for the benefit thereof"* (*Laws of North Dakota*, 1897, p. 124).

In 1901 the state legislature proposed and passed a concurrent resolution to amend the constitution, changing the language from creating a penitentiary at Grafton, to developing an institution. Subdivision 8 of section 215 of the constitution was amended to read, *"...and there shall be located at or near the city of Grafton, in the county of Walsh, an institution for the feeble minded, on the ground purchased by the secretary of the interior for a penitentiary building"* (*Laws of North Dakota*, 1901, p. 90).

In 1901 a five member Board of Trustees was created to furnish a bond running to the state of North Dakota in the sum of $5,000. Each member of the board received full compensation for his services, three dollars per day and five cents per mile for travel.

In 1903, the Institution for Feeble Minded needed additional support as management and development expenses rose. The Institution needed to be finished and the buildings needed furnishing. An appropriation of $57,765 was provided by the state. Support and management was provided by establishing a permanent location near the city of Grafton to be known and designated as "The Institution for Feeble Minded." The Institution was to be controlled by a board of five trustees, each member serving for four years. The Board of Trustees annually selected a president and secretary, who held office for two years and until their successors were chosen and qualified. Trustees had general management and superintendency of the institution; they prescribed all rules and regulated admission of pupils. Generally, they performed all acts necessary for the operation of the institution. Legislation clearly indicated the purpose for which the institution was established, *"For the relief and instruction of the feeble minded and for the care and custody of the epileptic and idiotic of the state, and they may introduce and establish such trades and manual industries as in their judgment will best train their pupils for future self-support"* (*Laws of North Dakota*, 1903, p. 142). The board of trustees also appointed a superintendent who was required to be a *"physician skilled in caring for, and in instructing the class of unfortunates to be provided for by this act"* (*Laws of North Dakota*, 1903, p. 143).

At this time, all feeble minded persons who were resident of the state were to be admitted to and receive the benefits of the institution free of charge. When pupils of the institution were not provided appropriate support, they received clothing from the superintendent, who made out an account against the parent or guardian. The Board of County Commissioners of each sending county provided expenses for transportation to and from the institution.

On or before the first day of November 24, 1904, and biennially after that, the superintendent, secretary, and treasurer were to submit full and complete reports to the board of trustees. On or before the first day of December, members of the board were to furnish the governor a printed report of the institution for the two years ending on the preceding June 30th. These reports served as biennial accounts of the institution and presented the case for continuation or expansion of services throughout the years.

As early as 1907, the expenses and improvements in the institution continued to grow such that the institution asked for and received $86,600 from the state legislature (see S.B. 108, 1907, p. 18). Admission into the institution was no longer free of charge and a semi-annual payment of $50 was required to be paid to the superintendent in Grafton. If family members were unable to pay this fee, it was charged upon the county that was required to make payment. Because so many indigent citizens were being sent to Grafton, clothing expenses began to be drawn from the maintenance fund. By 1913, expenses had reached the stage where a payment of $15 per month was required by the person legally responsible for the support of any person admitted to the institution.

Developing Rules for Control of Residents

By 1909 the superintendent of Grafton, Dr. LaMoure realized that a critical mass of residents was needed for economic survival at the institution. Family members, and even residents themselves, often revoked their admission and left the institution. The constant coming and going of residents made efficient operation of the facility difficult. During the 1909 legislative session, LaMoure urged the state to give control of entrance and exit to the superintendent. Senate Bill 264 was passed, ensuring that feeble minded residents were not to be removed from the institution, except upon written request by the parents or guardian, which then had to be approved by the superintendent (*Laws of North Dakota*, 1909, p. 318).

In 1913, the level of social control reached a peak. Dr. Wylie, the new superintendent at the institution, had worked with the new Board of Control of Institutions to make necessary changes at Grafton. In conjunction with the Board of Medical Examiners, House Bill 342 was passed, *"An Act to Prevent Procreation of Confirmed Criminals, Insane, Idiots, Defectives, and Rapists; Providing for a Board of Medical Examiners and Making Provisions for Carrying Out of Same"* (*Laws of North Dakota*, 1913, p. 63). This law gave broad powers of control relating to the sterilization of individuals in state institutions. The law stated that, *"Whenever the warden, superintendent, or head of any state prison, reform school, state school for feeble minded, or of any state hospital or state asylum for insane shall certify in writing that he believes that the mental or physical condition of any inmate would be improved thereby, or that procreation by such inmate would be likely to result in defective or feeble-minded children with criminal tendencies, and that the condition of such inmate is not likely to improve, so as to make procreation by such person desirable or beneficial to the community, it shall be lawful to perform a surgical operation for the sterilization of such inmate as hereafter provided"* (*Laws of North Dakota*, 1913, pp. 63-64). While Wylie was a staunch proponent of this law, it was not significantly implemented at the institution until the late 1920s and early 1930s.

During this same time, the legislature also passed Senate Bill 166. This bill expanded the definition who was feeble minded, and thus who was a likely candidate for the institution. This definition included those properly classified as feeble minded or one *"who is offensive to the public peace or to good morals, and who is a proper subject for classification and discipline in the institution"* (*Laws of North Dakota*, 1913, p. 222). This refinement of the definition of feeble-mindedness reflected the philosophy of Wylie, but also reflected the understanding of mental retardation of the time. In later years, Wylie would use this typology of retardation to discuss the need for increased incarceration and institutionalization of the indigent, orphans, the poor, and criminals (see Wylie's discussion of an individual named Metro in the 10th Biennial Report, 1922).

During the next 14 years, Wylie continued to press for greater control of individuals in the institution. In 1915 the legislature expanded the definition of feeble-mindedness to include those *"whose defects prevent them from receiving proper training in the public schools"* (*Laws of North Dakota,* 1915, p. 208). By 1921, the law was further expanded to allow admission temporarily for observation and diagnosis of feeble mindedness without the normal regulations imposed by normal admission proceedings (see *Laws of North Dakota*, 1921, p. 123).

Finally, in 1927 the state passed a new law regarding sterilization. Senate Bill 136, sponsored by Senator Kretschmar, was designed to promote the cause of social control. This bill effectively expanded the 1913 sterilization law by broadening the scope of potential patients. This was clearly evident in the descriptive title of the bill; *"An Act to Prevent the Procreation of Feeble-minded, Insane, Epileptic, Habitual Criminals, Moral Degenerates and Sexual Perverts, Who may be Inmates of State Institutions..."* (Laws of North Dakota, 1927, p. 433). Wylie and his staff, especially the social worker H. Safely, promoted use of this new law, and effectively increased the sterilization rates at Grafton. In 1932, Ms. Safely reported that only 11 institutional residents had been sterilized in all the prior years at Grafton. However, her new Department of Social Services actively promoted the practice such that by 1940 North Dakota ranked number two in the nation in the per capita rate of sterilization, second only to California.

While laws were passed to prohibit marriage of or to persons with mental retardation, perhaps none would have been as devastating as a law that was passed in South Dakota, and was promoted by the Grafton superintendents. Although defeated by the North Dakota legislature, the law would have required a state registry for individuals deemed mentally defective. All persons with such a designation would be listed in a card catalog in each county clerk's office. This list would then be used to restrict various legal acts, such as land purchases, lawsuits, and most specifically marriage. No person listed in the card catalog would be allowed to purchase a marriage license. One can only wonder what other restrictions such a list would have brought forth.

Using Legislation for Expansion of Facilities

In many cases the superintendents were aggressive in using state legislation to building new facilities. Generally the only source of consistent income was the state appropriation. Frequently the individual guardian and county assessments of $15 per month were insufficient to operate the institution. This was due both in part to continually rising costs of doing business and the abysmal record of collections from guardians and the counties. Even state legislative action had little effect on counties that refused to pay the admission and enrollment fees of its residents.

During the 1920s Dr. Wylie obtained funding for several new buildings including the refectory (1921), the east section of North B (1923), spiral fire slides for Main (1924), Pleasant View dormitory (1926), an addition to the laundry building (1928), and the west section of North B (1928). Wylie also obtained over $267,700.00 for general maintenance, improvements, and repairs during the mid 1920s. This was a considerable amount of money, but much needed as the number of institutionalized residents increased during this time.

Throughout the years various superintendents used legislative action to continue the expansion and improvement of facilities. Additional dormitory space was constructed in 1937 (Sunset Hall), 1957 (West Hall, now New Horizons), and 1960 Prairie View Wylie Hall), and 1982 (Maplewood and Cedar Grove) from state appropriations. Further, six staff cottages were built on state appropriate funds between the mid 1950s and the early 1960s. State dollars were also used to expand support facilities on the campus including a new cattle barn (1930), a farm utility building (1936) the Health Service Center (1950), machine and repair shops (1957 and 1958), a new barn and carpenter shop (both 1963), Collette Auditorium (1967), the Food Service Center (1973), and the Professional Services Building (1978). In later years Dr. Archer would use federal funding to improve facilities such as the remodeling of Midway for use as a women's training program using Vocational Rehabilitation funds.

Legislative Support for Improving Services

One might argue that all of the laws passed related to Grafton were intended for the improvement of services for residents with mental retardation. And to an extent, that is true. Generally the administrators who promoted the legal changes, and the legislators who sponsored and passed the laws felt that they were doing the best possible actions for the residents. However, beginning in the late 1950s and throughout the present day, most of the legislative action has centered on service delivery systems and service provision to citizens with developmental disabilities

The first example of such an action was the passage of Senate Concurrent Resolution O-O. This resolution required the legislative research council to study the institutional revolving fund, and to look for more stable ways of providing payment for services at the institution. As mentioned previously, many individuals and counties neglected to pay their assigned costs for enrollment of residents at Grafton. The study expressly was conducted to see if the use of general funds could alleviate some of the continual funding emergency problems faced each legislative session by the institution.

In 1963, the North Dakota legislature passed House Bill 886. This established a state coordinating committee on mental retardation using federal pass through funds authorized by President Kennedy and his initiative on improved research and services for persons with mental retardation. This coordinating committee was given the responsibility of *"making or providing for such studies and surveys of the needs of retarded persons in North Dakota as it may deem necessary, and shall coordinate the activities of all state departments, divisions, agencies, and institutions having responsibilities in the field of mental retardation"* (*Laws of North Dakota*, 1963, p. 359).

This committee had far-reaching effects. It established an advisory committee that completed three planning reports, one each in 1966, 1968 and 1970. These reports provided wide-sweeping recommendations for services for persons with mental retardation, including reducing the institutional population, creating professional training programs, creating community-based services, and examining a system of regionalized services for persons with developmental disabilities. In fact, many of these recommendations were implemented when the state established the regionalized human service support systems in the early 1980s.

Pressure for Community-Based Services

The state began a significant move away from institutions with the passage of several laws in 1967. Senate Bill 249 was passed *"to provide for the purchasing of residential care, custody, training, treatment or education of the mentally retarded by the state from private, nonprofit, charitable organizations"* (*Laws of North Dakota*, 1967, p. 468). The Senate also proposed and the legislature passed Senate Bill 390, *"An act to provide for the establishment, administration, organization, and management of sheltered workshops"* (*Laws of North Dakota*, 1967, p. 465). Together these two laws signaled the impact of the advisory committee on mental retardation. The recommendations for greater community-based services had been heard. (It is interesting to note that at about this same time, the legislature considered another bill that would have established a second institution for persons with mental retardation, this one located in Minot. While this seems somewhat disparate from the passage of laws concerning community-based programs, it was still in line with one recommendation from the advisory committee, that being that the Grafton institution's overcrowding could be alleviated by the construction of a second facility in the western half of the state. The bill for the second institution failed.)

However, the state legislature was not yet quite convinced that community-based service was a viable option for many persons with mental retardation. During this same legislative session, House Bill 538 was passed. This bill amended the state law on sterilization, specifically residents of the institution. *"An act authorizing the superintendent of the Grafton state school to recommend a sterilization operation for a resident of such school upon receiving the approval of a board of professional personnel and the written consent of a relative or guardian, specifying the manner of obtaining and granting consent, prohibiting the superintendent from acting as guardian, providing for compensation of physicians and surgeons and limiting liability, and providing that parents may initiate such procedure"* (*Laws of North Dakota*, 1967, p. 443). Thus, while they provided supports for community-based programming, they still had latent concerns about the procreative abilities of persons with mental retardation.

In 1973 the tuberculosis sanatorium at San Haven discontinued, and the facility passed to Grafton State School. The facilities at San Haven had long housed individuals with mental retardation, some as early as 1938 when a small number of Grafton residents with tuberculosis were sent there for treatment. In the late 1950s a more formalized arrangement was developed between Grafton and San Haven. The TB hospital at Dunseith was losing residents as local hospitals and physicians were using more aggressive treatments. As the numbers of TB patients declined, the number of institutionalized residents at Grafton grew. San Haven was used for many residents who were elderly, or needed significant medical and nursing treatments. By 1973 San Haven housed nearly 150 residents from Grafton; thus the transfer in operation from a TB sanatorium to a branch of the Grafton State School was easily done.

The final push for greater community inclusion hit Grafton in 1972 and again in 1980. Dr. Ron Archer reported that Grafton State School had been named as a defendant in a lawsuit in December 1972. Archer stated that *"the suit is being brought on grounds of constitutionality which follows a trend in our nation which was begun in September of 1971 when a group of parents in Pennsylvania brought suit against the Commonwealth declaring that although the Constitution declared that children shall receive a free and pubic education, that there was in fact discrimination against mentally retarded children, in that the school districts did not have to provide educational services for them if they chose not to"*. Further, *"The parents of the one resident of the Grafton State School named in the suit are in essence saying that 'our youngster has not received any educational opportunity and that he has regressed or deteriorated in intellectual development.' The feel that this is due to possibly the lack of facility and staff and that those in charge of running the School should secure more legislative support and funding to rectify that situation"* (*The Ambassador*, December 1972, p. 1). One sees that the effect that this had on the institution, as the school newspaper, *The Ambassador*, reports a number of new teacher hires, and a new school principal over the next three years. This issue was ultimately put to rest by the passage, and then the state implementation, of Public Law 94-142, the Education for All Handicapped Children's Act of 1977. This federal law required that all children, regardless of the severity or nature of their disability, were entitled to a free and appropriate public education, and an individualized education program specifying the nature and duration of the educational services. Numerous documents show the institutional administration and staff attempting to meet those educational requirements while simultaneously attempting to prepare some residents for community placement. However, this process became a peak concern of parents, advocates, lawyers, and legislators in 1980.

The ARC Lawsuit

The filing of the 1980 lawsuit, ARC vs. ND, was a major event in the shaping of the institution at Grafton and of services for ND citizens with mental retardation. The story of the filing is quite interesting. In late spring 1980, Earl Pomeroy was contacted by Perry Groutberg, ND ARC president. The ARC was concerned about the proposed state budget for San Haven. Apparently, the state budget included a line item of approximately $1 million for an aquatic center at the San Haven facility, and the ARC wanted to know if Mr. Pomeroy, a new lawyer in eastern ND, would be willing to conduct an attack on this budget. The ARC felt that the funds could be more appropriately used to support persons with mental retardation in the community. Since Mr. Pomeroy was a state legislator, he could not wage a legal battle against the state government. However, he did refer the ARC to his friend, Mike Williams of Bismarck.

Mike Williams had been a law student at the UND law school with Earl Pomeroy. In fact, they were moot court partners in a constitutional law course. In that course, they prepared a fictitious case that examined the rights of persons who had been committed to public mental health facilities. Their law school partnership was a good match, as Williams was an excellent writer, and Pomeroy was the superb speaker. Mr. Pomeroy remembered this moot course case as he made the ARC referral to Mr. Williams.

Mike Williams was a new lawyer for the Kapsner and Kapsner law firm in Bismarck. The ARC referral was something new for him, and he approached it with considerable gusto. Another friend of Williams, Mary Deutsch Schneider, was a lawyer for Legal Assistance of North Dakota. For several years Ms. Schneider had been in contact with the institution and several families regarding instances of possible abuse and lack of services. However, as a legal assistance agency, she could not bring forward a lawsuit if there was probable action for fees. In other words, if a lawsuit could likely be handled by a private lawyer or firm, for remuneration, then Legal Assistance could not file the case on its own. But the material that Ms. Schneider had was of paramount interest to Williams, and helped shape the initial complaint. In fact, Ms. Schneider and Legal Assistance were listed as attorneys for the plaintiffs in the original complaint and subsequent actions of the case.

Once Mr. Williams received the call from Pomeroy and spoke to the ARC representatives, he was hired to examine the steps needed to combat the proposed aquatic center. However, as he reviewed the case and met with Ms. Schneider, it was clear that a much larger issue was at stake.

In July of 1980, Mike Williams was asked to present his strategy for action to the ND ARC Board of Directors. For over an hour Mr. Williams presented an outline, not for attacking the Human Services budget for the aquatic center, but rather for suing the state of North Dakota for "failure to fulfill their statutory and constitutional duties" to ND citizens with mental retardation and other developmental disabilities. The ARC Board had not been expecting this presentation, and sat stunned for several minutes. What followed has been described as a very animated and frank discussion of the Board's possible options. Before the end of the day, the Board held a sealed vote on a motion to pursue action against the state on behalf ND citizens with mental retardation. The vote was unanimous, and the Board gave Mike Williams the nod to pursue legal action against the state.

The Initial Complaint

On September 26, 1980, Williams and Schneider filed a complaint in the United States District Court for the District of North Dakota, Southwestern Division. The case was listed as

> "*Association for Retarded Citizens of North Dakota; Lindley Black, by his father, Sidney Black; Bradley Cossette, by his mother, Denise Cossette; Richard Schneiderhan, by his mother and guardian, Elira Schneiderhan; Naomi Jordison, by her father, Timothy Jordison; Kelli Moriarty, by her mother and guardian, Jacquelyn Moriarty; and Philip Dechant, by his mother and guardian, Lois Dechant; on behalf of themselves and all others similarly situated, Plaintiffs v. Arthur A. Link, Governor of the State of North Dakota; Edward Klecker, Director of Institutions; Milton Wisland, Superintendent of Grafton State School,; Richard Charrier, Assistant Superintendent of Grafton State School and Chief Administrative Officer of San have Division; Joan Griggs Babbott, State Health Officer and Administrative Officer of the Department of Health; Sam Ismir, Director of Mental Health and Retardation Division of Department of Health; Darvin Hirsch, Director of Office of Developmental Disabilities of Department of Health; Carroll Burchinal, Director of Department of Vocational Education; Howard Snortland, Superintendent of Public Instruction; Gary Gronberg, Director of Special Education Division of Department of Public Instruction; T.N. Tangedahl, Executive Director of Social Services Board; James O. Fine, Executive Director of Division of Vocational Rehabilitation of Social Services Board; Marcellus Hartze, Director of Division of Community Services of the Social services Board; and the State of North Dakota, Defendants.*"

This complaint alleged that the state and the institution deprived the plaintiffs of their statutory and constitutional rights. In particular the suit stated, "*The named plaintiffs and their class allege that they have been, and continue to be, gravely harmed by their confinement at either Grafton or San Haven. The design and physical condition of the buildings at the institutions deprive plaintiffs of privacy, dignity, and a normal, home-like environment and endanger their safety*" (*ARC Complaint*, 1980, p. 2).

The suit was brought forward to Judge Bruce Van Sickle who ordered that the lawsuit be categorized as a "class action" lawsuit. Essentially, this meant that any judgments for the plaintiffs would be applicable to any and all citizens who received or were eligible to receive services from the state due to their disability.

Over the next two years, the ARC lawyers Williams and Schneider prepared their case. They invited disability experts to examine the institution, the residents and the documentation of services. The state also prepared its case, and attempted to avert further legal action through various state legislative actions. In 1981 the legislature passed several laws that it hoped would show good intent toward remedying the ARC situation. For example House Bill 1009 appropriated over $26 million for services and improvements at Grafton. House Bill 1418 created a new Department of Human Services and established a firm link between the Department and state developmental disability services. The legislature also passed House Concurrent Resolution 3058, a study of the rights of persons with developmental disabilities, and set forth an examination of guardianship laws and commitment procedures.

The state's lawyers used these laws to show that sufficient effort toward the cause of disability services and that good intentions were being made by the defendants. The state then proposed that the lawsuit be dismissed. Judge Van Sickle denied the motion to dismiss and the case went to trial. After 31 days of testimony over five months, and several additional months of reflection on the evidence, Van Sickle issued the base order on August 31, 1982.

The base order was a 43-page document that outlined the case history, findings of fact, and statutory and constitutional grounds for the judge's decision. The order granted the plaintiffs relief on 13 specific issues. Several of these included the right to written individualized habilitation plans (IHPs); appropriate care, education and habilitation; environments that assured privacy and dignity; prohibition of chemical and physical restraints used in place of appropriate programming; and the expansion and maintenance of a state-wide service delivery system for persons with developmental disabilities. Van Sickle also established his continual oversight on the case until all issues were resolved.

After further study and additional motions by both sides, Van Sickle issued an implementation order in March 1984. This 65-page document listed nearly 100 actions to be implemented by the state. Among these actions were orders to provide the institutional residents with IHPs; services in a least restrictive environment; normalized living conditions; freedom from harm and abuse; education or habilitative programming; confidentiality of records; appropriate staffing levels; staff training; and an infrastructure for community placement and support. Most of these orders had specific timelines for implementation.

These sweeping changes were to be overseen by a court appointed monitor. Van Sickle stated, *"The monitor will be responsible solely to the Court and will serve at the discretion of the Court or until this order has been fully implemented. The monitor shall review and report to the Court on the progress towards implementation of this order, in accordance with procedures and schedules established by this and related orders. The monitor shall, as advisable, review and evaluate all staffing requirements necessary to implement this and related orders. Specific staffing ratios, when necessary, may be appended as amendments to this order. Defendants shall pay the fees and expenses of the monitor and assistants and appropriate consultants as necessary and shall provide necessary clerical support"* (Implementation Order, 1984, p. 58).

Amendments, clarifications, and further stipulations to the initial implementation order were provided by a supplemental order issued by Judge Van Sickle on September 18, 1985. This 6-page order with multiple exhibits addressed numerous points of the initial order that needed clarification and explanation. Van Sickle based these clarifications upon a memorandum of agreement that had been submitted by both the plaintiffs and the defendants. Thus, there was general agreement on the issues of the order.

Some of the more interesting issues were addressed immediately, including a plan to accelerate the Title XIX and Accreditation Council accrediting processes. As part of the initial order, the state was to assure that Grafton State School and any community providers met the standards of care outlined by these two accrediting bodies. However, the process was sometimes complex and frequently time consuming, in some cases drawing staff away from direct service provision to residents with mental retardation. Thus, this new order specified a plan to hire up to eight more staff to assist providers in meeting the standards of care.

Staff training was a required component of the implementation order. However, no detailed plan had been outlined for the provision of this training. This new order specified that all full time staff were required to have 40 hours of staff training prior to any contact with residents. Then, staff were required to complete 100 hours of additional training within a year of employment, unless they were otherwise able to demonstrate competence addressed by the in-service training.

Among the other issues detailed in this new order were requirements for staff recruitment and compensation, uniformity of compensation between providers and the institution, a client appeals process, a plan for supported and minimally supervised living arrangements, respite care eligibility calculations, and admission procedures for Grafton State School.

Judge Van Sickle, the plaintiffs and the defendants engaged in several more legal wranglings for the next few years. In 1992 Van Sickle appointed a five-member panel to review the lawsuit, the past court proceedings, and other relevant materials to determine if the state had met the standards of care required by North Dakota's constitution. The panel heard testimony in this matter from November 1992 through August 1993. Then, on November 14, 1994 the panel produced a report stating that North Dakota had indeed met the constitutional requirements addressed in the initial lawsuit. On January 11, 1995, Van Sickle dismissed most of the case and ended his injunction over the state for failure to provide adequate services to persons with mental retardation and other developmental disabilities.

Summary

An examination of Appendix C of this book will show that the North Dakota legislature passed over 200 separate pieces of legislation regarding the institution and persons with mental retardation. This is more than two per year, or more than four each time the legislature met. Perhaps no other state facility or program has received such attention.

It is interesting how the laws reflected either specific requests of the Grafton superintendents, or the philosophy of practice of the time. While one must assume that all of the laws were passed with good intention for the residents, many were of detriment to the rights and dignity of individuals with mental retardation. Perhaps none exemplify this more than the numerous laws on sterilization and prohibition of marriage. At least 10 separate times the state examined the issue and passed laws and amendments on these issues.

Clearly the impact of the ARC lawsuit is evident in our current system of services and supports for persons with developmental disabilities. The impact was also felt at Grafton, where in a period of less than 15 years, the resident population decreased from nearly 1,000 to approximately 150. Subsequent state legislation has formed and refined those services so that today North Dakota ranks as one of the few states with less than 200 residents in state supported institutions.

Chapter Seven

The Institutional Farm

Most institutions built in the late 1800s or early 1900s were located in relatively rural areas. Part of the reason for this was that the residents were to be separated from society, and thus society would be protected from them. For more practical reasons, however, the rural locations allowed superintendents to operate farms and thus raise the necessary produce and livestock necessary to support a large population. Scheerenberger (1983) describes how the prevalent thought of the time was for superintendents to press for large acreage so that the institution could become fairly self-sufficient, and not place a great burden on the rest of the state. One superintendent expressed his confidence in the ability of farming to reduce the burden on his state as follows, "*If the State would give him one thousand acres of land, they could take care of all their custodial cases free of further expense*" (Scheerenberger, 1983, p. 126).

While the farms were necessary for supplying food for the staff and residents, they were also useful operations for keeping the residents active. This fit the early philosophy of institutions as training facilities. Residents were taught to tend chickens, milk cows and perform various other agricultural duties. Often they did this for little or no pay. As institutions transformed from training centers in the early 1900s to agents of social control of mental defectives in the 1930s, residents often looked forward to opportunities to work in the farm programs simply as a way to stay active and move out of the residence hall for at least a portion of the day.

Early Farming at Grafton

The institution at Grafton was no different that most institutions of the time. Almost as soon as the institution was opened, the land surrounding the facility was put into farm production. The institution was originally built on 40 acres of land just west of the community of Grafton. The soil was rich, and had long been prime farmland for the local area farmers. As the institution was initially being constructed in 1902 and 1903, the institution land surrounding the building site was leased to a local farmer. This allowed the state and the Board of Trustees to gather some small investment on the land. This investment was returned to the state fund previously set aside for the operation of the facilities.

The Board of Trustees and the new superintendent knew that the success of the institution depended upon their ability to use the allotted and the surrounding farmland for the good of the facility. They also knew that 40 acres was inadequate to provide for the original 125 residents for which they planned. Thus, in the first biennial report to the Governor, the Board of Trustees asked for funds for additional land. They stated that "*in order that the institution may be economically managed, more land should be added to the institution tract, and we accordingly urge that the legislature in providing for the maintenance of the institution for the next biennial period bear in mind and provide for these absolute necessities*" (First Biennial Report of the North Dakota Institution for Feeble Minded at Grafton, 1904. p. 4). Superintendent Baldwin concurred, and in his accompanying report stated "*More land is required for the economical maintenance of the institution. The prospective grounds about the building take up nearly fifteen acres, leaving only twenty-five for cultivation. There should be at least one acre of land for each inmate. Thus, with a population of 150, including employees, there should be 150 acres of land. A portion of this should be suitable for pasture, and cows should be kept....All the vegetables consumed should be raised on the premises, thus affording outdoor occupation for a portion of the male inmates"* (First Biennial Report of the North Dakota Institution for Feeble Minded at Grafton, 1904, pp. 7-8).

The first institutional budget request to the Governor and the legislature included $1,000 for a barn, $300 for a root cellar (for potatoes and other vegetables), $750 for stock, and $6,000 for additional land. To illustrate how important Baldwin thought the farming operations were to the success of the institution, compare these figures to the total of $650 for training school supplies and amusements for the residents. Clearly the farming operation was viewed as a primary part of the institution.

In 1905, ND Legislature voted upon the recommendation of the superintendent and the Board of Trustees to purchase 100 acres of additional land for the institution. The Governor vetoed the purchase; however, he allowed for the building of the barn and purchase of livestock. In spite of the veto, the Board entered into a long-term agreement with a local farmer to lease with the option to buy some surrounding land. This land was put into production with labor from outside the institution, and it produced millet, hay, barley, oats, potatoes, and garden produce. Further, eight cows were purchased and they produced sufficient milk for the institution. A hog house, originally constructed just to the rear (west) of the main building, was moved to the farmland north of the institution. The superintendent was rather proud of the hog production, as they were fed and then sold for a profit of $490.82.

During the 1906 – 1908 biennium, the superintendent hired a full time farmer for the newly purchased 120 acres of land, just north of the institution buildings. The farmland contained an icehouse, granary, barn, machine shed, and farmhouse that needed extensive work for habitation. Grain and hay were raised for the stock and for sale. The institution netted over $800 during this biennium on grain and hay. Also, hog production was good, with the sales netting over $800. An additional 12 acres of land were rented for production.

At the inception of the institution, the superintendent hired local farm help to tend the land. However, by 1914, the institutional population was 223 residents, with 47 employees, most who had room and board at the facility. The farm was extremely important to the viability of the institution, as many counties were not paying the required monthly fees for residents from their areas. Thus, there were two farm hands in full employment; T.C. Johnson, and Fred Ledwich. Both received board (meals and room) for their work, along with $60 per month salary for Johnson and $30 per month for Ledwich. Their work was important in assuring the viability of the institution. Following a difficult few years, the production of the 1912- 1914 biennium was rather good. Johnson and Ledwich reported a total of 3,800 bushels of oats, 3,800 bushels of potatoes, 2,500 heads of cabbage, nearly 400 pounds of dressed chicken, and 2,300 pounds of dressed beef. Cash sales on the farm raised $370.55 during the biennium.

While the farm production was excellent for the time, Superintendent Wylie made it clear that the farming situation needed to improve. He continually asked for remodeling or new construction of the farmhouse, and the purchase of new land. *"The Farm House to*

*which attention has been called in a number of previous reports still remains a disgrace.
to the State. It is not fit to house human beings."* Also, *"We have been unable to raise the
necessary produce on the land we now own and we have been compelled to rent fifty
acres additional. Land is this section of the State is rising in value, so the State should
not wait in increasing its holdings."*(Sixth Biennial Report, 1914, p. 401).

The urgency of the farm situation escalated quickly. By 1916, the institution was
required to sell 20 acres of farmland to the city of Grafton for a park. This sale netted the
institution $2,200 which Dr. Wylie wanted to use for farmland investment. By this time
they were renting over 100 acres of land, owning only slightly more than 40 acres. The
institutional farmers also wanted to modernize their production, and thus make the
operations more efficient. Wylie requested funds for a greenhouse to get an earlier start
on the garden plants. Also, the dairy operations needed work. *"We have been continually
criticised (sic) by the inspectors as to our handling of the milk. Our present methods are
as good as they can be with the present equipment. A separate milk house fully equipped
should be erected near the dairy barn"* (Seventh Biennial Report, 1916, p. 1196).

Over the next six years, things did not improve greatly. No additional land was
purchased, the milk production facilities were not improved, and the farmhouse was not
renovated. Obviously World War I had impacted the state and the institution. State
funding was low and supplies and labor were scarce. While appropriations were made for
most of these farm items, the funds were so meager that nothing substantial could be
done. The institution was still renting land, and farm production was good, but the land
available was sparse. The 1920 superintendent's report shows a total of 183 acres in
production (both rented and owned land). There were only four acres in wheat, 65 acres
in oats, 25 acres of potatoes, 30 acres of corn, 18 acres of oats hay, 8 of Timothy hay, 25
acres of alfalfa, and an 8-acre garden. For stock, they owned 25 milk cows, 40 pigs, 10
work horses and 2 driving horses. With the rising prices of produce purchased for the
institution (for example canned wax beans rose over 30% and molasses by nearly 300%
during the biennium), the institution needed to make a major change in their farm
operations.

Improving the Farm

In 1922 Superintendent Wylie made one of the best investments in farming
operations for the institution, he hired Walfred Anderson. At $80 per month he was one
of the highest paid employees in the Grafton facility, and one of four farm and garden
workers. In less than ten years Anderson increased the 25 cow herd to nearly 60 cows of
fine breeding. By 1928 the institution owned 140 acres of land and rented an additional
654 acres. A dairy barn was built in 1926, and a milk house was connected to the barn. A
silage silo was built in 1924 and a poultry house built around 1922. A brooder house for
raising chickens was built about 1925.

During the depression the farm operations became increasingly important to the
survival of the institution. Buildings, farm production, and efficiency increased again
during the 1930s. A hog house was built in 1931, and a farm implement shed was built
from used institutional garage framing. Another dairy barn and silo were built in 1930. A
one-story granary was constructed about 1932 and was used for small grain storage. A
potato pit was built on the farm for storage, although this would prove a mistake in later
years due to excessive ground moisture and spoilage.

By 1938 the farm was no longer using horses and wagons but was using trucks and tractors, most notably the 22-36 McCormick-Deering tractor that was now badly in need of repair. The dairy herd was increased and produced nearly enough milk for the 868 residents. The once 8-acre garden was now 50 acres, and tilled by tractor and cultivator. There were 300 laying hens and over 1500 chicks being raised in brooder and hens houses on the former Worthing estate now belonging to the institution. By now the institution owned 260 acres and rented an additional 932, for a total of 1,192 acres in crop production, building sites, stock lots and general grounds.

Farming in the 40s and 50s

The institutional farm went through great fluctuations during the 1940s and 1950s. Weather, economic conditions, the war, and varying farm investments caused huge fluctuations in the bottom line on the farm at Grafton. By this time Walfred Anderson was keeping rather detailed records and reporting these in the Biennial Reports. Every two years he would add a Farm Report to the superintendents' reports. These farm reports provide a nice insight into the farm operations during this period.

In the 1940 Biennial Report, Anderson reports that the institution had a capital investment of nearly $71,000 in the farm. This included the 260 acres of land, equipment, stock, feed, and other farm goods. The institutional land alone was worth $15,648. The institution also rented nearly 1,000 additional acres. These 1,200 acres resulted in 9,600 bushels of oats, 1,580 bushels of barley, 5,120 bushels of potatoes, 500 tons of silage for the cattle and 125 tons of hay. The dairy herd produced 63,368 gallons of milk. Using the current price of $0.25 per gallon, Anderson estimated that the farm saved the institution nearly $16,000 in milk purchase alone. Overall the farm brought in a profit of $4,795.02 to Grafton State School.

Anderson's 1942 report shows an increase in the capital investment to $84,029 and that the overall farm profit was $11,026.03. Production increased in many crops. There were 14,000 bushels of oats harvested, along with 2,000 bushels of barley, 800 bushels of wheat, 6,500 bushels of potatoes, 800 bushels of corn, and 600 tons of silage. Milk production increased to 70,353 gallons for the year. Anderson's staff also sold the pig and cow hides that resulted from the butchering, netting several hundred more dollars for the institution.

In the fall of 1942 a new poultry building was constructed. Later reports show that the poultry operations were located on the south edge of the campus, while the dairy and crop production operations were on the north edge along the Park River. Several construction projects were completed during the 1942 – 1944 biennium including a new basement and remodeling of the farmhouse, reconstruction of the dairy barn, and the purchase of a milk pasteurizer. Prior to this time most milk consumed at the institution was raw or separated milk directly from the farm. However, the new pasteurizing machine, placed in the Refectory Building, allowed for better and safer handling of the milk. The overall farm profit rose again to $14,038.83 in 1943. The dairy herd produced 65,697 gallons of milk, over 5,500 bushels of various vegetables, 6,000 pounds of pumpkins, and 28,000 pounds of cabbage.

Labor and production costs rose significantly during the mid and late 1940s. These costs, along with the post-war pressures on the state, forced the institutional staff to increase their use of residents as paid laborers. Anderson's 1946 report shows that inmates (residents) were indeed paid for most or all of their work on the farm, including work in the greenhouse, on the poultry farm, in the large farm garden, and in the fields. While the capital investment (net worth) of the farm rose to over $100,000, the farm profits shrank dramatically to just over $5,000 per year.

Dr. Lamont was concerned about the abrupt turn-around of the farming operations. In his 1948 biennial report, he gives an indication of his thoughts about the viability of the farm. "*Rapid changes in labor and feed costs, and in rental rates, have changed the institutional farm outlook. Rental costs have doubled and new machinery is expensive. All products are returned to the institution in the form of food. Inmate labor is gradually being replaced by new machine tools. Higher costs of concentrates for swine, poultry and daily cows, have reduced the profit margin and placed budget estimates in the 'red' for the first time in years. Whether it will pay to continue our present farm program during a ten year period of declining values, is a question for Budget Committees. As the matter stands, the School has a large investment in our present farm program, and eggs, milk, meat and garden produce are a very important maintenance asset, which cannot always be purchased on the market in sufficient quantity at any price*" (Twenty-Third Biennial Report, 1948, p. 1039).

In 1950 Dr. Lamont again wrote a brief narrative describing the bleak farm picture. This time, however, he appealed for a greater state investment as the method for turning things around. He wrote, "*In the circumstances it would seem best to purchase tillable land of known production value within close range of the institutional property. The acreage suggested for purchase is from half a section to one section. On the tax-exempt basis this would keep our farm program operating without loss of present investment in stock and equipment*" (Twenty-Fourth Biennial Report, 1950, p. 1703).

These comments came at a time when Anderson was able to show a huge increase in the farm profits, giving the institution a positive balance of over $19,000. The dairy herd had increased in size, additional machinery had been purchased, and the institution was still farming nearly 1,000 acres of land. Anderson also began a differentiated accounting system for various parts of the farm. The records show that he divided the income statements into four categories, one for the main farming/crop operations, one for the dairy, one for the poultry farm, and one for the institution garden. He and Lamont would later be able to use these separated accounts to more finely tune the operations into the profitable side of the institution budget.

The 1950s decade was again plagued by fluctuating profits and weather patterns, and rising equipment and feed costs. In 1952 Lamont reported that 300 acres of land previously rented by the institution had been sold, and it was unlikely that they would have access to the land in the future. Again, he proposed the purchase of 1,000 acres. The capital investment had risen to nearly $150,000 yet the profits had decreased to $3,399.83, partly due to the increased land rental costs.

Apparently Lamont's plea for more land worked. In October of 1953 the institution purchased 80 acres from the Hegranes estate. The institution had a long history with the Hegranes family, as the original warrant records for 1904 show that the first institutional purchase of milk for the residents was from the Hegranes farm. Then in April of 1954 an additional 236 acres was purchased from Herman Fisher. These purchases allowed the institution to maintain, with their rental land, about 1,000 acres of production. This included a 60-acre vegetable and fruit garden.

Anderson also increased the cattle and hog operations. In 1953 he had 120 registered Holsteins, 240 young hogs, and 48 production sows. The dairy herd produced 91,348 gallons of milk, and the hogs were fed the garbage from the institution, carefully following state and federal health codes in the process. However, the bottom line on profit is unclear, as the biennial reports no longer listed farm profits as separate accounts.

In 1955 Superintendent Charles Rand promoted Walfred Anderson to the position of Farm Manager. Previously Anderson had served as head farmer, but worked with several department managers on the farming operations. As Farm Manager, Anderson now had the capability to move staff and equipment around the institution to become more efficient.

Rand's 1956 biennial report included a long farm report. This was his first foray into the farm operations, and the report served both to instruct him in the overall picture of the operations, as well as update the governor and state legislators on the agricultural aspects of Grafton. Rand's report had several statements that serve to illustrate the importance of the farm and yet educate the citizens about the needs of the institution. It is especially noteworthy how Rand incorporates the operation of the farm into the overall mission of resident education and transition into society. *"The farm is an important division of Grafton State School. We have 14 paid employees on the farm and there are 20 patients or students working there. Our state is primarily an agricultural state and we train our boys on the farm in practical farm work. More boys are paroled from the farm than any other training department. There is one thing to note, too, that we do not have as many boys admitted to the school with intelligence high enough to work on the farm as in the past years. None of our farm power equipment is operated by student or patient help. It is too dangerous."* Rand also stated, *"In the past year the school has lost 80 acres of very good productive land in that it has been sold by McDonalds, from whom we rented it. I have been given to understand that we will lose another 40 acres of our best land this fall or next spring. We will get the crop off most of this land this fall; however, we will feel this land loss in the fall of 1957 when our yields will be down. There should be money appropriated for the purchase of more land so that we would be assured of enough land to raise our own feed as well as providing training for future parolees"* (Twenty Seventh Biennial Report, 1965, pp. 2016-2017).

By 1956 the institution owned 652.69 acres and rented another 429.81 acres. The farm had 163 cattle, 288 hogs, 2 horses, 841 laying hens, 500 broilers, and 1,835 pullets. The male cattle were now being kept for slaughter rather than selling them at the market. Milk production was over 91,000 gallons per year, and Anderson began listing a more comprehensive listing of production, especially for the 60-acre garden. The variety and production are amazing. For example the garden harvest included 95 bushels of lettuce, 409 bushels of carrots, 932 bushels of onions, 268 bushels of beets, 48 bushels of rhubarb, 1,248 bushels of tomatoes, and 5 tons of squash.

Anderson's 1958 report shows further increases in farm production, with over 106,000 gallons of milk produced in 1958. He also reports that nearly 1,000 pounds of chicken were required for one meal for the institution. Grafton continued to supply the School for the Blind and the School for the Deaf with potatoes and other vegetables as were available. In addition to the produce, the farm greenhouse was growing a number of plants and flowers for the institutional grounds. These included mums, petunias and snapdragons, and made the institution a more visually appealing place.

The Farm in the 1960s

The farm in the early 1960s continued the prosperity of the 50s. By 1960 the farm harvest was valued at nearly $300,000 per biennium. The milk production was up to 129,115 gallons per year in 1961, and over $10,000 worth of produce was sent to the School for the Deaf, the School for the Blind, the Tuberculosis Hospital at San Haven, and to the State Penitentiary in Bismarck.

In 1963 milk production was about 119,000 gallons per year, but the milk handling and pasteurization processes had come under scrutiny by the State Health Department. The Department was concerned about the transportation of raw milk from the barn, to a storage tank and then again to the Refectory. It recommended a new milk processing and storage facility to be attached to the main dairy barn.

By legislative action there was a shortened version of the total biennial report in 1966, so no farm records are available. The next report, 1968, showed several major changes. The new milk house had been built in 1966, but Walfred Anderson retired on March 31, 1967.

The End of the Farm

Anderson's retirement as Farm Manager after 45 years at Grafton signaled the death knell for the farm. During this time he changed the operations completely, taking a small herd of "scrub cows" and developing a regionally recognized herd of registered Holsteins. The farming operations expanded to several sections of land, both owned and rented. Building were constructed and remodeled, making the facilities pleasing to view as well as more functional for operations. Dr. Rand reported Anderson's retirement as follows; "*Mr. Anderson has made our farm operation very profitable to the State of North Dakota. Through his work we have been transferring produce from our institution to other institutions. Devils Lake has been obtaining all the pork that they consumer from the Grafton State School as well as potatoes and many of the vegetables that we raise. We have given all of the pork to the Grand Forks School for the Blind that they need as well as provided them with potatoes and vegetables. We have also transported potatoes to the San Haven Institution. The Grafton State School has received live beef from the Penitentiary which we butcher here and feed to our residents. We have given the Penitentiary oats whenever available so that they can use it for feed for their livestock. This trading back and forth and providing other institutions with farm products has helped the budgets of all institutions*" (Thirty Third Biennial Report, 1968, pp. 74-75).

For nearly 70 years the farming operations had provided food and work for the residents and the staff. However, changing economies and state and federal regulations made it difficult to operate the farm. During the 1972 – 1974 biennium, the farm operations were phased out. Some land was sold, and other land rented. Buildings and equipment were sold, and the proceeds put into an emergency fund for use in other institutional areas. Grafton State School no longer farmed.

Chapter Eight

Science and Research at the Institution

One does not generally associate science or scientific study with institutions. However, there is a long history of the study of individuals with mental retardation in institutions, particularly in the US. Since the early 1800s researchers (usually physicians) have studied people with disabilities (Rosen, Clark, & Kivitz, 1976). For example Eduouard Sequin and his colleagues developed and refined the physiological methods for instructing persons with mental retardation. Sequin's work led to research by others who tried to classify the various types and causes of mental retardation. This led to later work to refine intellectual assessment instruments that could more finely distinguish amongst clinical syndromes.

Shortly after the Civil War in the United States, the public characterized people with mental retardation as socially and morally corrupt (Rosen, Clark, & Kivitz, 1976). This led to an increase in mental testing and the idea that, since mental retardation was a permanent and untreatable condition, such individuals were to be isolated. The result was a large increase in institutions throughout the country. Certainly the eugenics movement and the national concern over the growing number of "morally corrupt" immigrants fed into these thoughts. (The eugenics movement was a set of proposals forwarded by researchers and policy makers in the early 1900s that sought the segregation of persons of differing nationalities and abilities, as well as the limitation of immigrants into the US.)

As institutions were established and grew, much of the early research focused on effective methods for training individuals. Certainly the introduction of Sloyd work at Grafton was related to this. However, the growing public concerns over the "mentally defective" and the necessity of efficient and cost effective operations led the institutional staff to conduct their own studies. Often these studies were influenced by noted researchers such as Goddard, Barr and Schwartz. Their work set the model for how research with people with mental retardation should be conducted, and what types of findings would be most evident. Goddard (1914) for example used the Kallikak family as an example of the study of heredity and the cause of mental retardation. Barr (1902) urged institutional directors to lobby for segregation and sterilization to protect individuals with mental retardation, and perhaps more importantly to protect society from the "menace of feeble-mindedness". Schwartz, a reverend and avid author on mental retardation, argued that the laws of nature called for restrictions on marriage and for sterilization and institutionalization. These early authors clearly set the agenda for early 20th century research, especially through the study of select individuals.

Early Ideas about Feeblemindedness

Much of the early research depended upon the early conceptualization of intelligence. Goddard and others used the relatively new instruments such as the Binet tests to measure mental abilities. This research led to the belief that intelligence was stable and non-variable. Thus, once someone was labeled mentally defective, nothing could change the result. This idea led to the presentation of two ways to protect society from the feeble-minded, institutionalization and sterilization.

From the 1920s through the 1950s several researchers challenged the inviolability of intelligence, and present a more malleable concept of the impact of mental retardation. In 1924 Edgar Doll argued against the use of IQ testing only as a means for diagnosing mental disorders. He thought that social adaptability was important and conducted several major studies at the Vineland Institution in New Jersey. Fernald's (1919) seminal study of the community adjustment of persons with mental retardation set the stage for nearly 40 years of work on instruction and rehabilitation. Also, Haskell (1944) presented a 15-year series of studies at the Wayne County Training School that further supported the work of education and training for people with mental retardation.

Refining and Re-defining

Research in the 1960s and 1970s emphasized the advocacy movement toward rehabilitation and treatment. Certainly Marc Gold's "Try Another Way" research had a profound impact on how persons with were taught. Parent-led efforts for appropriate education had their foundations in legislation and litigation. Also, President Kennedy's personal interest in mental retardation fostered public support for federally funded research and training activities.

Basic educational research often utilized B.F. Skinner's behavior theories. Also researchers began to examine structures of public education and the role of families in habilitation. Of course the concepts of deinstitutionalization and normalization prevailed, making their impact on the function and feasibility of institutions.

Deinstitutionalization

For the past 20 years, much of the research in mental retardation has focused on community supports and services for individuals. As states closed institutions, service providers have worked to define their roles and responsibilities toward people with disabilities. Much has been written lately about concepts like person-centered planning and self-determination. Clearly institutions have had to refocus their efforts toward community-based services.

Research and Science in the North Dakota Institution

The early superintendents were as current with the common day research as could be expected. For example, Baldwin, LaMoure and Wylie all had frequent interactions with other institutional superintendents, most frequently those in Minnesota. However, they also attended national meetings of the Association of Medical Officers of American Institutions for Idiots and Feeble-minded Persons (later known as the American Association on Mental Deficiency; today, the American Association on Mental Retardation). At these meetings this listened to presentations by Lewis Terman of Stanford University of California, Fred Kuhlmann of the research department at Fairbault, MN state institution and Henry Goddard from Ohio State University.

In fact, many of the superintendents' ideas on institutional operation and services for persons with disabilities were greatly shaped by these researchers. For example, in Wylie's biennial report to the ND Board of Control of State Institutions (6th Biennial Report of the Institution for Feeble Minded, 1914), he stated, *"By means of investigations carried on by the Eastern Institutions, particularly, the causes of feeble mindedness are becoming more clearly determined. On account of special appropriation they are enabled to send out 'Field Workers' who investigate the families of inmates of the different Institutions. And they have found the hereditary element very markedly in evidence. In fact from two-thirds to eighty per cent of feeble mindedness is due to heredity" (p. 394).*

The operations of the ND institution have long held much fertile ground for research. For example, in May 1904, as the first residents were admitted to the institution, the superintendent began an admissions ledger (later called the Patient Record, State Historical Society of ND, State Archives, Series 30292). In this ledger, admission was recorded on a separate ledger sheet, which listed a multitude of information including the rank of admission, nationality, date of birth, place of residence, parent/guardian names, cause of retardation, and county or party responsible for support. In addition, the superintendent recorded important information such as the degree of deficiency at admission, the person's "disposition" (most often characterized as apathetic or agitated), speech, motor and education abilities, and the superintendent's opinion as to condition (classification) at admission. In total these ledgers compiled a critical set of information on the first 825 admissions into the institution, spanning a period from 1904 – 1922. Later, the institution implemented a daily census report of resident movement, listing the number of residents in each building and ward, and categorized by gender and degree or type of disability (State Historical Society of ND, State Archives, Series 30803).

In 1929 the ND Institution for the Feebleminded/Grafton State School began a purposeful process for examining the conditions and causes of individuals served in the institution. The aforementioned resident records were the basis for the studies. In his June 31, 1930 report to the Board of Administration of State Institutions, Superintendent Wylie reported on the hire of a social worker. Her primary job was to "investigate the histories of our children in their homes and communities" (14th Biennial Report, p. 2957). She was also available in investigate new case referrals to the institution. Similarly, she was to go into communities throughout the state and work with local physicians and other professionals to determine if there were individuals who might be served at the institution.

It appears that Wylie's intention was to develop a systematic process to review the existing cases in the institution, and thus develop a set of critical features that might be used in his institution. While the institution was using Binet IQ scores as a means of categorizing residents, there was little information on the residents as to possible causes of their conditions. Frequently, the Patient Records listings in the ledger listed "unknown cause" or "congenital" as the reason for the disability. It seems that Wylie's employment of the social worker was intended to get a better grasp on who had been admitted to the institution, and thus better understand how they might be served.

The social worker's role came about as a direct result of work done in 1929-1930 with a traveling clinic. As part of a community service initiative, the institution held Mental Hygiene Clinics in Jamestown, Wahpeton, Mandan, and Bismarck. These cities had asked Dr. Wylie for assistance with school children who had been labeled problem children. Institution staff worked with doctors, dentists, psychologists, nurses, and even local women's clubs to determine the appropriate methods for handling these children.

In 1930, Dr. Wylie described his plan for continuing these traveling clinics. He stated "The Institution should be a center or source of information for the use of the schools and communities of this state. There are probably about six thousand feeble minded in this state. There is hardly a school that does not have at least one, and in every community there are problem children of this type. The Institution should be able to offer them the service of its knowledge and experience." (14th Biennial Report, p. 2957).

During the 1930 – 1934 period, the superintendents more fully developed the duties and responsibilities of the social worker. In 1932, Superintendent Wylie established a social service department. Miss Henrietta Safley, the director of the department, began extensive work on the histories of persons who were and who had been served in the institution. Her partial report is shown in the 15th and 16th Annual Reports of the Board of Administration to the Governor, while the entire report has been obtained from the state historical archives (State Historical Society of ND, State Archives, Series 30795). The report is interesting in its content and purpose. The following is a description of the complete report.

Social Service Department Report – 1932-1934

In 1934 the head of the Grafton State School Social Service Department, Henrietta Safley, wrote a report detailing the department's long-term study of mental defectives. Safley and her colleagues developed and implemented a study of the histories and characteristics of all of the 738 residents of Grafton State School. Her report, produced in part in the 15th and 16th Annual Reports of the Board of Administration to the Governor (1934), and fully in an unpublished draft of this document (State Historical Society of ND, State Archives, Series 30292, p. 29 of draft of 1934 report) details the results. There are several interesting features of the report, which are summarized here.

Categorization of disability. Safley and her colleagues used the science of the day, mental testing, to categorize individuals in the institution. According to the records, individuals who were feeble-minded could be classified into three types. *"namely: (1) The "Idiot", who mental age ranges from less than one year to three years; (2) the "Imbecile", whose mental age ranges from three to seven years; and (3) the "Moron", whose mental age ranges from seven to twelve years"* (15th/16th Annual Report, pp. 599-600). While these classifications had been used throughout the 1920s at Grafton, it was here where the social service department first began using them as categories for their study. Thus, using a classification system of mental age was a step forward in their research.

One must remember that researchers and staff during this time period were convinced that persons with mental retardation were imbued with the disability due to genetic or moral reasons. The heredity of mental retardation was the over-arching theory of the time and was so prevalent that in 1927 the Grafton superintendent pushed for, and the ND legislature passed House Bill number 135, Act – Sterilization of Feeble-Minded. This was "an act to prevent procreation of feeble minded, insane, epileptic, habitual criminals, moral degenerates and sexual perverts"…for the purpose of the "betterment of the physical, mental, neural, or psychic condition of the insane, or to protect society from the menace of procreation."

Financial impact. Safley calculated that from January 1, 1922 to January 1, 1934 a total of $1,467,336 was used to support individuals with disabilities at Grafton. The counties provided approximately $1,100,000 in individual payments for residents from their counties, and the remainder came from state appropriations. The social workers at Grafton determined that these were reasonable expenses, and in fact, probably were a savings to the counties and the states. They reached this conclusion after examining the "deplorable conditions under which many of these families exist due to the limited mental ability of one or both parents..." (State Historical Society of ND, State Archives, Series 30292, p. 29 of draft of 1934 report). The social workers felt that individuals with mental retardation, left on their own in such conditions, would place an even larger burden on counties due to their poverty and welfare needs. They thus concluded that money spent on institutionalization was a wise investment.

Heredity of mental retardation. The social services department staff at Grafton State School conducted a study of all 738 residents of the institution. This study incorporated procedures of medical and intake file review, local community visits, and community interviews. The staff examined the family characteristics of the residents, with particular attention to hereditary traits. A summary of their findings suggests:

- Fully 50% (369 of 738) of the residents inherited their mental retardation.
- Residents have many siblings, most of which could be classified as mentally defective.
- The community living conditions were impoverished.
- Residents with mental retardation would invariably produced children with mental retardation.

Specifically the staff found that their residents have produced 278 children of which 72 had been institutionalized. Further the staff prepared a Mendelian explanation for such results.

"In the mating of a mental defective, there are three possibilities; (1) mate with a normal, (2) with a hybrid, or (3) with another mental defective. The results would be:
(1) aa (mental defective) plus AA (normal) equals all Aa (hbrid.
(2) aa (mental defective) plus Aa (hybrid) equals ½ Aa – aa.
(3) aa (mental defective) plus aa (mental defective) equals all aa."
(State Historical Society of ND, State Archives, Series 30292, p. 30 of draft of 1934 report)

The social services staff then went on to use these data to justify the institutionalization of persons with mental retardation, and the sterilization of those who might produce "defective" offspring. It is important to understand the relevance of this report, given only in part to the Governor and the citizens of North Dakota at the time. Safley argues that the 1927 sterilization law has not been used enough (i.e., "Little use was made of this law, in so far as the feeble-minded were concerned..., p. 33), and that future use is necessary to protect the citizens economically (remember the financial impact), and socially (i.e., these individuals live and procreate in poverty situations). In fact, Safley promotes the sterilization law as follows:

"North Dakota has provided a law for the eugenic sterilization of feeble-minded, insane, epileptics, moral degenerates and social perverts, who are potential to producing offspring, who, because of inheritance of inferior or anti-social traits probably would become a social menace or wards of the state." (p. 33)

It is important to note again that this social service report was presented only in part to the Governor in the final report to the Board of Administrators in 1943. What was left out of the final report is interesting, and likely this is first time anyone has presented the data publicly.

Sterilization was particularly prevalent in the early and mid 1930s at the institution. In an effort to support the law, and promote sterilization, the staff examined the records and family background of 71 individuals who had been sterilized. On pages 38-39 of the 1934 draft report, Safley presents *Table 1 – Showing Mental Background of Family*. Apparently this table was presented to show the overall influence of familial inheritance of mental retardation. The table is reproduced here in full.

TABLE 1
SHOWING MENTAL BACKGROUND OF FAMILY

			SIBLINGS			
CASE NO	FATHER	MOTHER	Apparently Normal	Borderline	FM	No Data
1	No data	FM	4	(unstable	and sex	problems)
2	FM	Normal				3
3	No data	No data		5		
4	Borderline	FM & E	2		2	
5	No data	Borderline		3	1	
6	Borderline	FM	2		2	
7	Normal	Normal	4	1		
8	Borderline	FM			2	5
9	Normal	Normal	5			
10	FM	FM		4	2	
11	Borderline	Borderline	1	6	2	
12	Normal	Borderline	3		2	
13	FM	Normal	1	1		
14	No data	FM			1	2
15	No data	FM			1	2
16	Psychotic	FM	1		3	
17	No data	FM				1
18	FM	Borderline	1		5	
19	Normal	FM	7		1	
20	Borderline	Borderline		1	3	
21	Borderline	Borderline		1	3	
22	Borderline	Borderline		1	3	
23	Borderline	FM	2		1	5
24	Borderline	FM			8	2
25	Borderline	FM			8	2
26	Normal	Borderline	4	1		
27	Normal	FM			1	2
28	Borderline	Normal				4
29	No data	No data		(2 insane)		6
30	Borderline	FM			1	
31	FM	FM			1	1
32	No data	FM & E		7	5	

33	FM	FM	2	1	5	1
34	Borderline	FM		2	2	
35	No data	No data	0	0	0	0
36	No data	FM			3	
37	Borderline	FM	2	3	1	
38	No data	FM		2	1	4
39	Borderline	Borderline				4
40	No data	No data			1	6
41	No data	FM	0	0	0	0
42	No data	No data	6	5		
43	No data	No data	4			2
44	Normal	Normal	9			1
45	No data	No data	4			2
46	FM	Insane			2	
47	FM	No data	0	0	0	0
48	Normal	Normal	9			1
49	Normal	Insane			2	1
50	Borderline	FM		3		
51	Normal	No data	1	2	1	(1 insane)
52	No data	No data	3	1		3
53	Borderline	Insane (?)			1	
54	Borderline	Borderline		3	1	
55	No data	FM	1		3	4
56	No data	No data	2		2	
57	Borderline	Borderline		3	1	
58	Normal	Normal	10			
59	Borderline	Borderline	8			
60	Normal	Borderline	8			
61	Borderline	Normal	3	1		
62	Dull Normal	FM	1	1	2	
63	FM	FM	(1 insane)	2	3	2
64	No data	No data			1	
65	FM	FM	2	1	2	
66	No data	FM				
67	No data	No data	4			
68	No data	No data			1	
69	FM	Normal	4	2	2	
70	Normal	Normal	4			
71	No data	No data				
		TOTALS	124	59	95	70 (4 insane)

The results from this table are interesting. First, let's see what Safely has to say. *"The data in Table I shows the mental status, as near as can be determined, of the parent and siblings of each case involving sterilization. In stances where no information is given, the individuals are deceased, have moved from the state or were away from home at the time the visit was made. In such instances it has been impossible to secure reliable information from other sources. This table illustrates nicely the following points: that feeble-minded tend to marry on their own level, and that the mental status of their off-spring is dependent on the type of union made."* Further in the report she says, *"the tendency of the moron to procreate legitimately and illegitimately is very evident."*

It is apparent that Safely is promoting institutionalization and sterilization based on the data from Table I. However, a closer look at the data is revealing. First, 28% of the 71 cases have parents with no known predilection to or diagnosis for feeble-mindedness. Only five cases are presented where both parents have definitive diagnoses of feeble-mindedness. From these parents, fully 56% have no diagnosis of a disability.

Next, the table shows that there are no adequate data on over 20% of the siblings. Although four of the siblings may have been classified as insane, the remaining 66 are presumed to be fine.

Also, the diagnosis of "borderline" at that time was ill defined. Rather than a particular score on a test, the label was given to those individuals whose test scores were fine, but "showed a predilection toward feeble-mindedness". In other words, it was a rather loose clinical judgment.

If we assume all of the borderline siblings, and those with no data on their abilities, are not feeble-minded, and then further add those who are diagnosed as normal, we find that fully 73% of the siblings of these individuals are not feeble-minded. Clearly, Safely's presumption of the heredity of feeble-mindedness is weakened. Her contention that 50% of the 738 residents had hereditary causes of mental retardation is supported only by the intake (Patient Record) ledger data, not test results. Her statement that most siblings could "be classified as mentally defective" is no supported. However, the research of the 1920s and early 1930s continued to promulgate the notion that heredity was the primary contributor to mental deficiency. Also, the institution was continuing to ask the state legislature for additional funding for buildings and operations. There was a need to continue the line of thought that institutions were important in protecting individuals with disabilities, and perhaps more importantly, protecting society from these people.

The Science of Classification at the Institution

In their earliest reports the superintendents gave the resident census and the classification of the residents. In 1904, in his first report, Dr. Baldwin showed that 75 people had been admitted to the institution between May 2 and November 1, 1904. These individuals were classified by gender and by level, using the terminology of the day, moron, imbecile, and idiot. The table below is reproduced from the First Biennial Report, page 9.

The Classification of those admitted is as follows:	High Grade	Middle Grade	Low Grade	Moral Imbeciles	Idio Imbeciles	Idiots
Males	1	13	17	1	6	9
Females	0	8	10	1	3	6
Total	1	21	27	2	9	15

Taken from the First Biennial Report of the North Dakota Institution for Feeble Minded at Grafton, 1904.

The classification labels referred to the system typically used at the turn of the century. Namely, high-, middle-, and low-grade were levels in the category of moron, which referred to individuals with mental abilities from seven to 12 years of age. The imbecile label was given to those with mental age abilities from three to seven years, and the idiot label for those with mental age abilities from less than one year up to three years.

Initially, these labels were rather unscientifically assigned. Often, the admitting personnel would interview the parents or referring agent (often a physician), and ask about the individual's education level or mental ability. Based on that information, a classification might be assigned in the Patient Record ledger. Later, the institution's social workers (and later psychologists) would administer tests to determine a mental age and assign classification.

Not all classifications had to do with mental age. Frequently people were admitted to the institution with simply a diagnosis of epilepsy, often with no indication of mental retardation. Thus, one will often see classifications by gender, mental ability, and by presence of epilepsy. For example, the Fourth Biennial Report (1910) presents a record of resident movement and shows that "29 epileptics" were admitted from July 1908 through June 1910.

By 1912, the institution staff was using the Binet-Simon tests to classify the residents by mental age. Initially developed in 1905 in France by Alfred Binet and his student, Theodore Simon, the 30 item test was designed distinguish between subnormal and average ability children on characteristics such as visual coordination, following simple instructions, weight discrimination, and differentiation between abstract terms. Early versions of the test just differentiated between the normal and subnormal children, while the 1908 and 1911 versions divided children's abilities by mental age, between ages one and twelve (Scheerenberger, 1983).

The following is an example of a table produced for the Fifth Biennial Report on the institution (1912):

FEEBLE-MINDED

Mental Age

Physical age	1	2	3	4	5	6	7	8	9	10	11	12
Birth to 5 years – Boys	1	1		1								
Birth to 5 years – Girls		2										
5 to 10 years – Boys	3	3										
5 to 10 years – Girls	2	1										
10 – 15 years – Boys	7	1		1			3	1				
10 – 15 years – Girls	1	3			2	1	1					
15 – 20 years – Boys		5	1									
15 – 20 years – Girls	3				1		3		1			
20 – 25 years – Boys	2			1	1	2	3		1			
20 – 25 years – Girls			1	1		1		1		1		
25 – 35 years – Boys	1			1		1	2	1				
25 – 35 years – Girls	8	1	1	1	1	1	2		1	1		
35 – 45 years – Boys					2		1					

35 – 45 years – Girls	3	1		1	1	1	2	1		1		
45 years up – Boys	2	1		1		1	1					1
45 years up – Girls	2	1		1		1	1	1	1	2		1
Total	35	20	3	9	9	9	21	5	4	5	0	2

Taken from the 5ᵗʰ Biennial Report of the Institution for the Feeble Minded at Grafton, 1912.

Later, the reports would become more sophisticated. For example in 1944, the superintendent's report included 12 tables related to residents' movement, abilities, mental status, age of admission, citizenship, marital condition, environmental condition, discharges and deaths related to mental and chronological age, and county of residence at time of placement.

These methods of classification and reporting continued until 1962, when Paul Witucki, director of the Psychology Department of Grafton State School reported on the use of a more recent classification system by intelligence quotient (IQ). He stated, *"The former classifications of idiot, imbecile, and morons have become obsolete due to their adverse connotations and we are presently using the terminology of mildly retarded, moderately retarded, severely retarded, and profoundly retarded. This new classification system was advocated by the American Psychiatric Association and the American Association of Mental Deficiency."* (Thirtieth Biennial Report of the Grafton State School, 1962). He presented the following table to Superintendent Rand:

A. Retardates tested: July 1, 1960 to June 30, 1962

Admissions Total	Borderline IQ 70 – 84 Code 1	Mild IQ 55 – 69 Code 2	Moderate IQ 40 – 54 Code 3	Severe IQ 25 – 39 Code 4	Profound IQ below 25 or untestable Code 5 & 9
New 195	2	30	70	43	50
Old 277	1	30	88	87	71
Total 472	3	60	158	130	121

Taken from the Thirtieth Biennial Report of the Grafton State School, 1962.

These terms continued to be used until the 1980s when the term developmentally disabled became commonplace. Later the language changed to be "people first" and the terminology generally used was "persons with developmental disabilities".

Case Studies

The development of and analysis of case studies within the institution was an important method of science and research for institutional staff. As early as 1910 the superintendents used case examples in their biennial reports to either educate or coerce the Board of Trustees, the Governor, and the ND Legislature into action. Dr. LaMoure, in writing about the necessity of institutions to relieve the states' families from the stress and burden of feeble-minded children wrote: "In many of these homes everything that tends to uprightness and morality is lacking. To illustrate this I cite the case of a little girl who was admitted to this institution about three years ago. She was a child of a brother and sister. The boy was seventeen years and the girl fifteen. I leave it to your imagination to picture the social conditions existing in the home where this occurred. It *(sic)* think it is an established fact that at least 80 per cent of the cases of feeble minded are born in families in which the history shows a hereditary taint which has expressed itself in cases of feeblemindedness, epilepsy, insanity, criminality or other nervous diseases" (Fourth Biennial Report of the Institution for the Feeble Minded at Grafton, 1910).

In 1914, Dr. Wylie, Superintendent of the institution, presented a two-page "family tree" showing the genetic relationship of families and feeble mindedness. This genetic paradigm of three diagrams showed the progeny of a couple with suspected feeble mindedness, and showed how their children were likely to be immoral, insane, or feeble minded.

In 1922 Dr. Wylie introduced two case studies of individuals in the institution attempting to show the benefit of institutionalization. His two cases, *The Improvement of Metro*, and *The Story of Ottne*, describe how two young children made impressive gains at Grafton. He describe Metro as a little boy with "blue eyes, light hair and rather pitiful face" who quickly learned some basic academic skills, became proficient with weaving, basketry and woodwork, and learned to play the cornet in the school band. Overall, he advanced 3 years 1 month on the Simon-Bent test.

Ottne was a girl who "grew up without any training whatever. Mentally defective, she was allowed to run wild." Apparently she was forced to live in the family barn prior to institutionalization, and was finally arrested and sent to Grafton. There she learned to iron in the laundry, learned the value of coins and money, and learned to sew. Wylie finishes the story by saying, "From a useless low grade girl in the home, a nuisance in the neighborhood, a menace to society, Ottne has become a good member of our Institution family; a happy woman, able to take personal care of herself under supervision and to be of real help to others."

Perhaps the most compelling story is Wylie's 1928 *The Story of Barbara and Her Family*. In 1927 the ND Legislature passed HB 135 allowing for the sterilization of the feeble minded. Wylie's story attempted to confirm to the legislators that their decision to pass the law and then to further support the institution with funding appropriations was a correct decision. Barbara is described as a 16 year old "tall, slender rather delicate looking" young woman who was admitted to the institution. During her four years in the institution, she apparently made gains in her speech, and academic skills, learned to sew, cook, and do laundry. However, her parents removed her from the institution, had her quickly married to a farm hand, and then had her move out of the house. Wylie describes how the young Barbara then divorced her first husband, married another man, and then had four children. The school then reported how Barbara's children were dirty, under weight, and did poorly in school. The suspicion is that Barbara's children will all be classified as feeble minded, and will likely end up in the institution. Wylie concludes with "*From all appearances there is little hope that any of Barbara's children will develop normally. The city will eventually have to support the family. The moral to the story is plain*" (Thirteenth Biennial Report of the Institution for Feeble Minded, 1928).

Other Research at the Institution

Mental hygiene. In the early 1920s Dr. Wylie was a member of a national research group that examined the mental health of North Dakota's poor, feeble minded and other indigent citizens. This study was conducted by the National Committee for Mental Hygiene, Inc. and was presented in the 1923 text, *Report of the North Dakota Mental Hygiene Survey with Recommendations.* The committee members traveled to family homes throughout the state and interviewed parents, siblings, and other relatives who had individuals with mental deficiency or mental illness. The committee's report was disconcerting. The findings suggested that, for a rural state, North Dakota had a significant number of citizens with mental health issues. Of course, much of the report was focused on those with mental retardation, and many of the recommendations suggested that the state implement strategies to limit the spread of mental deficiency. These strategies included institutionalization, limitations of who might be permitted to marry, and selective sterilization of individuals with undesirable habits and character traits. One rather innovative recommendation was that the state develop a department of mental hygiene, and fully staff and fund the efforts to improve the mental health of its residents. This recommendation was never implemented.

Pharmacological treatments. In the 1940s and 50s, U.S. scientists were developing and testing a variety of drugs designed to change the behavior of unruly or unresponsive residents of institutions. Without the oversight now provided by governmental agencies like today's Federal Drug Administration (FDA), scientists and institutional medical staff designed and implemented their own studies to test the drugs' effectiveness. The institution at Grafton participated in some of these drug tests.

In 1958, Charles Thomson, the staff pharmacist, reported on such tests at the institution. *"We are indebted to some of our Pharmaceutical Manufacturers, such as Smith, Kline & French Co., E.R. Scuibb & Sons, Wyeths, Ciba, Schering Co. and others for their liberal supply of tranquilzer preparations for free trial on our patients"* (Twenty-Eighth Biennial Report, 1958, p. 2494). Thomson's report further shows that drugs such as Thorazine, Compazine, Vesprin, Sparine, Equanil, Rserpine, Sandril and Moderil were used on the residents. These powerful drugs were used to moderate problem behaviors and calm unruly residents. Thomson's finishes his report for a plea for a budget increase in medications for the next biennium.

Preventive medicine. In the mid 1950s the institution's medical staff battled several contagious outbreaks amongst the residents. Diseases such as influenza, measles and mumps, while treatable, took considerable time from the staff and many beds in the hospital. This was also a time where staff were concerned with the disease polio.

During the 1956-58 biennium Dr. Margaret Chandler from the U.S. Public Health Service office in Georgia spent several months at Grafton studying the effects of polio vaccine on the children in the institution. Some children had been inoculated with polio vaccine whereas others had not yet received the treatment. Chandler's studies examined the effects of the vaccine on the blood chemistry of the children.

While Chandler was conducting her studies at Grafton, an Asiatic flu epidemic began to spread across the county. With her connections in the public health channels, Chandler was able to obtain enough vaccine to inoculate over 1,000 residents, thus preventing a likely devastating outbreak in the institution.

Education and treatment programs. The superintendent's reports over the years hint at numerous research and training partnerships with both the University of North Dakota and North Dakota State University. Apparently numerous university students in the medical, allied health, psychology, social work and education programs visited Grafton. In some cases these students conducted training, treatments, or behavioral interventions with the residents as part of their practical internships at the institution. While the reports provide little detail about rigorous scientific studies, staff have reported over the years that several student projects, theses or dissertations were conducted with residents.

Summary

Research studies often require large groups of rather homogeneous subjects for conducting scientific study. In some instances, the resident population of institutions is a convenient group for study. In other cases, the nature of medical, education, or social treatments affords opportunities for the examination of interesting cases. Like many institutions across the country over the last 100 years, Grafton was the site of several research studies. Some of these included rather serendipitous benefits, like the access to the Asiatic influenza vaccine. Others were of probably dubious benefit, such as the rather loose study of free tranquilizer medications from major pharmaceutical companies.

Certainly many of these historical and rather crude studies of persons with mental retardation would not meet today's standards for research rigor, nor for human subject protections. But one must remember that while these actions could not be condoned in our current practice, these professionals rarely harbored ill will toward their subjects. In fact, one might argue that these studies were often done in search of better, more effective means of treating and supporting persons with mental retardation. Thus, the actions taken to better understand and serve the institution's residents were done with good intentions, often using the best available methods of the time. Hopefully we can learn from our predecessors and gain both valuable scientific and sociological information to best support persons with disabilities in the future.

Appendix A

Site Plan of the North Dakota Developmental Center

The following site plan was developed in the 1990s as part of the mission examination and reorganization process at the Developmental Center. The original document is courtesy of the North Dakota Developmental Center Centennial Committee.

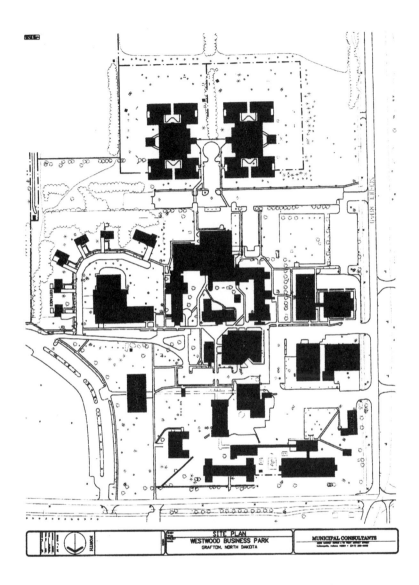

SITE PLAN
WESTWOOD BUSINESS PARK
GRAFTON, NORTH DAKOTA

MUNICIPAL CONSULTANTS

Appendix B

Photographs of the
North Dakota Developmental Center

The following photographs were selected to illustrate various portions of the North Dakota Developmental Center. Unless otherwise specified, these are courtesy of the State Historical Society, ND State Archives. Special thanks to Allen Olson, Shannon Dove, and Susan Anderson for formatting these digital files for inclusion in this book.

J.L. Cashel, Walsh County State Senator
Photo Courtesy of the State Historical Society of North Dakota, item name "Cashel"

Institution for Feeble Minded, about 1912
Photo courtesy of the ND Developmental Center Centennial Committee

First hospital at institution, built in 1911
Photo Courtesy of the State Historical Society of North Dakota, #C1134

Midway (old hospital), January 2003
Photo by Brent A. Askvig

Farm plots at Institution for Feeble Minded
Photo Courtesy of the State Historical Society of North Dakota, #C1132

Dining room at Institution for Feeble Minded
Photo Courtesy of the State Historical Society of North Dakota, #C1144

Merry-go-round, purchased in 1958
Photo Courtesy of the State Historical Society of North Dakota, #30804-001-005

Early institutional fieldwork
Photo Courtesy of the State Historical Society of North Dakota, #30804-024

Sloyd work, basket weaving, about 1908
Photo Courtesy of the State Historical Society of North Dakota, #30804-027

Boys network class, about 1908
Photo Courtesy of the State Historical Society of North Dakota, #C1129

Sitting room in Main building, about 1908
Photo Courtesy of the State Historical Society of North Dakota, #C1142

Kindergarten class, about 1908
Photo Courtesy of the State Historical Society of North Dakota, #C1139

Nursery school class, about 1960
Photo Courtesy of the State Historical Society of North Dakota, #30804-002-01

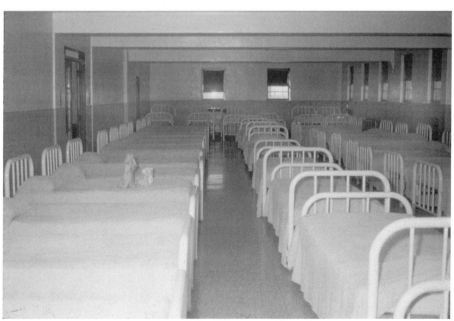

Women's residential ward, early 1960s
Photo Courtesy of the State Historical Society of North Dakota, #30804-004-02

Main building, winter 1962
Photo Courtesy of the State Historical Society of North Dakota, #30804-011

Men's canteen, Main building, early 1960s
Photo Courtesy of the State Historical Society of North Dakota, #30804-006-02

Appendix C

List of State Laws and Resolutions Concerning the North Dakota Developmental Center: 1897 – 2003

The following appendix lists nearly all of the laws and resolutions passed by the North Dakota legislature from 1897 through 2003 concerning the institution at Grafton. In most cases the descriptions here are verbatim excerpts from the Laws of North Dakota texts. Readers are urged to read the entire laws for the full text of the laws for a full understanding of the intricacies of the legislation. Many thanks to Ana Novosel, Terri Senger, and Gina Fradette for assistance in compiling this appendix.

1897
S.B. No. 157, Act
An act providing that the means derived from the fund known as the school for the feeble-minded at Grafton shall be credit to such funds. All interest and means derived from the congressional appropriations for a federal penitentiary was to be credited in the state treasurer's office in the fund for the feeble-minded school

1901
S.B. No. 186, Act
An act creating a board of trustees for an institution for the feeble-minded located at or near the city of Grafton, Walsh County, ND. This act created a board of trustees that would oversee the funds previously designated for the federal penitentiary in Grafton. The board of trustees was charged with obtaining plans, and then constructing a building for the institution for feeble-minded.

1901
Concurrent Resolution
A Senate and House concurrent resolution was passed to amend the North Dakota constitution, specifically subdivision 8 of section 215 to read as "…and there shall be located at or near the city of Grafton, in the county of Walsh, an institution for the feeble minded, on the ground purchased by the secretary of the interior for a penitentiary building".

1903
S.B. No. 30, Appropriation
An act to provide an Appropriation for the finishing and the furnishing of the building for the current and contingent expenses of the Institution for the Feeble Minded at Grafton. Appropriated $59,765 to cover expenses related to the finishing and furnishing of the institution at Grafton. Also, included was an emergency plan that stated that if work should be commenced on finishing the building long before July 1, 1903; then an act providing additional funds was available.

1903
H.B. No.103, Act
An act to make it mandatory that every school district is to make an enumeration each year of all unmarried persons of school age, being over six and under twenty years of age, having their legal residence in the district as of June 1st. The names, ages and post office addresses of parents and/or guardians having the care of custody of each deaf and dumb, blind and feeble-minded person between the ages of five and twenty-five years of age, residing in the district; including all individuals deemed too deaf or feeble-minded to acquire an education in the common school.

1903
H.B. No.143, Appropriation
An act stating that if anyone was to bring any child into the state of North Dakota, for the sole purpose of being placed in a family home, by adoption or otherwise, should first file

a $2000 bond in favor of the state. The child is to have no contagious or incurable disease, has no deformity, or is not feeble minded, or of vicious character; the state of North Dakota will seize and remove the child if they are brought up on a public charge within five years of being brought to the state.

1907
S.B. No. 108, Act
An act appropriating money from the state treasury, for paying the 'current and contingent' expenses for improvements to the state institution for the feeble-minded at Grafton. The total sum appropriated was $86,600.

1907
S.B. No. 109, Amendment
Section 1165; all feeble-minded residents, and residents who are idiotic and epileptic of the state who are of suitable age and capacity to receive instruction in the institution, and whose defects prevent proper education in the public schools, may be admitted to and receive benefits of the institution.
Section 1167; the person legally responsible for the support of any person admitted to the institution shall pay semi-annually to the superintendent $50 for care of the individual in the institution.
Section 1168; the paid money goes to credit for the resident in the institution, to be expended on clothing. The excess will be placed in a maintenance fund for the institution. In case of death or removal of the individual from the institution, the money will be reimbursed for the year, pro rata.

1909
S.B. No.56, Appropriation
An act appropriating money from the state treasury, for paying the 'current and contingent' expenses for improvements to the state institution for the feeble-minded at Grafton. The total sum appropriated was $78,850. A Partial Veto was executed by the Governor.

1909
S.B. No.264, Amendment
Section 1165; Who may receive benefits of school. All feeble-minded residents, as well as those who are idiotic and epileptic, of the state of North Dakota, who in the opinion of the superintendent, are of suitable age and capacity to receive instruction in the institution for the feeble-minded at Grafton, and whose defects prevent them from receiving an education in the public schools; may be admitted to the institution, subject to payment to the sums provided and to such rules and regulations as may be made by its board of trustees. No inmate of such institution shall not be removed, except upon a written request of the parent, parents, guardian or custodian of such inmate.

1911
H.B. No.297, Amendment
Section 1168; Payments, how applied. The superintendent quarterly, during the months of January, April, July and October shall cover the state treasury all sums paid the same to be credited to the maintenance fund of the institution.

1913
H.B. No.252, Amendment
An amendment to Section 8 of chapter 62 of the session laws of 1911. The Board of Control is to have full power to manage, control and govern, subject only to the limitations stated in the act, the State Hospital for the Insane, the State Penitentiary, North Dakota Blind Asylum, the School for the Deaf and Dumb, the School for the Feeble-minded, the State Reform School, the North Dakota State Tuberculosis Sanitarium, and other charitable institutions. The State Board of Control is to have access to all state institutions previously mentioned, and to all books, accounts, vouchers, supplies and equipments.

1913
H.B. No.342, Act
An act to prevent procreation of confirmed criminals, insane, idiots, defectives, and rapists. Whenever the warden, superintendent or head of any state prison, reform school, state school for the Feeble-minded, or any state hospital or state asylum for the insane should verify in writing that they believe that the mental or physical condition of any inmate would be improved there-by or that procreation by the inmate would likely result in a defective or feeble-minded child with criminal tendencies; or if the condition of such inmate is not likely to improve, as to make procreation by such person desirable or beneficial to the community, it shall be lawful to perform sterilization.

1913
H.B. No.104, Act
An act to provide for the maintenance of inmates of the Institution for the Feeble-minded, and to Amend Section 1 of Chapter 165 of the Laws of 1911. The person legally responsible for the support of any person admitted to such institution shall pay $15 per month during all the time such person is an inmate of said institution to support the inmate.

1913
S.B. No.94, Act
An act to amend Section 1 of Chapter 213 of the Laws of 1909, Relating to the Inmates of the Institution for the Feeble-minded. All Feeble-minded residents of the state, who in the opinion of the superintendent, are of suitable age and capacity to receive instruction in the Institution for the Feeble-minded and whose defects prevent them from receiving proper training in the public schools.

1913
S.B. No.373, Act
An act to amend and to re-enact Section 1904 of the Revised Codes of North Dakota for 1905. Proceedings for release of persons alleged not to be insane. On a statement in writing verified by affidavit addressed to the county judge of the county in which the hospital is situated, or in which any person confined in the hospital has residence, alleging that such person is not insane.

1913
S.B. No.94, Act
An act to amend Section 1 of Chapter 213 of the Laws of 1909, Relating to the Inmates of the Institution for the Feeble-minded; Who may receive benefits of school. All feeble-minded persons residing in the state, who, in the opinion of the superintendent are of suitable age and capacity to receive instruction in the institution for the feeble-minded, and whose defects prevent them from receiving proper training in the public schools of the state, and all idiotic and epileptic residents of the state may be admitted to and receive benefits of the institution, subject to payment; provided that any inmate of such institution shall not be removed there from except upon a written request of the parent, guardian or custodian of such inmate, said request must receive the approval of the superintendent before such inmate can be removed.

1915
H.B. No.263, Act
An Act regulating the care of the feeble-minded, providing that the cost of keeping patients in the institution for the feeble-minded shall be a charge against the county sending such patient; that persons liable to support such defective person shall, when able pay the expense of treatment; and amending Section 1717 of the compiled laws of 11913 and repealing section 1718 of the compiled laws of 1913.

1915
S.B. No.141, Appropriation
An act making an appropriation for maintenance, new buildings, improvements and repairs, and equipment for the Institution for the Feeble-minded at Grafton. Appropriated was $54,700.

1917
H.B. No.244, Act
An act to amend and re-enact Section 1714 of the Compiled Laws of North Dakota for the year 1913, relating to the Commitment of Feeble-minded Persons to the Institution for the Feeble-Minded. All feeble-minded persons residing in the state, who, in the opinion of the superintendent are of suitable age and capacity to receive instruction in the institution for the feeble-minded, and whose defects prevent them from receiving proper training in the public schools of the state, and all idiotic and epileptic residents of the state may be admitted to and receive benefits of the institution, subject to payment; provided that any inmate of such institution shall not be removed there from except upon

a written request of the parent, guardian or custodian of such inmate, said request must receive the approval of the superintendent before such inmate can be removed.

1917
S.B. No.202, Act
An act to amend and re-enact Section 1717 of the Compiled Laws of North Dakota for the year 1913, as amended by Section 4 of Chapter 113 of the Session Laws of 1915, relating to the Support of Feeble-minded persons in the Institution for the Feeble-minded. Person legally responsible for the feeble-minded person is to pay $15 monthly to the County Treasurer, if the person liable to make payments fails or neglects to do so the Board of County Commissioners must direct the state attorney to bring an action in the name of the state against such person.

1921
S.B. No.6, Act
An act to amend and re-enact Section 1714 of the Compiled Laws of the State of North Dakota for the year 1913, as amended by Chapter 143 of the Session Laws of 1914. All feeble-minded residents of the state, who in the opinion of the superintendent are of suitable are and capacity to receive instruction in the institution for the feeble-minded, and whose defects prevent them from receiving proper training in the public schools of the state and all idiotic and epileptic residents of the state shall receive the benefits of the institution subject to the payment of the sum provided. Any inmate of such institution shall not be removed from the institution, except on written request of the parent, guardian or custodian, approval must be granted by the Board of Administration and Superintendent.

1923
S.B. No.97, Appropriation
An act making an appropriation to provide the payment of an existing deficit in the maintenance fund of the institution for the feeble-minded. Appropriated was $14,486.73 for the purpose of paying an existing deficit in the general maintenance fund.

1923
H.B. No.88, Appropriation
An act making an appropriation for maintenance, improvements, and repairs, and equipment for the Institution for the Feeble-minded at Grafton. Appropriated was $188,400.

1923
S.B. No.272, Act
An act relating to the method of levying tax for the care of patients at the Hospital for the Insane, Institution for the Feeble-minded, and the State Tuberculosis Sanatorium; providing the method of settlement between county and state; providing a penalty for failure to pay; providing a method of settling disputed claims and repealing Sections 2572 and 2573, Compiled Laws of 1913 and all acts or parts in conflict therewith.

1923
S.B. No.172, Act
An act granting to and imposing upon the Board of Administration certain powers and duties with reference to the Welfare of Children, and the administration of laws relating thereto.

1925
H.B. No.36, Appropriation
An act making an appropriation for maintenance, improvements and repairs, new building equipment and miscellaneous items for the Institution for the Feeble-minded at Grafton. Appropriated was a total of $267,700.

1927
S.B. No.136, Act
An act to prevent the procreation of Feeble-minded, Insane, Epileptic, Habitual criminals, Moral Degenerates and Sexual Perverts, who may be inmates of state institutions, authorizing and providing for the Sterilization of such persons and providing appeals to the District Court in certain cases; and repealing Sections 11429 to 11438 inclusive to the Compiled Laws of North Dakota for 1913.

1929
S.B. No.34, Appropriation
An act making an appropriation for the care of feeble-minded whose residence cannot be determined and whose care must be borne by the state. Appropriated was a total of $8,000.

1929
S.B. No.36, Appropriation
An act making an appropriation for the general maintenance, improvements and repairs, new buildings, equipment and miscellaneous items for the Institution for the Feeble-minded at Grafton, North Dakota. Appropriated was a total of $199,400.

1931
S.B. No.40, Act
An act defining a feeble-minded person and providing for his removal from this state. Definition of 'feeble-minded person' in this act means, any person, minor or adult, other than an insane person, who is so mentally defective as to be incapable of managing himself and his affairs, and to require supervision, control and care for his own, or the public's welfare.

1931
S.B. No.181, Act
An act to authorize the juvenile court to commit to the Institution for the Feeble-minded any feeble-minded, dependent, neglected or delinquent child.

1931
S.B. No.14, Appropriation
An act making an appropriation for the care of feeble-minded whose residence cannot be determined and whose care must be borne by the state. An appropriation for a total of $2,000.

1933
S.B. No.41, Appropriation
An act making an appropriation for the care of feeble-minded whose residence cannot be determined and whose care must be borne by the state. An appropriation for a total of $1,500.

1933
S.B. No.80, Appropriation
An act making an appropriation for the general maintenance, improvements and repairs, equipment and miscellaneous items for the Institution for the Feeble-minded at Grafton, North Dakota. Appropriated was a total of $128,044.

1933
S.B. No.121, Act
An act to amend and re-enact Section 1709 of the Compiled Laws of the year 1913, changing the name of the Institution for the Feeble-minded. The Institution for the Feeble-minded is to known and designated as "Grafton State School".

1933
S.B. No.287, Act
An act regulating the practice of courts in the prosecution of insane or mentally deficient persons or persons whose mental capacity is in issue; providing for examinations and hearings to determine their mental conditions; providing for commitment of such persons to the State Hospital for the Insane during such disability, and for the resumption of prosecution after the restoration of mental capacity; providing for the appointment and examination of experts by the court and fixing their fees and repealing Sections 11064 to 11071 inclusive of the Compiled Laws of 1913.

1935
H.B. No.15, Appropriation
An act making an appropriation for the care of feeble-minded whose residence cannot be determined and whose care must be borne by the state. An appropriation for a total of $1,080.

1937
H.B. No.107, Act
An act to amend and re-enact Section 2572a of the 1925 Supplement to the Compiled Laws of North Dakota for 1913, providing for the settlement of the expenses of patients in the Hospital for the Insane, the Institution for the Feeble-minded and State Tuberculosis Sanatorium, between the various Counties, the State and such Institutions,

providing for disputed claims, repealing all Acts in conflict therewith, and declaring an emergency.

1939
H.B. No.27, Appropriation
An act making an appropriation for the care of feeble-minded whose residence cannot be determined and whose care must be borne by the state. An appropriation for a total of $1,080.

1939
S.B. No.4, Appropriation
An act making an appropriation for general maintenance, improvements and repairs, equipment and miscellaneous items for the Grafton State School at Grafton, North Dakota. An appropriation of a total of $335,000.

1939
H.B. No.153, Act
An act amending and re-enacting Chapter 123 if the Session Laws of 1931, authorizing the juvenile court of commit to the Institution for the Feeble-minded any dependent, neglected or delinquent child who is feeble-minded or whose mental condition is found a subject of inquiry.

1941
S.B. No.155, Act
An act authorizing the Bank of North Dakota to transfer funds for necessary operation and maintenance expenses of the Grafton State School, the State Hospital for the Insane and the State Tuberculosis Sanatorium, subject to the supervision of the Industrial Commission; and declaring an emergency.

1941
S.B.No.19, Appropriation
An act making an appropriation for the care of feeble-minded whose residence cannot be determined and whose care must be borne by the State. An appropriation total of $1,080.

1943
S.B. No.25, Appropriation
An act making an appropriation for the payment of salaries for employees of the Grafton State School, and declaring an emergency. Appropriated was $26,500.

1943
S.B. No.23, Appropriation
An act making an appropriation for the general maintenance, improvements and repairs, new building, equipment and miscellaneous items for the Grafton State School. Appropriated was $725,630.

1944-1945
H.B. No.42, Appropriation
An act making an appropriation for the payment of the City of Grafton for water consumed by the Grafton State School, and declaring an emergency. Appropriated was $3,198.36.

1944-1945
H.B. No.16, Appropriation
An act making an appropriation for the general maintenance, improvements and repairs, new buildings and miscellaneous items for the Grafton State School at Grafton, North Dakota. Appropriated was $1,177,725.50.

1944-1945
H.B. No.33, Appropriation
An act to make an appropriation for the payment to the City of Grafton for water consumed by the Grafton State School, and declaring an emergency. Appropriated was $3,000.

1944-1945
S.B. No.9, Appropriation
An act making an appropriation for the care of feeble-minded whose residence cannot be determined and whose care must be borne by the state. An appropriation for a total of $1,080.

1944-1945
S.B. No.67, Act
An act to amend and re-enact Section 25-0825 of the North Dakota Revised Code of 1943, relating to recovery of expenses for institutional care from patients, and from Veterans, and declaring an emergency.

1947
S.B. No.274, Amendment
To amend and re-enact Section 25-0409 of the North Dakota Revised Code of 1943, relating to the expense of care of inmates at the Grafton State School.

1947
H.B. No.135, Authorization
Authorizing the Board of Administration to enter into reciprocal agreements with other states for the exchange, return, and transportation of insane, feeble-minded, or epileptic persons.

1947
S.B. No.57, Appropriation
Making an appropriation for the general maintenance, improvements and repairs, new buildings, equipment and miscellaneous items for the Grafton State School at Grafton, North Dakota. Appropriated was $1,406,500.

1947
S.B. No.111, Appropriation
Making an appropriation of $201.29 to the Grafton State School for the payment of a deficiency in the State at Large appropriation.

1947
H.B. No. 66, Appropriation
Making an appropriation for the care of feeble-minded whose residence cannot be determined and whose care must be borne by the State. Appropriated was $3,080.

1949
County Expense for care of state hospital patients
S.B. No.9, Amendment
To amend and re-enact section 25-0214 of the North Dakota Revised Code of 1943, relating to the expense for care of patients at the state hospital and declaring an emergency.

1949
Recovery county care institutional patients
H.B. No.127, Amendment
To amend and re-enact section 25-0825 of the 1947 Supplement to the North Dakota Revised Code of 1943, relating to recovery of expenses for institutional care from patients, estates of patients, and from veterans, authorizing County Auditors to collect such expenses for the county and the state, providing that the statute of limitations shall not bar the collection of such expenses.

1949
S.B. No.8, Amendment
Compulsory school attendance of deaf, mute, blind or feeble-minded persons
To amend and re-enact section 15-3402 of North Dakota Revised Code of 1943, relating to compulsory school attendance of deaf, mute, blind, or feeble-minded persons.

1949
H.B. No.65, Appropriation
Grafton State school
Making an appropriation for the general maintenance, improvements and repairs, new buildings, equipment and miscellaneous items for the Grafton State School at Grafton, North Dakota. Total appropriated was $797,000 out of the county care and institutional funds and $1,140,050 out of the state treasury.

1949
S.B. No.62, Appropriation
Feeble-minded- state at large
An act making an appropriation for the care of feeble-minded whose residence cannot be determined and whose care must be borne by the State. Appropriated was $3,080.

1949
H.B. No.86, Appropriation
An act making an appropriation for the general maintenance of the Grafton State School, and declaring an emergency. Appropriated was $85,000.

1951
S.B. No.4, Appropriation
An act making an appropriation for the general maintenance, improvements and repairs, new buildings, equipment and miscellaneous items for the Grafton State School at Grafton, North Dakota. Appropriated were $560,000 out of the County care and Institutional collections funds and $1,060,900 out of the State Treasury.

1951
H.B. No.511, Appropriation
An act making an appropriation for the care of feeble-minded whose residence cannot be determined and whose care must be borne by the state. Appropriated was $2,000.

1953
S.B. No.65, Appropriation
An act making an appropriation for the use of special education of exceptional children. Appropriated was $164,000 out of the state equalization fund in the state treasury.

1953
H.B. No.504, Appropriation
An act making an appropriation for the general maintenance, improvements and repairs, equipment, miscellaneous items and new buildings and special projects for the Grafton State School at Grafton, North Dakota. Appropriated was $2,169,416.

1953
S.B. No.11, Appropriation
An act making appropriations for the care of feeble-minded whose residence cannot be determined and whose care must be borne by the state. Appropriated was $3,360, from the state Treasury.

1953
S.B. No.219, Amendment
To amend and re-enact section 25-0403 of the North Dakota Revised Code of 1943, relating to qualifications of Superintendent of the Grafton State School for the Feeble-minded.

1955
S.B. No.4, Appropriation
An act making an appropriation for the general maintenance, improvements and repairs, equipment, miscellaneous items and new buildings and special projects for the Grafton State School at Grafton, North Dakota, and declaring an emergency. Appropriated was $2,305,100.

1957
H.B. No.617, Act
An act authorizing the Board of Administration to convey certain property now owned by the state and under the control of the Grafton State School.

1957
H.B. No.504, Appropriation
An act making an appropriation for the general maintenance, improvements and repairs, equipment, miscellaneous items and new buildings and special projects for the Grafton State School at Grafton, North Dakota, and declaring an emergency. Appropriated was $3,252,600.

1957
H.B. No.536, Amendment
To amend and re-enact sections 11-1524, 11-1525, 12-4727, 12-4728, 12-4729, 12-4730, 14-0307, 25-0101, chapters 25-02 and 25-03, sections 25-0404, 25-0411 subsection 1 of 25-0808, subsection 2 of section 25-0811 sections 25-08091, 25-0815, 25-0826, 54-2301, 54-2316, 54-2321 and 54-2322 of the North Dakota Revised Code of 1943, as amended, relating to the admission, transportation, care, treatment, and discharge of patients at the state hospital and elsewhere, the powers and duties at the county mental health board, the administration of the state hospital, and the care, treatment and rights of epileptic persons; providing penalties; and repealing Chapter 50-05 and section 54-2310 of the North Dakota Revised Code of 1943, section 25-02051 of the 1953 Supplement thereto, and chapters 184 and 185 of the North Dakota Session Laws of 1955, relating to the treatment of alcoholics and the mentally ill.
25-0201; State Hospital for the Mentally Ill
25-0202; Additional Hospital for the Mentally Ill located at Rugby
25-0203; Object of State Hospital
25-0204; Superintendent to possess certain qualifications, employees
25-0205; Superintendent to furnish forms and bylaws to County Mental Health Boards
25-0206; Nonresidents admitted to State Hospital
25-0207; Disposition of mentally ill non-resident
25-0208; Expense for care of patient
25-0209; Care of patients to be impartial, exceptions
25-0210; Attorney General to bring action against county
25-0211; County Mental Health Board: members, appointment, term, quorum
25-0212; Oath required of appointive members
25-0213; Meetings of County Mental Health Board
25-0214; Duties of Chairman of County Mental Health Board
25-0215; Absence of member of Mental Health Board, substitute
25-0216; Powers of Mental Health Board
25-0217; Compensation and expenses of Mental Health Board
25-0218; Non-liability of certain officers for detention of Mentally Ill persons
25-0301; Authority to receive voluntary patients
25-0302; Voluntary Admittance of Alcoholics and other patients
25-0303; Payments by voluntary patients

25-0304; Inability to pay costs: investigation
25-0305; Discharge of Voluntary Patients
25-0326; Right to release of Voluntary Patients
25-0307; Authority to receive involuntary patients
25-0308; Hospitalization, emergency procedure
25-0309; Notice of hospitalization
25-0310; Right to release, application for Judicial Determination
25-0311; Hospitalization upon order of Mental Health Board, Judicial Procedure
25-0312; Hospitalization by an Agency of the United States
25-0313; Transportation, Temporary detention
25-0314; Transfer of patients
25-0315; Discharge
25-0316; Convalescent Status, re-hospitalization
25-0317; Petition for re-examination of order of hospitalization
25-0318; Right to humane care and treatment, penalties and civil liability for mistreatment
25-0319; Mechanical Restraints
25-0320; Right to communication and visitation, exercise of civil rights
25-0321; Patients entitled to writ of habeas corpus
25-0322; Disclosure of information, penalty
25-0323; Detention pending Judicial determination, detention without proper authority prohibited
25-0324; Escape of patient from hospital
25-0325; Reports to and additional powers of state Board of Administration
25-0326; Expenses of Stutsman County Mental Health Board
25-0327; Filing with County Judge sufficient
25-0328; Unwarranted hospitalization or denial of rights
11-1524; Transportation of prisoner
11-1525; Fees for transporting persons committed to penitentiary or state hospital
12-4727; Transfer of penitentiary inmate to state hospital, report to warden, order by Board of Pardons
12-4728; Copy of order of Board of Pardons delivered to Superintendent of state hospital, Superintendent to receive inmate, filing of receipt
12-4729; Recovery of person transferred, duty of Superintendent, return or release, allowance on discharge
12-4730; Expense of Transferring inmates to and from state hospital
25-08091; Reciprocal exchange of mentally ill or feeble-minded persons
25-0815; Allocation of moneys in the charitable Institutions revolving fund to various institutions, basis for allocation
54-2301; Institutions under control of Board of Administration
54-2316; Power of Board to Investigate Mental Health of patients
54-2321; Collection of information by board, investigation of treatment of mentally ill and feeble-minded
54-2322; Transfer of inmates from one institution to another
14-0307; Marriages prohibited
25-0404; Who may receive benefits of state school

25-0411; Disposition of feeble-minded non-resident
25-0826; County Auditor Authorized to collect expenses

1957

H.B. No.533, Appropriation and Act

An act to appropriate money for the construction of a tuberculosis sanatorium to be located at Grand Forks, and for expenses for the renovation to the facilities of San Haven for the care of the feeble-minded, and directing the state health department and the state health planning council to exert efforts to obtain federal funds for the construction of the tuberculosis sanatorium, to create and en-act subsection 12 of section 25-0101, and to amend and re-enact sections 25-0401, 25-0501, and 25-0512 of the North Dakota Revised Code of 1943 and section 25-0102 of the 1953 Supplement to the North Dakota Revised Code of 1943, relating to state schools for the feeble-minded and the North Dakota state tuberculosis sanatorium.

25-0102; General supervision over state hospital, state school, state sanatorium, blind asylum and school for deaf
25-0401; State School for the Feeble-minded, maintained, name
25-0501; North Dakota State Tuberculosis Sanatorium, maintained, location
25-0512; Electric power may be furnished to city of Dunseith from state school power plant

1959

S.B. No.4, Appropriation

An act making an appropriation for the general maintenance, improvements and repairs, equipment, miscellaneous items and new buildings and special projects for the Grafton State School at Grafton, North Dakota. Appropriation was $3,149,085.91.

1959

L.R.C. Study of Institutional Care and Revolving Funds

A concurrent resolution directing the legislative research committee to study the feasibility of depositing all moneys presently deposited in the institutional revolving fund that are received from the state liquor tax into the general fund and relieving the counties of their responsibility for paying and collecting the expenses of institutional care in the state hospital, Grafton state School and tuberculosis sanatorium and to authorize the state board and administration to collect the cost of institutional care in certain instances from responsible relatives and patients' estates.

1959

H.B. No.723, Act

An act authorizing and directing the legislative research committee to study existing mental health facilities in North Dakota for the purpose of reorganizing and coordinating the same and authorizing necessary expenditures for professional assistance in making the study and to make an appropriation.

1961
H.B. No.504, Appropriation
An act making an appropriation for the general maintenance, improvements and repairs, equipment, miscellaneous items and new buildings and special projects for the Grafton State School at Grafton, North Dakota. Appropriated was $3,796,080.

1961
H.B. No.542, Amendment
An act to amend and reenact sections 23-08-03 and 23-08-06 of the North Dakota Century Code, relating to sterilization of persons in state institutions.
23-08-03; Heads of State Institutions report persons who should be sterilized to Board of Examiners
23-08-06; When sterilization ordered

1961
H.B. No.543, Amendment
An act to amend and reenact section 25-04-06 of the North Dakota Century Code, relating to voluntary admission to the Grafton State school.
25-04-06; Patients admitted to state school temporarily for observation

1961
S.B. No.51, Act
An act providing for a transfer of all funds in the charitable institutions revolving funs and the institutional support funds and providing that all collections from liquor taxes be deposited in the general fund and to relieve the counties of any share of costs of operation and administration of the state hospital, state school, and tuberculosis sanatorium, and further providing for the collection of expenses incurred by the state for care and treatments of patients at such institutions to create and enact chapter 25-09 of the North Dakota Century Code, and to amend and reenact sections 5-03-09,5-03-11, 25-03-15, 25-03-26, 25-04-04, and 25-05-34 of the North Dakota Century code, and to repeal sections 25-01-14, 25-02-07, 25-02-08, 25-02-10, 25-03-03, 25-03-04, 25-04-09, 25-04-10, 25-05-08, 25-05-09, and 25-05-10 and chapter 25-08 of the North Dakota Century Code, relating to institutional care and treatment and expenses thereof and the disposition of liquor taxes.
25-09-01; Operational and Administrative expense of institutional care and treatment
25-09-02; Expenses chargeable against patient or his estate-filing claims-duties of County Judge
25-09-03; Expenses chargeable against guardianship estate of patient-restrictions
25-09-04; Responsible relatives shall pay for care and treatment- definition
25-09-05; Inability to pay all or part of expenses
25-09-06; Application for review of ability to pay
25-09-07; State's Attorneys to bring action for expenses
25-09-08; Disposition of funds collected
25-09-09; Statutes of limitations not bar to recovery
25-09-10; Disposition of non-resident—reciprocal agreements
5-03-09; Disposition of tax moneys

5-03-11; Disposition of tax
25-03-15; Discharge
25-03-26; Expenses of Stutsman County Mental Health Board
25-04-04; Who may receive benefits of State School
25-05-34; Transfer of Tubercular Persons to the Sanatorium

1963
S.B. No.4, Appropriation
An act making an appropriation for the general maintenance, improvements and repairs, equipment, miscellaneous items and new buildings and special projects for the Grafton State School at Grafton, North Dakota. Appropriated was $4,237,480.

1963
H.B. No.886, Act
An act to create a coordinating committee on mental retardation, providing for the membership and officers thereof, and prescribing its powers, duties, and responsibilities.

1963
S.B. No.59, Amendment
An act to amend and reenact subsection 25-01-01, sections 25-01-02, 25-04-01 and 25-04-03 of the North Dakota Century Code, relating to the name of the institution for the feeble-minded at Grafton, North Dakota.
25-01-02; General supervision over state hospital, state school, state sanatorium school for the blind, and school for the deaf
25-04-01; State school-maintained name
25-04-03; Qualifications of Superintendent

1963
S.B. No.116, Act
An act to create and enact section 25-09-06.1 of the North Dakota Century Code Supplement, limiting certain claims for the costs of care at certain state institutions.
25-09-06.1; limitations on certain claims

1963
S.B. No.234, Amendment
An act to amend and reenact sections 25-09-02, 25-09-04, 25-09-05, 25-09-06, 25-09-07, 25-09-09 of the North Dakota Century Code, deleting reference to tuberculosis sanatorium and to provide for payment by the state of all costs of care and treatment for persons suffering from tuberculosis or suspected of having tuberculosis.

1963
H.B. No.580, Act
An act to create and enact section 25-09-11 of the North Dakota Century Code, providing for the reduction of and limitations upon claims for the expense of care and treatment at the Grafton State School.

1963
S.B. No.224, Act
An act to provide for an interstate compact on mental health, assuring care and treatment of mentally ill persons in any member state, permitting the transfer of patients, and providing for after care services for mental patients released from the state hospital in any member state.

1965
LRC Study of Laws pertaining to the Mentally Retarded
A concurrent resolution directing the legislative research committee to study and review laws pertaining to the care and treatment of the mentally retarded and to consider the enactment of a new code of laws embodying modern methods of care and treatment.

1965
Senate Concurrent Resolution "H"
LRC Study of Grafton State School Facilities
A concurrent resolution directing the legislative research committee to study the facilities of the Grafton State School and consider the establishment of a second school in the state of North Dakota for the treatment and care of mentally retarded children and adults.

1965
H.B. No.664, Amendment
An act to amend and reenact section 25-04-05 and section 25-04-08 of the North Dakota Century Code, providing for commitment to and discharge from the state school at Grafton and to create and enact section 25-04-08.1 of the North Dakota Century Code providing for the temporary release of inmates of the state school under the supervision and control of the Superintendent of such school.
25-04-05; Commitment to State School upon order of County Mental Health Board-Judicial Procedure
25-04-08; Discharge of inmate from institution
25-04-08.1; Temporary Release

1965
S.B. No.87, Act
An act to authorize the establishment of mental health and retardation service units, to provide for their administration and for state aid and assistance from mental health division of the state department of health, to authorize a mill levy of not to exceed three-quarters of one mill for such purpose, and providing for an appropriation.

1965
H.B. No.504, Appropriation
An act making an appropriation for the general maintenance, improvements and repairs, equipment, miscellaneous items and new buildings and special projects for the Grafton State School at Grafton, North Dakota. Appropriated was $4,790,750.

1967
H.B. No.534, Act
An act to create and enact sections 25-04-05.1 and 25-04-13 of the ND Century Code, providing for the transfer, visiting, release placement, and guardianship of mentally deficient persons, and to amend and reenact subsection 3 of section 12-02-01, section 14-03-07, subsection 3 of section 14-03-17, section 15-34-02, subsection 4, 5, and 6 of section 15-34-03, section 15-34-07, subdivision b of subsection 1 of section 15-39-01, subdivision I of subsection 2 of section 15-39-01, sections 15-47-13, 15-47-26, subsections 2, 3, and 5of section 25-01-01, sections 25-04-01, 25-04-02, 25-04-04, 25-04-05, 25-04-06, 25-04-07, 25-04-08, 25-04-08.1, 25-04-11, subsection 4 of section 27-16-08, sections 29-20-01, 29-20-02, subsection 4 of section 54-01-19, and subsection 14 of section 54-21-13 of the ND Century Code relating to terminology of laws pertaining to the mentally deficient, admission of mentally deficient persons to a state institution, cost agreements, custody of minors who are mentally deficient, mentally deficient defendants, discharge of mentally deficient persons, nonresident mentally deficient persons, and examination of defendants appearing mentally deficient.
14-03-07; Marriages Prohibited
15-34-02; Compulsory attendance- deaf, mute, blind or mentally deficient persons
15-34-07; Preparation for religious duties- absence from public schools- deaf, blind, mentally deficient may not be paid transportation
15-47-13; School census
15-47-26; Definitions
25-04-02; Purpose of State school
25-04-04; Who may receive benefits of state school
25-04-05; qualifications for admission to state facility- temporary admission, payment agreement
25-04-05.1; Transfer of residents-visiting privileges, release and placement of patients
25-04-06; Juvenile Court Commitment of Defendant, neglected or delinquent mentally deficient, commitment for observation, appeal
25-04-07; Mentally Deficient Defendants
25-04-08; Discharge of resident from institution
25-04-08.1; Notification prior to discharge
25-04-11; Disposition of Mentally Deficient Person who is not a legal resident
25-04-13; Guardianship of person and estate-Superintendent and Board of Admission to act as guardians in lieu of court appointment or assumption by parent
29-20-01; Examination of Defendant's mental condition to determine whether he shall be tried
29-20-02; Commitment to state hospital or Grafton State School-rehearing, trial or commitment

1967
H.B. No.538, Act
An act authorizing the Superintendent of the Grafton State School to recommend a sterilization operation for a resident of such school upon receiving the approval of a board of professional personnel and the written consent of a relative guardian, specifying the manner of obtaining and granting consent, prohibiting the Superintendent from acting

as guardian, providing for compensation of physicians and surgeons and limiting liability, and providing that parents may initiate such procedure.

1967
H.B. No.537, Amendment
To amend and reenact sections 25-09-04, 25-09-05, 25-09-06, 25-09-07,25-09-08, and 25-09-11 of the ND Century Code, relating to charges for the care and treatment of residents of the Grafton State School, methods of determining actual liability and disposition of revenue, and to repeal section 25-09-06.1, relating to limitations on certain claims.
25-09-04; Responsible relatives shall pay for care and treatment-definition
25-09-05; Inability to pay all or part of expense
25-09-06; Application for review of ability to pay
25-09-07; State's Attorneys or Attorney General to bring action for expenses- contract for collections
25-09-08; Disposition of funds collected
25-09-11; Reductions in claims against resident patients of the Grafton State School and their responsible relatives-voluntary payments, termination of billings

1967
S.B. No.74, Amendment
An act to amend and reenact section 25-09-07 of the 1965 Supplement to the ND Century Code, relating to the collection of expenses of care and treatment of patients at the state hospital and state school.

1967
S.B. No.51, Amendment
An act to amend and reenact sections 25-09-09 and 25-09-10 of the ND Century Code, relating to the manner of billing patients of state institutions and their responsible relatives, and the disposition of nonresident patients at the Grafton State School.
25-09-09; Statute of limitations not bar to recovery
25-09-10; Disposition of nonresidents-exceptions, reciprocal agreements

1967
H.B. No.691, Amendment
An act to amend and reenact section 25-12-01 of the ND Century Code, relating to establishment of mental health and retardation service units.

1967
S.B. No.390, Act
An act to provide for the establishment, administration, organization and management of sheltered workshops.
Legislative intent:
1. to improve rehabilitation services for the seriously handicapped including the mentally retarded of ND by providing for the development and continuation of long-term sheltered workshops

2. To provide for licensure and standard setting for sheltered workshops, and to establish responsibility for development and continuation of a statewide program by the division of vocational rehabilitation.

1967
S.B. No.249, Act
An act to provide for the purchasing of residential care, custody, training, treatment or education of the mentally retarded by the state from private, nonprofit, charitable organizations.

1967
S.B. No.324, Act
An act to authorize the Board of Administration to accept donations, gifts, grants, and bequests for the construction of a chapel at Grafton state school, and providing for a special fund in the state treasury for such purpose, and making an appropriation.

1967
S.B. No.52, Act
An act to provide for the testing and treatment of the disease phenylketonuria and other metabolic diseases causing mental retardation, providing for an educational program concerning such diseases under the direction of the department of health, and requiring physicians attending newborn infants to subject such infants to tests for phenylketonuria and other metabolic diseases.

1967
S.B. No.6, Appropriation
An act making an appropriation for the general maintenance, improvements and repairs, equipment, miscellaneous items and new buildings and special projects for the Grafton State School at Grafton, North Dakota. Appropriated was $5,309,515 out of the Grafton State school operating fund.

1967
H.B. No.566, Appropriation
An act to make a deficiency appropriation pay salaries and wages of the Grafton state school, and declaring an emergency. Appropriated was $61,000.

1969
S.B. No.131, Amendment
An act to amend and reenact section 54-23-28 of the ND Century Code, relating to care and custody of funds belonging to inmates of state institutions.

1969
H.B. No.32, Act
An act providing coordination by the board of administration of institutional farm activities providing for transfer of products between institutions, and requiring a biennial report to the governor and legislature.

1969
H.B. No.128, Act
An act to repeal chapter 54-25 of the ND Century Code, relating to the regulation as to sale and use of dairy products by state institutions.

1969
S.B. No.483, Amendment
An act to amend and reenact chapter 387 of the 1967 Session Laws, relating to the construction of a chapel and vocational rehabilitation facility at the Grafton State school, and declaring an emergency.

1969
S.B. No.425, Act
An act to create and enact section 54-21-06.1 of the ND Century Code, relating to the definition of the term 'board of administration' in the ND Century Code; to amend and reenact sections 54-21-06, 54-21-07, 54-21-09, 54-21-10, 54-21-11, 54-21-12, 54-21-18, 54-21-19, 54-21-20, and 54-21-24 of the ND Century code relating to establishment of a director of institutions and abolishment of the board of administration; and to repeal sections 54-21-01, 54-21-02, 54-21-03, 54-21-04, 54-21-05, and 54-21-08 of the ND Century Code, relating to the membership, powers, and duties of the board of administration.
54-21-06; Director of institutions-appointment, term, additional employees, compensation, removal, expenses
54-21-06.1; Director of institutions to be substituted for board, members of board and secretary of board
54-21-07; Bonds required of director and his employees who have control of money
54-21-09; Reports of Director of institutions to Governor and Secretary of State
54-21-10; Contents of report-daily record
54-21-11; Governor may require additional report
54-21-12; Suggestions for legislation included in report
54-21-13; Child welfare-mentally deficient persons, powers and duties of Director of Institutions
54-21-18; Custody of office building-considered part of capital building, director has control of public property
54-21-19; Director to furnish supplies to capital, state of offices, and executive mansion
54-21-20; Director authorized to acquire property for Capital park
54-21-24; Additional office space may be obtained outside of state capital

1969
S.B. No.80, Act
An act to create and enact subsection 4 of section 20-03-02 of the 1967 Supplement to the ND Century Code, relating to fishing license exemption. Any patient of the Grafton state school for the mentally deficient and any student at the state industrial school may fish without first having obtained a resident fishing license as prescribed in this chapter.

1969
H.B. No.38, Amendment
An act to amend and reenact section 12-45-07 of the ND Century Code, relating to the disposal of effects of deceased persons by the warden of the penitentiary and the superintendent of the state training school.

1969
H.B. No.9, Appropriation
An act making an appropriation for the general maintenance, improvements and repairs, equipment, miscellaneous items and new buildings and special projects for the Grafton State School at Grafton, North Dakota. Appropriated was $5,287,860.

1969
H.B. No.119, Act
An act authorizing the board of administration to lease certain property owned by the state and currently part of the Grafton State school.

1971
H.B. No.1342, Act
An act authorizing the director of institutions to convey certain land owned by the state of ND to the Grafton park district.

1971
S.B. No.2122, Act
An act to create and enact sections 25-09-02.1, 25-09-02.2, 25-09-03.1, 25-09-04.1, and 25-09-11.1 of the ND Century Code; to amend and reenact sections 25-09-02, 25-09-03, 25-09-04, 25-09-05, 25-09-06, subsection 2 of section 25-09-07, and section 25-09-08 of the ND Century Code; and to repeal section 25-09-11 of the ND Century Code, all relating to the expenses of care and treatment of patients at the Grafton state School and the state hospital.
25-09-02; Expenses chargeable against patient or his estate-filing claims
25-09-02.1; Reduction and write-off of accounts- reports required
25-09-02.2; Filing of claims- notice of department
25-09-03; Expenses chargeable against guardianship estate of patient-restrictions
25-09-03.1; Claims against estates of resident responsible relatives
25-09-04; Responsible relatives shall pay for care and treatment-definition
25-09-04.1; Nonresident patients
25-09-05; Inability to pay all or part of expenses
25-09-06; Application for review of ability to pay
25-09-08; Disposition of funds collected
25-09-11.1; Reductions in claims against resident patients of the Grafton State School and their responsible relatives

1973
S.B. No.2344, Amendment
An act to amend and reenact section 25-09-04 of the ND Century Code, relating to liability of relatives for expenses of care and treatment of patients of the state hospital, state school and San Haven state hospital.

1973
S.B. No.2180, Amendment
An act to amend and reenact section 25-05-02 of the ND Century Code, relating to the qualifications of the Superintendent of San Haven state hospital.

1973
S.B. No.2178, Amendment
An act to amend and reenact section 25-04-03 of the ND Century Code, relating to the qualifications of Superintendent of Grafton State school.

1973
S.B. No.2172, Amendment
An act to amend and reenact section 25-05-01 of the ND Century Code, relating to the administrative placement of the San Haven state hospital as a division of the Grafton State school.

1973
H.B. No.1007, Appropriation
An act making an appropriation for defraying expenses of various departments and various divisions thereof of the state of ND and which are under the supervision of the director of institutions, and declaring an emergency.

1973
H.B. No.1040
An act to create and enact relating to guardianships at the Grafton state school, and appeals in probate cases; relating to the authority of trustees, personal representatives, guardians, and conservators, to estate tax filing and collection procedures, to payment of deposits by financial institutions, to the powers and duties of public administrators, to minors' rights, to the jurisdiction of county courts, to appointment of guardians or conservators for orphans, statutes of limitations, to homestead estates, to appeals in probate proceedings, to testimony concerning transactions or conversations with the decedent, and to duties and powers of the soldiers' home commandant regarding deceased members' estates; relating to probate procedures, wills, and trusts, to the jurisdiction of county courts, to disposition of joint deposits by certain financial institutions, to guardians consenting to partition of real property, to satisfaction of real property mortgages, to mineral leasing by personal representatives, and to the acquisition of rights-of-way by public utilities; to provide penalties; and providing an effective date.

1973
House Concurrent Resolution No. 3089, Resolution
A concurrent resolution calling for a legislative council study to determine how ND can best care for and educate the deaf-blind children of the state.

1973
H.B. No.1263, Act
An act authorizing the director of institutions to lease certain land owned by the state of ND to the park district of the city of Grafton for a period of 25 years.

1975
House Concurrent Resolution No.3002
A concurrent resolution directing the legislative council to carry out a study of mental health and retardation commitment procedures and the in-hospital procedures relating to the custody and treatment of persons hospitalized because of mental deficiency.

1975
H.B. No.1468, Act
An act to provide for a conditional transfer of funds to a state capital construction funds, and providing an appropriation for the construction, additions to, remodeling, and equipping of buildings at state agencies, departments, and institutions.

1975
S.B. No.2007, Appropriation
An act making an appropriation for defraying expenses of various departments and various divisions thereof, of the state of ND, and which are under the supervision of the director of institutions, and declaring an emergency.

1975
S.B. No.2110, Appropriation
An act making an appropriation defraying expenses of the various departments of the government of the state of ND and declaring an emergency.

1975
S.B. No.2301, Amendment
An act to amend and reenact section 15-47-26 of the ND Century Code, to extend the definition of teacher or include section 15-47-38. Teacher is used to define teachers, principals, and superintendents in all public school districts, and all persons employed in teaching in any state institution, except institutions of higher learning.

1975
H.B. No.1530, Amendment
An act to amend and reenact sections 25-04-05, 25-09-02, 25-09-02.2, 25-09-03, 25-09-04, 25-09-04.1, 25-09-05, 25-09-06, subsection 1 of section 25-09-07, and section 25-09-10 of the ND Century code, relating to provisions for the charging of expenses for care and treatment of patients of the Grafton State school; and to repeal sections 25-09-03.1

and 25-09-11.1 of the ND Century Code, relating to claims against estates of responsible relatives and reduction of claims against responsible relatives.

25-04-05; Qualifications for admission to state facility-temporary admission, care and treatment of persons under 21 years of age

25-09-04; Responsible relatives shall pay for care and treatment-definition

25-09-04.1; Nonresident patients

25-09-05; Inability to pay all or part of expenses

25-09-06; Application for review of ability to pay

25-09-10; Disposition of nonresidents-exceptions, reciprocal agreements

1977
Senate Concurrent Resolution No.4077
A concurrent resolution directing the legislative council to conduct a study of the internal organization, policies, and programs of human service and mental health and retardation centers.

1977
H.B. No.1007, Appropriation
An act making an appropriation for defraying expenses of various departments and various divisions thereof of the state of ND and which are under the supervision of the director of institutions; and declaring an emergency.

1977
S.B. No.2010, Appropriation
An act making an appropriation for defraying expenses of various departments and various divisions thereof, of the state of ND.

1977
S.B. No.2059, Amendment
An act to amend and reenact sections 14-03-07 and 14-03-12 of the ND Century Code, relating to prohibited marriages and marriage prohibition if a person is infected with syphilis in communicable form.

1977
S.B. No.2164, Act
An act to create a new chapter of the ND Century Code dealing with the emergency, voluntary, involuntary commitment of individuals to the state hospital or other treatment facilities; to amend section 27-20-04 of the ND Century Code, relating to concurrent jurisdiction of the juvenile court with county mental health boards; and to repeal sections 25-02-05, 25-02-11, 25-02-12, 25-02-13, 25-02-14, 25-02-15, 25-02-16, 25-02-17, and 25-02-18 of the ND Century Code, relating to forms furnished by the superintendent of the state hospital, the establishment, powers, duties, and authority of county mental health board, and the liability of certain officers for detention of mentally ill persons, and to repeal chapter 25-03 of the ND Century Code, relating to the custody and release of the mentally ill.
Section 1: Definitions

Section 2: Jurisdiction
Section 3: Legislative Intent
Section 4: Voluntary Admission
Section 5: Discharge of Voluntary patients
Section 6: Right to release on application-exception, Judicial proceedings
Section 7: Involuntary admission
Section 8: Petition for involuntary treatment
Section 9: Review of petition for involuntary treatment-probable cause established, respondent notified, rights, investigation
Section 10: Involuntary Treatment, court ordered examination
Section 11: Involuntary treatment, examination, report
Section 12: Notice of hearings
Section 13: Right to counsel-indigency, waiver
Section 14: Duty of State's Attorney
Section 15: Respondent's attendance at hearings
Section 16: Medication pending hospitalization order
Section 17: Involuntary Treatment, preliminary hearing
Section 18: Involuntary Treatment, release
Section 19: Involuntary Treatment hearing
Section 20: Involuntary Treatment hearing-findings and dispositions
Section 21: Alternatives to hospitalization
Section 22: Involuntary hospitalization orders
Section 23: Petition for subsequent hospitalization orders
Section 24: Right to treat
Section 25: Detention or hospitalization-emergency procedure
Section 26: Emergency procedure-acceptance of petition and individual, notice, court hearing set
Section 27: Notice and statement of rights
Section 28: Records and proceedings
Section 29: Appeal
Section 30: Discharge of hospitalized patient
Section 31: Review of current status of continuing hospitalization
Section 32: Periodic hearing and petition for discharge-continuing hospitalization
Section 33: Legal incompetence-presumption-finding-adjudication neglected
Section 34: Transfer of patients
Section 35: Hospitalization by an agency of the United States
Section 36: Escape of patient from treatment facility
Section 37: Reports to and additional powers of department
Section 38: Expenses of Stutsman County Court
Section 39: Transportation-expenses
Section 40: Rights of patients
Section 41: Limitations and restrictions of patient's rights
Section 42: Limitations of Liability-penalty for false petition
Section 43: Confidential Records
Section 44: Records of disclosure
Section 45: Expungement of records

Section 46: Rules and regulations-preparation of forms
Section 47: Amendment—27-20-04, concurrent jurisdiction

1979
Grafton Indemnification
S.B. No.2284, Appropriation
An act to provide appropriation to the Grafton state school to indemnify Mrs. Ray Holt, Mrs. Myrtle McDonald, Mr. Tim Holt, Nygard's Auto Inc., and Wally's Fairway Foods, all of Grafton ND, for property and other losses suffered due to the acts of residents of Grafton State school. Appropriated was the sum of $1,868.41.

1979
H.B. No.1060, Act
Mental Health and Retardation Service Units
An act to create and enact a new section to chapter 25-10 of the ND Century Code, relating to the authority of the mental health and retardation division; and to amend and reenact sections 25-12-01, 25-12-02, 25-12-03, and 25-12-04 of the ND Century Code, relating to the operation of mental health and retardation service units.

1979
H.B. No.1061, Act
Mental Health and Service Unit Collocation
An act to improve the quality and efficiency in delivery, of human services through the collocation of social services and mental health services in each of the eight regions of the state; providing for joint intake, interagency referral, and inter-program planning and coordination; encouraging regional collocation of other related human services; providing for a fiscal incentive for the collocation of county social services in the regional centers; providing for the ND social service board to reimburse qualifying mental health and retardation service units and human service centers for provision of clinical services to medical assistance individuals; and to amend and reenact section 50-24.1-03 of the ND Century Code, relating to medical assistance.

1979
Senate Concurrent Resolution, No.4060
Community Placement Program Study
A concurrent resolution directing a legislative council study of the community placement program at the Grafton State School.

1979
House Concurrent Resolution, No.3061
Deinstitutionalization Programs Study
A concurrent resolution directing the legislative council to conduct a study of deinstitutionalization programs for residents of the State Hospital, Grafton State School, and San Haven State Hospital.

1979
S.B. No.2383, Amendment
Vocational Rehabilitation Facilities
An act to amend and reenact sections 25-15-01, 25-15-02, 25-15-03, 25-15-04, 25-15-05, 25-15-06, and 25-15-07 of the ND Century Code, relating to vocational rehabilitation facilities for the handicapped.

1979
S.B. No.2057, Act
Transportation at Grafton and San Haven
An act to create and enact a new section of the ND Century Code, relating to transportation costs to and from the San Haven state hospital; and to amend and reenact subsection 3 of section 25-04-05 of the ND Century Code, relating to transportation costs to and from Grafton state school.

1979
H.B. No.1279, Amendment
State Council on Developmental Disabilities
An act to amend and reenact section 25-01-01.1 of the ND Century Code, relating to the coordinating committee on mental retardation.

1979
S.B. No.2009, Appropriation
Grafton State School and San Haven
An act making an appropriation for defraying the expenses of the Grafton state school and the San Haven state hospital of the state of ND. Appropriated was $17,950,634 for the Grafton state school, $7,120,885 for San Haven.

1979
S.B. No.2042, Appropriation
Deficiency Appropriations
An act to amend and reenact section 1 of chapter 4 of the 1977 Session Laws of ND, relating to the appropriation for the personal property tax replacement and homestead tax credit; and making an appropriation for defraying the expenses of various departments and institutions of the state of ND; and declaring an emergency.

1981
House Concurrent Resolution, No.3058
Developmentally Disabled Rights Study
A concurrent resolution directing a legislative council study of guardianship and conservatorship laws and commitment procedures affecting developmentally disabled persons.

1981
H.B. No.1418, Amendment
Department of Human Services
An act to create a department of human services; to amend and reenact sections of the ND Century Code, relating to the developmental disabilities council, the superintendent of the state hospital, care of patients at the state hospital, the mental health and retardation division of the state health department, local mill levy for support of mental health and retardation service units, the state you authority, penalty for driving under the influence of intoxicating liquors or controlled substances, definitions of state county social service boards, the creation of multi-county welfare districts, powers and duties of the social service board, use of federal funds for clinic services, the division of vocational rehabilitation, definition of state agency for administration of aid to dependent children, definition of state agency for aid to crippled children, county share of medical assistance, the governor's council on human resources, governor's power to appoint majority of certain board members, the division on alcoholism and drug abuse, human service centers, agencies subject to the merit system, and authority of merit system board to provide service to cities and political subdivisions.

1981
H.B. No.1009, Appropriation
Grafton State School and San Haven
An act making an appropriation for defraying the expenses of the Grafton state school and San Haven of the state of ND; providing for a transfer of oil extraction tax funds; and declaring an emergency.

1981
S.B. No.2021, Appropriation
Deficiency Appropriations
An act making an appropriation for defraying the expenses of various departments and institutions of the state of ND; and declaring an emergency.

1981
H.B. No.1435, Amendment
State Institution Resident's Travel Reimbursements
An act to amend and reenact section 15-59-07, subsection 3 of section 25-04-05, and sections 25-04-05.2, 25-06-04, and 25-07-04 of the ND Century Code, relating to transportation costs to and from state institutions.

1981
H.B. No.1050, Amendment
Facilities for the Developmentally Disabled
An act to amend and reenact section 1 of House Bill No.1614, as approved by the forty-seventh legislative assembly, relating to recognition by the division of vocational rehabilitation of physical plant licensing by other governmental entities; and to amend and reenact sections 25-15-05, 25-16-01, 25-16-02, 25-16-03, 25-16-03.1, 25-16-05, 25-16-06, 25-16-07, 25-16-08, 25-16-09, 25-16-10, 25-16-11, and 25-16-12 of the ND

Century Code, relating to the licensure of facilities for developmentally disabled persons by the developmental disabilities division, division of vocational rehabilitation, and the state department of health; to provide effective dates; and to provide expiration dates.

1981
H.B. No.1046, Amendment
Mental Health and Human Service Center Central Personnel Coverage
An act to amend and reenact section 54-44.3-19 of the ND Century Code, relating to the status of mental health and retardation service units and human service centers under the central personnel division classification and pay plan.

1983
S.N. No.2089, Act
Retirement Credit purchase by employees of Mental Health and Retardation Centers
An act to create and enact section 54-52-02.7 of the ND Century Code, relating to the purchase by certain employees of prior service credit for service with a mental health and retardation center prior to January 1, 1982.

1983
H.B. No.1581, Act
Claims for damage caused by residents of state institutions
An act relating to claims against the state resulting from activities of residents or inmates of state institutions.

1983
H.B. No.1002, Appropriation
Deficiency Appropriations
An act making an appropriation for defraying the expenses of various departments and institutions of the state of ND; and declaring an emergency.

1983
S.B. No.2009, Appropriation
Grafton State School and San Haven
An act making an appropriation for defraying the expenses of the Grafton state school, Grafton-deinstitutionalization, and San Haven of the state of ND; and providing for a transfer of oil extraction tax funds; and declaring an emergency.

1983
H.B. No.1057, Amendment
Guardianship Requirements
An act to amend and reenact sections of the ND Century Code, relating to requirements for the individual habilitation plan, to the superintendent of Grafton state school acting as a guardian, and a limited guardianship or conservatorship under the uniform probate code; to repeal section 25-04-13.1 of the ND Century Code, relating to the superintendent of Grafton state school acting as guardian; and to provide an effective date.

1985
S.B. No.2417, Amendment
Grafton State School Superintendent as Guardian
An act to amend and reenact sections 25-04-13.1, 30.1-01-06, 30.1-26-01, 30.1-28-03, 30.1-28-04, and 30.1-28-11 of the ND Century Code, and section 16 of chapter 313 of the 1983 Session Laws of ND, relating to the superintendent of Grafton state school acting as guardian and limited guardianship or conservatorship.

1985
H.B. No. 1209, Act
Grafton State School Name Change
An Act to change the name of the Grafton state school to the state developmental center at Grafton; to amend and reenact section 25-04-01 of the ND Century Code, relating to changing the name of the Grafton state school and to provide an effective date.

1985
H.B. No. 1062, Act
Grafton State School and San Haven Control to Department of Human Services
An Act to amend and reenact sections of the ND Century Code, relating to the transfer of control of Grafton state school and San Haven to the department of human services; and to provide an effective date.
Section titles:
State school – Maintained – Name
Purpose of state school
Qualification of superintendent
Biennial report – Assistant superintendent
Who may receive benefits of state school
Qualifications for admission to state facility – Temporary admission –Care and treatment of persons under twenty-one years of age without charge
Transfer of residents – Visiting privileges – Release and placement of patients
Discharge of resident from institution
Disposition of person who is not a legal resident
Expenses chargeable against patient or estate
Structure of the department
Institution under control of director of institutions
Effective date

1985
H.B. No. 1503, Act
MENTALLY ILL AND RETARDED, TUBERCULAR, BLIND AND DEAF:
Licensed Physicians at State Institutions
An Act to create and enact a new subsection to section 25-01-05 of the ND Century Code, relating to general powers and duties of institution superintendents; and to provide an effective date.

1985
H.B. No. 1446, Act
Commitment Proceedings
An Act to amend and reenact subsections 6, 7, and 9 of section 25-03.1-02 of the ND
Century Code, relating to independent expert examiners and mental health professionals
for commitment proceedings.

1985
H.B. No. 1289, Act
Venue of Emergency Commitment Proceedings
 An Act to amend and reenact subsection 1 of section 25-03.1-26 of the ND Century
Code, relating to venue for emergency commitment proceedings.
The state hospital or public treatment facility must immediately accept and a private
treatment facility must accept on a provisional basis the application and the person
admitted under section 25-03.1-25.

1985
S.B. No. 2007, Appropriation
Human Services, Penitentiary, Grafton State School, San Haven, Transition,
Governor-elect, Deinstitutionalization Court Monitor
An Act making an appropriation for defraying the expenses of various departments and
institutions of the state of ND, providing for a transfer; and declaring an emergency.

1985
H.B. No. 1010, Appropriations
Grafton State School, San Haven, Court Monitor, and Protection and Advocacy
Project
 An Act making an appropriation for defraying the expenses of the Grafton state school,
San Haven, protection and advocacy project, and deinstitutionalization court monitor of
the state of ND.

1985
H.B. No. 1662, Act
North Dakota Building Authority Powers and Funding
An Act to establish the industrial commission as the ND building authority and to set out
its powers and duties; to provide authorization for the issuance of evidences of
indebtedness and for the construction of various buildings and facilities for state
agencies, departments, and institutions; to provide a continuing appropriation; and to
declare an emergency.

1985
H.B. No. 1656, Act
Grafton State School and State Hospital Care Expenses
An Act to create and enact a new section to chapter 25-02, five new sections to chapter
25-04, and a new chapter to title 50 of the ND Century Code, relating to payment and
waiver of payment of expenses of care and treatment for patients at the state hospital and

Grafton state school and the imposition and collection of fees and expenses by the department of human services; and to repeal chapter 25-09 of the ND Century Code, relating to expenses for care of patients at the state hospital and Grafton state school.

1987
H.B. No. 1381, Act
Tax Credit for Employing Handicapped
An Act to create and enact three new subsections to section 57-38-01 of the ND Century Code and a new section to chapter 57-38 of the ND Century Code, relating to a tax credit for employers who hire developmentally disabled or chronically mentally ill employees; and to provide an effective date.

1987
H.B. No. 1028, Appropriation
Various Departments and Institutions
An Act making an appropriation for defraying the expenses of various departments and institutions of the state of ND; to provide for authorization to accept and expend income; to provide legislative intent regarding deinstitutionalization court monitor expenses; and declaring an emergency.

1987
H.B. No. 1902, Appropriation
Grafton State School – San Haven Revenue Transfer
An Act to provide authority to the Grafton State School to transfer excess revenue to San Haven; and to provide an effective date.

1987
S.B. No. 2016, Appropriation
Grafton State School, Court Monitor, and Protection and Advocacy Project
An Act making an appropriation for defraying the expenses of the Grafton state school, protection and advocacy project, and deinstitutionalization court monitor of the state of ND; authorizing the director of institutions to sell, lease, exchange, or transfer title or use of the properties of San Haven; to provide administrative supervision of the protection and advocacy project; to provide legislative intent regarding federally funded positions in the protections and advocacy project; to require emergency commission approval of new positions; and to provide an expiration date.

1987
H.B. No. 1421, Act
Work Activity Center Bids
An Act to require the office of management and budget and the state highway department to award contracts for the purchase of highway grade stakes to facilities for the physically handicapped, developmentally disabled, and chronically mentally ill; and to amend and reenact sections relating to competitive bidding procedures.

1987
S.B. No. 2362, Act
MENTALLY ILL AND RETARDED, TUBERCULAR, BLIND, AND DEAF:
Hospitalization Alternatives
An Act to amend and reenact section 25-03.1-21 of the ND Century Code, relating to alternatives to hospitalization for persons requiring treatment.

1987
S.B. No. 2068, Act
State Institution Care Expenses
An Act to create and enact two new sections to chapter 25-04 of the ND Century Code, relating to liability for care and treatment of nonresident patients at the reduction or write-off of accounts receivable by the Grafton state school; and to amend and reenact sections relating to payment of expenses for care and treatment of patients at the Grafton state school and the state hospital.
Sections Titles:
Who may receive benefits of state school
Care and treatment at the state school
Liability for care and treatment of nonresident patients
Expenses chargeable against patient of patient's estate
Expenses chargeable against guardianship estate of patient – Restrictions
Reduction or write-off of accounts
Expenses chargeable against patient, his estate or responsible relatives
Fees and expenses chargeable against patients
Liability for payment
Expenses chargeable against guardian ship estate or patient- Restrictions

1987
S.B. No. 2548, Act
State School Superintendent as Guardian
An Act to amend and reenact subsection 1 of section 25-04-13.1 of the ND Century Code, and section 16 of chapter 313 of the 1983 Session Laws of ND, relating to the superintendent of the Grafton state school acting as guardian of any resident.
The superintendent shall continue to act as guardian except if otherwise provided by the court or if resident is released or other exceptions.

1989
S.B. No. 2537, Act
PUBLIC WELFARE: Grafton State School Land Transfer
An Act to authorize the director of the department of human services to transfer title and convey certain land owned by the state of ND to job service ND for use as a job service office.

1989
H.B. No. 1229, Act
State Institutions Administration
An Act to create and enact new sections relating to the transfer of control of the school for the blind, school for the deaf, and the state library from the director of institutions to the superintendent of public instruction and institutions under the control of the director of institutions and to change the name of the state developmental center at Grafton; to require the governor to develop a plan for the transfer of the powers and duties of the director of institutions; and to provide an effective date.

1989
H.B. No. 1205, Act
MENTALLY ILL AND RETARTDED, TUBERCULAR, BLIND, AND DEAF:
Developmental Disability and Human Resource Programs
An Act to provide for a committee on protection and advocacy for persons with developmental disabilities or mental illnesses; to amend and reenact sections of the ND Century Code, relating to the placement of the state council on developmental disabilities and the governor's council on human resources within the office of the governor; and to provide a statement of legislative intent.

1989
H.B. No. 1127, Act
State Developmental Center Control
An Act to create and enact a new section to chapter 25-04 of the ND Century Code, relating to chapter limitations and to amend and reenact other sections relating to the state developmental center in Grafton. A facility for developmentally disabled persons shall be maintained at or near the city of Grafton in Walsh County. Also, the department of human services shall have administrative authority and control of the state developmental center at Grafton.

1991
S.B. No. 2284, Act/Appropriation
STATE GOVERNMENT: Developmental Center land Transfer
An Act to amend and reenact sections 54-01-05.2 and 54-01-05.5 of the ND Century Code, relating to sale or exchange of state land; to authorize the director of the department of human services to transfer title and convey certain land at the state developmental center at Grafton to the city of Grafton; and to provide an appropriation.

1991
S.B. No. 2121, Act
Developmental Center Patient Free Education
An Act to amend and reenact sections 25-04-05, 25-04-14, and 25-04-16 of the ND Century Code, relating to the provision of free educational services to developmental center patients who are twenty-one years of age or younger and to provide for the waiver of fees and expenses upon application by a parent of a patient or former patient under age eighteen.

1991
H.B. No. 1410, Act
Developmental Center Accreditation and Residency
An Act to create and enact a new section to chapter 25-04 of the ND Century Code, relating to accreditation of the developmental center at Grafton; and to amend and reenact sections or the ND Century Code, relating to who may receive services from the developmental center at Grafton.
Section headings:
Developmental center – Name – Administration and control
Purpose of developmental center at Grafton
Accreditation of developmental center
Who may receive benefits of developmental center
Qualifications for admission to state facility
Juvenile court commitment of dependent, neglected, or delinquent mentally deficient – Commitment for observation – Appeal
Disabled defendants
Discharge of resident from institution
Notification prior to discharge
Disposition of person who is not a legal resident
Disposition of nonresidents

1991
S.B. No. 2002, Appropriations
Department of Human Services
An Act making appropriation for defraying the expenses of the department of human services, making an appropriation from the lands and minerals trust fund to the common schools trust fund, and providing an appropriation from the revolving loan fund maintained in the Bank of ND; to provide authority for lease of real and personal property at the state developmental center and the state hospital; To provide alternative contingent appropriation; to allow the sale of surplus steam heat at the state developmental center; regarding administration of the child care block grant and at-risk child care programs; to create and enact new section and subsections, relating to insurance payments by the department of human services for persons with acquired immune deficiency syndrome, and operating margins and efficiency incentives for nursing homes.

1993
H.B. No. 1002 Appropriation
Human Service Funding Transfer
An Act to provide an appropriation for defraying the expenses of the department of human services, an appropriation from the lands and minerals trust fund to the common schools trust fund, an appropriation from the revolving loan fund maintained in the Bank of ND, and an appropriation from the state aid distribution fund; to provide for the transfer of appropriations between agencies and institutions and to require budget section approval of alternative programs at the state hospital to create new subsections to relating

to the duties of the ND health council, to the definition of long-term care facility, to the certificate of need program, to the lease of developmental center facilities or properties, to payment of services by county and state matching funds, and to aid to aged, blind, and disabled persons; to create and enact section 2 to House Bill No. 1274 as approved by the fifty-third legislative assembly, relating to residential care and services for the developmentally disabled and to provide an expiration date for that Act.

1993
S.B. No. 2026, Act
Day Care Property Lease from State
An Act to amend and reenact section 50-06-06.6 of the ND Century Code, relating to leases of real and personal property by the department of human services. The executive director also may enter further leases of real or property at the developmental center or the state hospital upon a specific finding that the granting of each such leasehold, except those relating to child care services.

1993
H.B. No. 1490, Act
Developmental Center Services and Records
An Act to create and enact a new section to chapter 25-04 of the ND Century Code, relating to services provided by the developmental center at Grafton; and to amend and reenact sections 25-04-02, 25-04-04, and subsection 1 of section 25-04-16 of the ND Century Code, relating to services provided by the developmental center at Grafton.
Purpose of developmental center at Grafton
Who may receive benefits of developmental center
Payment of services provided
Quality assurance review committees

1993
S.B. No. 2479, Act
Mental Disorder Insurance Services
An Act to amend and reenact subsection 2 of section 26.1-36-09 of the ND Century Code, relating to group health policy and services contract mental disorder coverage.

1995
S.B. No. 2506, Act
Protection and Advocacy Committee Membership
An Act to amend and reenact section 25-01.3-02 and subsection 13 of section 25-01.3-06 of the ND Century Code, relating to the members of the committee on protection and advocacy and the authority of the project; to provide for a report to the budget section of the legislative council; and to provide for application of this act.

1995
S.B. No. 2012, Appropriation
Human Services
An Act to provide an appropriation for defraying the expenses of the department of human services; to provide for the transfer of appropriations between agencies and institutions; to rename the developmental center the developmental center at westwood park, Grafton, county medical services for the poor, the state basic care program, and extending an appropriation from the lands and minerals trust fund to the department of human services for capital improvements or demolition of existing buildings at the developmental center at westwood park, Grafton.

1997
H.B. No. 1197, Amendment
Minimum Wage Special License Exception
An Act to amend and reenact section 34-06-15 relating to issuing special licenses to employ at less than minimum wage. Special licenses may be issued by commissioner to community rehabilitation programs for the handicapped and for other similar cases.

1997
S.B. No. 2059, Amendment
Disclosure of Commitment Records
An Act to amend and reenact a section relating to making confidential commitment records of the department of human services available to law enforcement in limited circumstances.

1999
S.B. No. 2266, Amendment
Committee on Protection and Advocacy Membership
An Act to amend and reenact section 25-01.3-02 relating to the membership of the committee on protection and advocacy of any state agency that provides treatment, services, or habilitation to persons with disabilities or mental illness.

1999
S.B. No. 2012, Appropriation
Human Services
An Act to provide appropriation for defraying the expenses of the department of human services; to create and enact new sections relating to a moratorium on residential treatment center and residential child care facility beds, the children's health insurance program, the county share of foster car costs and the limits of geropsychiatric nursing facilities, as well as Session Laws relating to appropriation for projects at westwood park assets management committee; appropriations between agencies and institutions; to provide an expiration date and to declare an emergency.

1999
House Concurrent Resolution No. 3016
Guardianship Services Study
A concurrent resolution directing the Legislative Council to study the qualifications, standards, and the monitoring requirements for guardianship services for incapacitated persons.

1999
Senate Concurrent Resolution No. 4045
Developmentally Disabled Services Funding Study
A concurrent resolution directing the Legislative Council to study alternative systems for the funding of services delivered to children and adults who are developmentally disabled.

2001
H.B. No. 1012, Appropriation
Human Services
An Act to provide an appropriation for defraying the expenses of the department of human services; to provide for the transfer of appropriation authority between agencies and institutions; to provide for legislative council studies to provide and exception to section 54-44.1-06 of the ND Century Code, relating to the preparation of the department of human services appropriations bill for the 2003-05 biennium; to provide exceptions and subsection to sections of the ND Century Code in many areas including eligibility for children's special health services and compensation for members of the state hospital governing body, county reimbursements, and assignment of support rights; to provide an effective date; and to declare an emergency.

2001
H.B. No. 1415, Act
Residential Treatment Center and Child Care Facility Moratorium
An Act to amend and reenact 25-03.2-03.1 and 50-11-02.3 of the ND Century Code, relating to a needs assessment and a moratorium on the expansion of residential treatment center for children and residential child care facility or group home bed capacity; to provide an expiration date; and to declare an emergency.

2001
S.B. No. 2034, Act
Sexual Predator Civil Commitment
An Act to create and enact three new sections and a new subsection of the ND Century Code, relating to the referral of inmates for civil commitment and rulemaking; and to amend and reenact sections of the ND Century Code, relating to the civil commitment of sexual predators.
Definitions
Jurisdiction and venue
Sexually dangerous individual – Petition
Referral of inmates to state's attorneys – Immunity

Appointment of guardian ad litem
Sexually dangerous individual – Procedure on petition – Detention
Sexually dangerous individual – Evaluation
Sexually dangerous – Commitment proceeding – Report of findings
Appeal
Rules
Individual rights

2001
H.B. No. 1118, Act
Fire Inspections

An Act to amend and reenact section 18-08-12 of the ND Century Code, relating to fire inspection of state buildings and institutions. All violations must be corrected with in the current budget of the responsible board, agency or commission and be initiated within 30 days of receipt of the report.

2003
S.B. No. 2153, Act
Provider Assessment for Mentally Retarded Care

An Act to create and enact a new chapter to title 57 of the ND Century Code, relating to a provider assessment for intermediate care facilities for the mentally retarded; and to provide a penalty.
Definitions
Impositions
Basis of assessment
Reports – Extension
Payment of assessment
Penalties – Offenses
Records required
Officer and manager liability
Commissioner to administer chapter
Lien of assessment – Collection – Action authorized
Commissioner may require bond
Correction of errors
Provider assessment fund

2003
S.B. No. 2047, Act
Trusts for Individuals with Disabilities

An act relating to trusts of individuals with disabilities.
Definitions
Third-party special needs trusts under state law.
Self-settled special needs trusts
Interpretation of enforcement – Reformation – Unenforceable trust provisions.

2003
House Concurrent Resolution No. 3037, Resolution
Human Services Delivery and Criminal Process Study

A resolution directing the Legislative Council to study the needs of individuals with mental illness, drug and alcohol addiction, and physical or developmental disabilities, including individuals with multiple needs, and how the state responds to those needs; the long-term plans for the State Hospital, the Developmental Center at Westwood Park, Grafton, state and county correctional facilities, and other state facilities and the relationships among those facilities; the impact and availability of community service.

2003
S.B. No. 2086, Act
Developmental Disability Care Fees
An Act to create and enact a new chapter to title 25 of ND Century Code, relating to implementation of a fee for service rate setting system for payment to treatment or care centers for individuals with developmental disabilities; to repeat sections 25-16-10, 25-16-10.1, 26-16-16, and 50-06-18 of the ND Century Code, relating to the purchase of services provided to individuals with developmental disabilities and allowing providers to services to individuals with developmental disabilities (IWDD)to transfer funds between budget categories and line items; and to provide an effective date.

2003
H.B. No. 1425, Amendment
Developmentally Disabled Record Confidentiality
An Act to amend and reenact section 25-16-07 of the ND Century Code, relating to the disclosure of individual records of a treatment of care center for developmentally disabled individuals.

References

Barr, M.W. (1902). The imperative call of our present to our future. *Journal of Psycho-Asthenics, 7* (1), 5-8.

Division of Mental Health and Retardation Services. (1966*). A plan for North Dakota's mentally retarded: A report to the governor, legislature, and citizens of North Dakota.*. Bismarck, ND: author.

Division of Mental Retardation Programs. (1970). *A plan for North Dakota's mentally retarded: A report to the governor, legislature, and citizens of North Dakota, 1970 revised edition.*. Bismarck, ND: author.

Fernald, W.E. (1919). After-care study of the patients discharged from Waverley for a period of twenty-five years. *Ungraded, 5* (2), 25-31.

Goddard, H.H. (1914). *The Kallikak family: A study in the heredity of feeble-mindedness.* NewYork: Macmillan.

Haskell, R.H. (1944). The development of a research program in mental deficiency over a fifteen-year period. *American Journal of Psychiatry, 101* (1), 73-81.

National Committee for Mental Hygiene, Inc. (1923*). Report of the North Dakota mental hygiene survey with recommendations.* New York, NY: author.

Rosen, M., Clark, G.R., & Kivitz, M.S. (1976*). The history of mental retardation: Collected papers, volume 1.* Baltimore: University Park Press.

Rosen, M., Clark, G.R., & Kivitz, M.S. (1976). *The history of mental retardation: Collected papers, volume 2.* Baltimore: University Park Press.

Scheerenberger, R.C. (1983). *A history of mental retardation.* Baltimore, MD: Brookes Publishing Company.

Trent, James, W., Jr. (1994). *Inventing the feeble mind: A history of mental retardation in the United States.* Berkeley, CA: University of California Press.

Vyzralek, F. (1996). *Registration form: National Register of Historic Places: North Dakota Institution for the Feeble Minded.* Unpublished document, available from the North Dakota Developmental Center.

Witmer, L. (1909). The study and treatment of retardation: A field of applied psychology. *Psychological Bulletin, 6*(4), 121-126.

Wylie, A.R.T. (1934). *Sixteenth Biennial Report of the State School for Feeble-Minded and Epileptics, draft.* Bismarck, ND: author. (State Historical Society of North Dakota, State Archives. Series 30795 Grafton State School, Subject Files.)

Chronological list of state documents

Board of Trustees, Institution for Feeble Minded. (1904). *First Biennial Report of the North Dakota Institution for Feeble Minded.* Bismarck, ND: author.

Board of Trustees, Institution for Feeble Minded. (1906). *Second Biennial Report of the North Dakota Institution for Feeble Minded.* Bismarck, ND: author.

Board of Trustees, Institution for Feeble Minded. (1908). *Third Biennial Report of the North Dakota Institution for Feeble Minded.* Bismarck, ND: author.

Board of Trustees, Institution for Feeble Minded. (1910). *Fourth Biennial Report of the North Dakota Institution for Feeble Minded.* Bismarck, ND: author.

Board of Control of State Institutions. (1912). *Fifth Biennial Report of the Institution for the Feeble Minded.* Bismarck, ND: author.

Board of Control of State Institutions. (1914). *Sixth Biennial Report of the Institution for Feeble Minded*. Bismarck, ND: author.

Board of Control of State Institutions. (1916). *Seventh Biennial Report of the Institution for the Feeble Minded*. Bismarck, ND: author.

Board of Control of State Institutions. (1918). *Eighth Biennial Report of the Institution for Feeble Minded*. Bismarck, ND: author.

Board of Administration of State Institutions. (1920). *Ninth Biennial Report of the Institution for Feeble Minded*. Bismarck, ND: author.

Board of Administration. (1921). *Third Annual Report of the Board of Administration to the Governor*. Bismarck, ND: author.

Board of Administration of State Institutions. (1922). *Tenth Biennial Report of the Institution for Feeble Minded*. Bismarck, ND: author.

Board of Administration of State Institutions. (1924). *Eleventh Biennial Report of the Institution for Feeble Minded*. Bismarck, ND: author.

Board of Administration of State Institutions. (1926). *Twelfth Biennial Report of the Institution for Feeble Minded*. Bismarck, ND: author.

Board of Administration of State Institutions. (1928). *Thirteenth Biennial Report of the Institution for Feeble Minded*. Bismarck, ND: author.

Board of Administration of State Institutions. (1930). *Fourteenth Biennial Report of the Institution for Feeble Minded*. Bismarck, ND. author.

Board of Administration of State Institutions. (1932). *Fifteenth Biennial Report of the Institution for Feeble Minded*. Bismarck, ND. author.

Board of Administration of State Institutions. (1934). *Fifteenth and Sixteenth Annual Reports of the Board of Administration to the Governor*. Bismarck, ND: author.

Board of Administration of State Institutions. (1936). *Seventeenth Biennial Report of the Grafton State School*. Bismarck, ND. author.

Board of Administration of State Institutions. (1938). *Eighteenth Biennial Report of the Grafton State School*. Bismarck, ND: author.

Board of Administration of State Institutions. (1940). *Nineteenth Biennial Report of the Grafton State School*. Bismarck, ND: author.

Board of Administration of State Institutions. (1942). *Twentieth Biennial Report of the Grafton State School*. Bismarck, ND: author.

Board of Administration of State Institutions. (1944). *Twenty-first Biennial Report of the Grafton State School*. Bismarck, ND: author.

Board of Administration of State Institutions. (1946). *Twenty-second Biennial Report of the Grafton State School*. Bismarck, ND: author.

Board of Administration of State Institutions. (1948). *Twenty-third Biennial Report of the Grafton State School*. Bismarck, ND: author.

Board of Administration of State Institutions. (1950). *Twenty-fourth Biennial Report of the Grafton State School*. Bismarck, ND: author.

Board of Administration of State Institutions. (1952). *Twenty-fifth Biennial Report of the Grafton State School*. Bismarck, ND: author.

Board of Administration of State Institutions. (1954). *Twenty-Sixth Biennial Report of the Grafton State School*. Bismarck, ND: author.

Board of Administration. (1956). *Twenty-Seventh Biennial Report of the Grafton State School*. Bismarck, ND: author.

Board of Administration. (1958*). Twenty-Eighth Biennial Report of the Grafton State School*. Bismarck, ND: author.

Board of Administration. (1960*). Twenty-Ninth Biennial Report of the Grafton State School*. Bismarck, ND: author.

Board of Administration. (1962*). Thirtieth Biennial Report of the Grafton State School*. Bismarck, ND: author.

Board of Administration. (1964*). Thirty-First Biennial Report of the Grafton State School*. Bismarck, ND: author.

Board of Administration. (1966*). Thirty-Second Biennial Report of the Grafton State School*. Bismarck, ND: author.

Board of Administration. (1968*). Thirty-Third Biennial Report of the Grafton State School*. Bismarck, ND: author.

Director of Institutions. (1970). *Thirty-Fourth Biennial Report of the Grafton State School*. Bismarck, ND: author.

Director of Institutions. (1972). *Thirty-Fifth Biennial Report of the Grafton State School*. Bismarck, ND: author.

Director of Institutions. (1973). *Annual Report of the Grafton State School*. Bismarck, ND: author.

Director of Institutions. (1975). *Thirty-Sixth Biennial Report of the Grafton State School*. Bismarck, ND: author.

Director of Institutions. (1977). *Thirty-Seventh Biennial Report of the Grafton State School*. Bismarck, ND: author.

Director of Institutions. (1979). *Fifth Biennial Report to the Governor*. Bismarck, ND: author.

Director of Institutions. (1981). *Sixth Biennial Report to the Governor*. Bismarck, ND: author.

Director of Institutions. (1983). *Biennial Report to the Governor of North Dakota*. Bismarck, ND: author.

Director of Institutions. (1985). *Biennial Report to the Governor of North Dakota*. Bismarck, ND: author.

Director of Institutions. (1987). *Biennial Report to the Governor of North Dakota*. Bismarck, ND: author.

Director of Institutions. (1989). *Biennial Report to the Governor of North Dakota*. Bismarck, ND: author.

North Dakota Department of Human Services. (1989). *1987-1989 Biennial Report*. Bismarck, ND: author.

North Dakota Department of Human Services. (1991). *1989-1991 Biennial Report*. Bismarck, ND: author.

North Dakota Department of Human Services. (1995). *1993-1995 Biennial Report*. Bismarck, ND: author.

North Dakota Department of Human Services. (1997). *1995-1997 Biennial Report*. Bismarck, ND: author.

North Dakota Department of Human Services. (1999). *1997-1999 Biennial Report*. Bismarck, ND: author.

North Dakota Department of Human Services. (2001). *1999-2001 Biennial Report*. Bismarck, ND: author.

Newsletters from Grafton State School
Grafton State School. (1965). *The Ambassador*, vol. 2, no. 11. Grafton, ND: author.
Grafton State School. (1969). *The Ambassador*, vol. 6, no. 7. Grafton, ND: author.
Grafton State School. (1969). *The Ambassador*, vol. 6, no. 8. Grafton, ND: author.
Grafton State School. (1969). *The Ambassador*, vol. 6, no. 9. Grafton, ND: author.
Grafton State School. (1969). *The Ambassador*, vol. 6, no. 10. Grafton, ND: author.
Grafton State School. (1969). *The Ambassador*, vol. 6, no. 11. Grafton, ND: author.
Grafton State School. (1969). *The Ambassador*, vol. 6, no. 12. Grafton, ND: author.
Grafton State School. (1970). *The Ambassador*, vol. 7, no. 2. Grafton, ND: author.
Grafton State School. (1970). *The Ambassador*, vol. 7, no. 3. Grafton, ND: author.
Grafton State School. (1970). *The Ambassador*, vol. 7, no. 4. Grafton, ND: author.
Grafton State School. (1972). *The Ambassador*, vol. 9, no. 6. Grafton, ND: author.
Grafton State School. (1970). *The Ambassador*, vol. 7, no. 2. Grafton, ND: author.
Grafton State School. (1984). *The Grafton State School Ambassador*, vol. 1, March-
    April. Grafton, ND: author.
Grafton State School. (1984). *The Grafton State School Ambassador*, vol. 1, May-June.
    Grafton, ND: author.
Grafton State School. (1984). *The Grafton State School Ambassador*, vol. 1, November-
    December. Grafton, ND: author.
Grafton State School. (1985). *The Grafton State School Ambassador*, vol. 2, March.
    Grafton, ND: author.
Grafton State School. (1986). *The Grafton State School Ambassador*, vol. 3, June.
    Grafton, ND: author.

Court documents
Initial complaint in ARC vs. North Dakota et al. (1980). Filed in US District Court for the
    District of North Dakota, Southwestern Division. Copy of original obtained from
    Mike Williams, January 2004.
Base order in ARC vs. North Dakota et al. (1982). Copy of original filed by Judge B. Van
    Sickle, Bismarck, ND. Obtained from Mike Williams, January 2004.
Implementation order in ARC vs. North Dakota et al. (1984). Copy of original filed by
    Judge B.Van Sickle, Bismarck, ND. Obtained from Mike Williams, January 2004.
Order in ARC vs. North Dakota et al. (1985). Copy of original filed by Judge B. Van
    Sickle, Bismarck, ND. Obtained from Mike Williams, January 2004.

Newspaper articles
Copeland, J. (September 21, 1993). Veterans home debate continues: Veterans home,
    satellite clinic top possible DC uses. *The Walsh County Record*, pp. 1, 13.
Lee, S.J. (June 21, 1995). Elder housing proposed for Grafton school. *Grand Forks
    Herald*, pp. 1B, 3B.
Morgan, T. (May 24, 2000). Developmental Center sees some changes: Schweitzer
    named superintendent. *Grand Forks Herald*, pp. A-1, A-9.
Sandsrom, S. (August 3, 1993). Legislature considers DC for women's correctional
    facility. *The Walsh County Record*.
Scaletta, S.E. (June 4, 1994). Fargo firm to run developmental center. *Grand Forks*

Herald, pp. 1A, 9A.

Scaletta, S.E. (August 2, 1995). House funds veterans clinic. *Grand Forks Herald.*

Scaletta, S.E. (March 18, 1997). Center makes case against cuts. *Grand Forks Herald*, pp. 1B, 3B.

Strand, J. (April 5, 1994). Kratochvil announces departure. *The Walsh County Record.*

Strand, J. (October 9, 1994). Cleanup planned for North A and North B. *The Walsh County Record*, pp. 1, 17.

Strand, J. (May 16, 1995). Lunski named DC superintendent. *The Walsh County Record*, pp. 1, 8.

Strand, J. (June 27, 1995). Retirement housing foundation gets nod. *The Walsh County Record*, p. A3.

Strand, J. (February 13, 1996). VA clinic gets funding nod. *Walsh County Record*, p. 1, backpage.

Wood, C. (March 30, 1994). Developmental Center may be turned over to private manager. *Grand Forks Herald*, pp. 1A, 7A.

The Author

Dr. Brent A. Askvig is a Professor of Special Education at Minot State University in Minot North Dakota, and serves as the Associate Director for the North Dakota Center for Persons with Disabilities, a University Center of Excellence in Developmental Disabilities. A native of Des Lacs, North Dakota, Dr. Askvig holds a doctorate in Education, Special Education and Educational Research from the University of Idaho, along with a master's degree in special education with an emphasis in severe disabilities from Minot State University. He also has a bachelor's degree in education with majors in elementary education and mental retardation, also from Minot State University.

A 17-year veteran of higher education, Dr. Askvig also taught students with significant disabilities in the Bismarck, North Dakota public schools, was the coordinator for a seven county program for infants and toddlers with disabilities and their families, and was a residential direct care provider in a community facility for adults recently released from the state institution. He has served on numerous state and national committees in early intervention, severe disabilities, and personnel training in special education. His most recent research has focused on professional development models for rural teachers as they educate children and youth with behavioral difficulties. Dr. Askvig lives in rural North Dakota with his wife Stacy.